STUDIES IN EATING DISORDERS
An International Series

Treating
Eating Disorders

Ethical, Legal and Personal Issues

Edited by

Walter Vandereycken and Pierre J. V. Beumont

THE ATHLONE PRESS
LONDON

First published 1998 by
THE ATHLONE PRESS
1 Park Drive, London NW11 7SG

© The Editors and The Athlone Press 1998
British Library Cataloguing in Publication Data
*A catalogue record for this book is available
from the British Library*

ISBN 0 485 24013 0 hb
0 485 24101 3 pb

Typeset by Ensystems, Saffron Walden
Printed and bound in Great Britain by
Bookcraft (Bath) Ltd

Contents

Preface

The treatment of eating disorders, particularly of anorexia nervosa, remains controversial, always difficult, usually protracted, and often unsuccessful. For this reason the editors believe that the time is appropriate for a book focussed on the burden of therapy in these disorders, in which colleagues from throughout the world examine some of the many impediments to the optimal care of their patients. This volume is the result. As discussed in the introductory chapter, the topic of this book can be summarized under the heading: Whose 'competence' are we questioning?

First, there is *the competence of the health care professionals*, especially with regard to their personal feelings and attitudes when working with eating-disordered patients. Why do some clinicians like these patients while others try to avoid them? Kathryn Zerbe discusses the issue from the viewpoint of a psychoanalytically oriented psychotherapist. A central element in the discussion is the gender of the therapist, as revealed in the dialogue between Melanie Katzman and Glenn Waller. How a male psychotherapist developed a feminist attitude is illustrated in the very personal disclosure by Joe McVoy. From a different angle, Jan Lackstrom and Blake Woodside describe the frustrations and rewards of working with eating disorder families.

Second, a series of ethical and legal questions deals with *the patients' competence*. Especially the right to refuse treatment can create a profound dilemma. Referring to international mental health laws, compulsory treatment for eating disorders is reviewed by Rosalyn Griffiths and Janice Russell. Focusing on forced feeding in psychiatric patients, Bridget Dolan illustrates the complexity of the issue within the legal context of England and Wales. Günther Rathner very decidedly argues against compulsory treatment in anorexia nervosa and warns that many treatments include coercive elements. For this reason some behavior modification programs have been criticized, and Stephen Touyz reports on his experiences with this approach.

Finally, we have to discuss *the competence of a society* in which a growing demand for specialized care is clashing with economic forces. According to Sue Robinson and colleagues, the treatment of eating disorders seems to be an attractive market. But on the other hand health care insurances are putting increasing limitations on the coverage of treatment costs. Arnold Andersen illustrates this conflict with the example of American 'managed care'.

Contributors

Arnold E. Andersen, M.D., Professor of Psychiatry and Director Eating Disorders Inpatient Unit, University of Iowa Hospitals and Clinics, Iowa City, USA

Pierre J.V. Beumont, M.D., Professor and Head, Department of Psychological Medicine, University of Sydney, Royal Prince Alfred Hospital, Sydney, Australia

Andrew Curry, B.A., manager in the communications industry, UK

Chris Dare, M.D., Senior Lecturer at the Institute of Psychiatry, London, UK

Bridget Dolan, Ph.D., C.Forensic Psychol., Barrister-at-Law, Hon. Senior Lecturer in Forensic Psychology, St. George's Hospital Medical School, London, UK

Rosalyn Griffiths, M.D., Senior Lecturer and Director of Clinical Training at the Department of Psychology, University of Sydney, Australia

Melanie A. Katzman, Ph.D., Senior Lecturer in Clinical Psychology, Eating Disorders Unit, Institute of Psychiatry, London, UK

Jan B. Lackstrom, M.S.W., Coordinator Family Therapy, Eating Disorders Ambulatory Clinic, Toronto Hospital, and Sessional Instructor, School of Social Work, York University, Canada.

Stuart Lieberman, M.D., Consultant Psychotherapist at Heathlands Mental Health Trust, Ridgewood, Camberley, Surrey, UK

Joseph H. McVoy, Ph.D., Clinical Psychologist at Virginia Highland Health Associates, Radford, Virginia, USA

Günther Rathner, Ph.D., Psychologist and Head of the Eating Disorders Unit, Department of Pediatrics, University of Innsbruck, Austria

Sue Robinson, M.A., was a research therapist at the Institute of Psychiatry, London, UK

Janice Russell, M.D., Senior Lecturer at the Department of Psychological Medicine, University of Sydney, Australia

Stephen W. Touyz, M.D., Professor and Head, Department of Psychology, University of Sydney, Australia

Walter Vandereycken, M.D., Ph.D., Professor of Psychiatry, University of Leuven, Belgium

Glenn Waller, Ph.D., Professor of Clinical Psychology, University of Southampton, UK

D. Blake Woodside, M.D., Director, Eating Disorders Inpatient Program, Toronto Hospital, and Associate Professor, Department of Psychiatry, University of Toronto, Canada.

Kathryn J. Zerbe, M.D., Jack Aron Chair in Education, Karl Menninger School of Psychiatry, and Training and Supervising Psychoanalyst, Topkepa Institute for Psychoanalysis, The Menninger Clinic, Topkepa, Kansas, USA

CHAPTER ONE

Challenges and risks for health care professionals

Pierre Beumont and Walter Vandereycken

In this chapter, we wish to provide an overview of the topic of this book and an introduction to the other chapters. We will first discuss some opinions about eating disorders and their influence on attitudes and reactions of health care professionals towards eating-disordered patients. Next we consider some delicate ethical and legal issues in the management of eating disorders. For example, has an anorectic patient the right to refuse treatment and eventually die? Fortunately, in the majority of cases one is not confronted with this type of life-or-death decisions but with other difficulties and pitfalls: in the interaction with the patient's family, in the collaboration with other health professionals, in the medical management or the implementation of a weight restoration programme. On the socio-economic level, we have to face increasing tensions in the market of 'supply and demand' of specialized treatments for eating disorders. After having discussed so many 'burdens' for the therapists, we finally address the question whether treating eating-disordered patients involves some health risks for the professionals concerned.

KNOWLEDGE AND OPINIONS

Eating disorders are 'Western' culture-bound syndromes (Vandereycken and Hoek, 1993). In non-Western countries, they occur in those segments of the population that are Westernised. In Western countries, they are now widespread throughout the community. They have become fashionable topics in the mass media, and the general public's knowledge about these disorders and its awareness of the psychosocial factors involved (Murray et al., 1996) are probably greater nowadays than that shown by physicians 20 years ago (Bhanji, 1979). Unfortunately, however, the general knowledge and attitudes of many physicians is closer to that of lay opinion than to the views of experts in the area (Vandereycken, 1993).

In the early 1980s American psychiatrists and psychologists acquired their knowledge of anorexia nervosa from clinical exposure rather than from formal teaching such as lectures and workshops (Whyte and Kaczkowski, 1983). In medical schools today, eating disorders are no longer overlooked: for instance, in the new Graduate Medical Programme that the University of Sydney in Australia launched in 1997, the very first case to which the students are introduced in week 1 of the first year is that of an adolescent girl with anorexia nervosa. However, this does not necessarily mean that the subject has sufficient attention paid to it, or that it is regarded with sufficient interest. Only 40 per cent of the residents from Canadian psychiatric training centres (more females than males) showed moderate to marked interest in working with eating-disordered patients, and only 22 per cent reported that knowledge on the topic had been adequately provided to them at medical school (Ghadirian and Leichner, 1990). A survey of therapists in Florida showed that one third (more males than females) did not want to treat eating disorders, mainly because of feelings of frustration and lack of empathy with these patients. Therapists who were reluctant to treat such patients thought that the prognosis of eating disorders was less favourable than those who wished to treat them (Burket and Schramm, 1995). Willingness to treat appeared to be related to the level of knowledge about the disorders, but another essential influence on the professionals' attitudes was the degree of responsibility for the illness they ascribed to the patients or to their environment (Fleming and Szmukler, 1992).

Therapists differ in their approach to eating disorders according to the theoretical view they adopt. More importantly, their actions are determined by the way they construct the notion of eating disorder itself (Vogler, 1993). Dickerson and Zimmerman (1995) have proposed the following *constructionist exercise* for therapists. Using anorexia nervosa as an example, they ask us to think about problems in three distinct ways: (1) as a diagnosis using a framework such as DSM-IV; (2) as patterns in a conversational process between therapist and client; and (3) as cultural and personal discourses that influence others in ways that promote the development of problem stories. They examine the effect each of these approaches may have: (1) on the way therapists think about clients; (2) on the way clients think about themselves; and (3) on the way therapists act towards clients. The authors briefly illustrate this exercise with the example of a student 'discussing the effects of the DSM label of anorexia on herself and her client. She discovered that it put her in a position where she, in effect, was controlling the client (a problem she was working hard to get the girl's parents to stop). She also imagined that it may have made her client feel incompetent and thus add to the problem. When the student further mapped out the effects of the pattern, which she constructed as criticism and incompetence, she was startled to see her own participation in it. When social discourse in the form of gender specifications for women (e.g. competency = thinness) was seen as the problem, she could relate from her own experience as a woman to the experience of her client. Now the client's desperation and her efforts to starve herself made sense' (Dickerson and Zimmerman, 1995, p. 41). Such a social constructionist perspective makes us aware that by putting a label on a condition, we turn it into a diagnosis, but perhaps lose the potential to understand it. This applies particularly to a culture-bound problem like an eating disorder (Vandereycken and Hoek, 1993).

ATTITUDES AND REACTIONS

An eating disorder may induce quite opposite reactions in clinicians: their therapeutic appetite may be either stimulated or suppressed. Faced with anorectic or bulimic patients some clinicians do not consider that they are dealing with a disorder worthy of professional care. They feel bored, angry, or even disgusted by these patients who, directly or indirectly, receive the message they already get from their social surroundings: their behaviour is incomprehensible, stupid and selfish; born out of vanity or envy their eating pattern has deteriorated because of stubbornness (anorexia) or lack of willpower (bulimia). A variant of such a rejecting attitude may be seen in clinicians, particularly psychiatrists or psychologists, who ignore, minimise, or even trivialise the eating disorder because the real issue is supposed to be something else. This attitude is often reflected by the parents, who seek a pathological secret that accounts for the disorder. Indeed, secrets there may be but they are only part of the complex process (Beumont, Russell and Touyz, 1993). At the other extreme are the therapists who feel strongly tempted to tackle the disturbed eating. They immediately want to act, to solve, to rescue: get the bingeing under control, stop the vomiting, make the patient gain or lose weight, send her to the hospital.... Pushed by a need to act, these therapists put all their efforts into controlling the symptoms rather than trying to discern what they express for the patients (Gutwill, 1994a).

Studying the emotional reactions of medical residents, Brotman, Stern and Herzog (1984) found that anorexia nervosa patients tend to generate more anger, stress and helplessness than do diabetic and obese patients. Compared to their colleagues in medicine and paediatrics, psychiatric residents reported more negative affects and a higher awareness that their dysphoric reactions affected the quality of care they delivered to anorectic patients. Fleming and Szmukler (1992) studied the attitudes of the medical and nursing staff within a large Australian teaching hospital. Patients with eating disorders were less liked than schizophrenic patients, and were seen to bear responsibility for causing their illness almost to the same degree as recurrent overdose takers.

Anorexia nervosa patients often evoke mistrust and even hostility in physicians who regard them as overprivileged manipulators and imposters because they have no genuine illness, deliberately harm themselves, and refuse to cooperate in treatment. The tactics that anorectic patients may display – from lying about food intake to manipulation of weight – are better regarded as strategies of self-defence rather than simply deceptions. For them it is a question of psychological survival and being-in-control, otherwise life becomes too threatening to endure (Vandereycken, 1993). The anorectic patients' desire for control relates both to the relationship with themselves (intra-active control) and with others (interactive control). Experienced therapists realise that this issue of control lies at the heart of the treatment process (Jarman, Smith and Walsh, 1997).

Resistance – any attitude, behaviour or feeling that opposes change – is part of every psychotherapeutic process. In the case of eating disorders it may take many forms, leading to varying reactions on the part of the clinician. Anorectic patients are often perceived as difficult: untrustworthy, obstinate, demanding, bothersome, manipulative, and likely to polarise family members and therapists (Tinker and Ramer, 1983). However, neither the punitive approach of sanctioning the negativism of the stubborn patient, nor the acceptance of her unrealistic statements about normality, will increase the patient's confidence. The cachectic condition evokes feelings of sympathy, worry and willingness to help. But soon the script of 'poor girl and caring rescuer' may change into that of 'naughty girl and angry doctor' (Vandereycken, 1993). The lack of cooperation, the disappointment caused by attempts at deception, and the patient's stubbornness and perceived arrogance may lead to anger and rejection (Cohen, 1978). Almost automatically the anorectic patient's behaviour and attitudes arouse tendencies to counteract them, whether through indulgence or punishment. Driven into a corner, the clinician is tempted to react as a superparent with covert displays of authoritarian power or superior knowledge, both towards the patient and to the real parents 'who did it all wrong' (Vandereycken, Kog and Vanderlinden, 1989). Feelings of aggression may also be disguised as therapeutic pessimism and/or the use of coercive methods, ranging from unnecessary hospitalisation to unnecessary tube feeding. In this way the struggle with the patient about food and weight – the *battle for control* – becomes a re-enactment of intrafamilial conflicts and reflects the frustration of the clinician.

Instead of looking at the treatment as a continuing battle, it is more constructive to view the therapeutic process as a series of crises. Analysing the kind of change of which the patient is afraid at each period of crisis will probably be more fruitful than searching for powerful tactics or counterstrategies to tackle resistance. In the latter instance, the protagonists are acting on an antitherapeutic battlefield! The anorectic patient's denial of being ill, the secretiveness of her eating habits, and her pseudo-happy attitude toward life must be viewed as a camouflage for helplessness and lack of basic trust. Resistance and lack of motivation should not be seen as oppositional behaviour, but rather as a reflection of a deep fear of change. The crux of the interaction is that we must trust eating-disordered patients if they are to trust us (Vandereycken and Meermann, 1987). Unfortunately, however, the health care professional's stance often appears to be quite ambivalent, if not contradictory. Nurses on an inpatient unit, for example, face the conflict between forming a trusting relationship with the anorectic patient while simultaneously showing distrust in respect to her behaviour by supervising meals and daily activities (Jarman, Smith and Walsh, 1997). It is in the resolution of this ambivalence of ideas that the skills of the true professional are displayed.

PERSONAL FEELINGS

The clinicians' behaviour is often similar to that of those surrounding the patient in her daily life. In many cases, however, the clinician's reaction is linked to some personal characteristic and may be described as a form of countertransference. This term belongs to a particular frame of reference (psychoanalysis or psychodynamic therapy; see chapter by Zerbe), but has been used in so many different settings that it is best to specify what exactly is meant by it. Each therapist may show a wide variety of emotional reactions within the treatment context (Vandereycken, 1993):

1. an affective response to the patient's feelings towards the therapist which reflect the patient's relationship with significant persons in his/her life (the patient's transference);
2. feelings based on the therapist's own prior life history and relationships with significant figures (unresolved intrapsychic and interpersonal problems);
3. the therapist's empathic response or sensitivity to the patient's distress;
4. common or characteristic reactions of the therapist in a personal encounter (eg sympathy, antipathy);
5. accidental or temporal reactions arising from particular situations or life events (not related to the therapy) with which the therapist has been recently confronted.

With this expanding notion of countertransference there comes a shift from the belief that it is necessarily something that obscures, to the recognition that it may also be something that illuminates the therapeutic process. According to Susan Gutwill (1994a), this reflects 'a democratization and feminization of the therapeutic profession'. Within the shared interactive reality of psychotherapy, patient and therapist evoke aspects of their own relational worlds, which for each is embedded in a larger sociocultural world. The therapist should always seek to be aware of the impact of these influences (e.g. gender, class, race, religion). Working with eating disorder patients requires a specially critical examination of the 'cultural countertransference', of the effect of cultural notions about eating and the ideal female body on the therapist as well as on the patient (Gutwill, 1994a).

Particularly in female clinicians, own body experiences may obstruct working with eating-disordered patients (Rabinor, 1995). Identification processes or projective mechanisms occur quite frequently in female therapists (Piran and Jasper, 1993; Steiner-Adair, 1991), as Kathryn Zerbe recognised in her own case: 'One savvy resident I supervised asked me if working with eating disorder patients had made me more aware of my own body image and size. At first I hastened to deny this interpretation. However, on reflection during the next few days, I realized that over the course of several months I had begun an exercise program and diet regimen on my own that was totally unlike my prior behaviour. The assumption that I had simply aspired to more healthful living was incorrect. Working with eating disorder patients had made me more cognizant of my own physique' (Zerbe, 1993, p. 173).

Since eating disorders occur primarily in women, the gender of the clinician can have a substantial impact on the form and content of the health care (see chapter by Katzman and Waller). In a large survey of American psychiatrists, women had a greater average number of patients with eating disorders in their caseloads than did men (Dial et al., 1994). Though this difference might be due to the fact that the female respondents were more likely to have taken a residency or fellowship in child or adolescent psychiatry, at every large conference on eating disorders one notices that the majority of attendants are women. Clearly female health care professionals feel more attracted to work with eating disordered patients. However, whether female therapists are actually better therapists for these patients than their male colleagues remains unproven (see Köpp, 1994, versus Stockwell and Dolan, 1994). Less than a third of the American therapists responding on a survey (23 per cent of the men, 35 per cent of the women) believed that female therapists are better at treating patients with eating disorders (Burket and Schramm, 1995). No outcome study has shown that therapist gender is a major determinant of the success of psychotherapy. Some may argue that therapists are better able to deal with gender-related issues when they are aware of them from their own prior experience – problems of body experience and sexuality, ambivalence about gender identity, the relationship with mother, and the need for a role model (Frankenburg, 1984; Wooley, 1991, 1994; Zunino, Agoos and Davis, 1991). But others may suggest that a degree of personal insulation allows the therapist greater objectivity. Indeed, this sort of argument in relation to doctors generally goes back to antiquity, and was raised in Plato's Republic! Since little has been written on male therapists' experiences (e.g. Kopp, 1994; Levine, 1994), McVoy's personal chapter in this volume is uniquely revealing.

ETHICAL AND LEGAL QUESTIONS

Fundamental to the management of any patient, but particularly perhaps of the anorexia nervosa sufferer, are two potentially conflicting responsibilities: the responsibility to treat the patient's illness effectively, and the responsibility to respect the patient's autonomy, her wishes and her personal values (Russell, 1995).

Eating disorder patients confront us with difficult ethical issues concerning informed consent, freedom of choice, and autonomy (Strasser and Giles, 1988). It has been suggested that the crucial issues of power and control inherent to the treatment situation should be negotiated in a contracting process between therapist and patient (Brown, 1993). However, the fundamental discussion of this matter, as illustrated in the chapters by Dolan and Rathner, centres around the judgment of the patient's *competence* (see also Dresser, 1984a+b, versus Fost, 1984). The right to refuse treatment in patients may create a profound dilemma that has to be evaluated and solved within the context of each individual: negative effects may be engendered when involuntary treatment is imposed, but what are the risks of an untreated eating disorder which bears the potential of chronic morbidity and even mortality (Goldner, 1989)? Up to now we have no solid data from controlled trials to answer these questions, and hence we are left with anecdotal accounts showing that compulsory treatment can be both an act of violation and of compassion (see, e.g. Lehmkuhl and Schmidt, 1986; Tiller, Schmidt and Treasure, 1993). By comparing the ideas of Griffiths and Russell with Rathner's the reader of this book can see how competent clinicians may hold opposite views on the ultimate implications of professional care for these patients. Griffiths and Russell's experience illustrates how difficult it is to study the issue objectively. There are legal restraints that are relevant in this context.

There is much diversity among various legislatures relating to the treatment of anorexia nervosa patients, as Griffiths and Russell describe in their chapter in this volume. In the State of New South Wales in Australia, the current Mental Health Act does not accept anorexia nervosa as a mental illness in the meaning of the Act. Some years ago this interpretation was confirmed by a decision in the Supreme Court, and a severely emaciated, resistant patient (J—) was discharged despite the protests of her doctors and of her family. This unfortunate young woman died some years later as a direct result of her undernutrition, but of course one can never know whether a period of enforced treatment would have altered this outcome. It is not that she ever fell out of treatment. The girl's sister, who was a child at the time of her death, recently came to see one of the authors to discuss her own reactions to her sister's tragedy, and said that the one thing that gave J— some comfort in the hell that was her anorexia nervosa was the knowledge that, despite all the arguments, all the failed attempts of treatment, her therapist had never given up on her. J—'s sister was grateful for that. It was some comfort for the therapist to know that, although unable to halt the inexorable progress of her illness, he had given his patient at least one thing of value.

In *Therapists' Dilemmas*, Dryden (1985) described an interview with London psychologist Fay Fransella. She asked her whether anorectic patients are 'free enough from emotional disturbance to make a decision that might be in their best interest'. Using Kelly's personal construct theory as framework, Fransella responded: 'In a way, these young people are personally "stuck", because they can't see outside their current constricted view of the world. It could therefore be argued that it is a good thing to try and give them an opportunity to see outside of it. But if you succeed in helping them see an alternative way of construing the world other than through thinness, and they then relapse, you are in an even worse situation. *They have seen the outside world and have decided that it is not as good as their present one* – so they return to the old familiar one where it is uncomfortable but safe' (Dryden, 1985, p. 129; italics added). Most therapists are probably able to recall patients whose stories illustrate this danger.

A decision to withhold further medical treatment does sometimes become an issue in the treatment of a patient with anorexia nervosa. At other times, it is forced on clinicians by the provisions of laws governing their ability to insist on treatment for their patients. A view expressed by one of the authors in a debate that focussed on such a patient some years ago is still pertinent: to speak of enforced treatment of anorexia nervosa is misleading. True therapy necessarily involves the patient's co-operation. At best, the fact of enforcement may help the patient abandon her non-compliance and begin to work with the therapist. At worst, it merely improves the patient's nutritional status, but at the cost of increased resentment and loss of trust (Mitchell et al., 1988). It is of interest to note what happened to the patient who was the subject of this debate. Some years after the paper was published, she returned to see one of the authors. Once freed of the constraint to accept treatment, she had carefully re-evaluated her own life and what she wanted from it – and made the decision to get better, which she had achieved on her own.

The decision to withhold treatment may become one of *passive euthanasia or palliative care*, as the authors, in common with many other clinicians, have become only too painfully aware. Many of us have been forced to face the same dilemmas as those recorded in the following case histories (see also Ramsay and Treasure, 1996). O'Neill and coworkers (1994), from Sheffield, UK, have reported on a 24-year-old woman who had anorexia since the age of 16. After several hospital admissions, the multidisciplinary team regarded her as incurable. The patient was then transferred to a hospice and managed symptomatically for pain due to a complication of her osteoporosis. She died within a week of admission. The authors conclude that this is an example in which a good standard of palliative care has been generalised to patients other than those with cancer. A similar case was reported in Canada (Hébert and Weingarten, 1994). A 22-year-old woman with an eight year history of anorexia nervosa with numerous hospitalisations and every known form of treatments was admitted in a state of extreme emaciation and cardiovascular collapse. As before, she resisted every effort directed at weight gain and pulled out the infusion line (as she had done in the past with nasogastric tubes). After a discussion with the ethics committee and the patient's parents, the physicians decided not to start further treatment and the patient died the next day. In their conclusion, the authors state: 'Forced feeding in anorexia nervosa is usually appropriate if patients are in danger of imminent death by inanition, but when a life of suffering is sustained only by more and more aggressive measures it may be appropriate to withdraw life-saving nutritional support' (Hébert and Weingarten, 1991, p. 144). In the debate on this case the question was raised 'whether the values of nutrition expressed by an anorexic patient can ever by the basis of competent decisions' (Kluge, 1991, p. 1123). Does this imply that compulsory treatment should be continued until she is again competent? How can we ever know?

The issue of *active euthanasia* is the most dramatic instance of the conflict between the obligation to treat and that to accede to the patient's wishes, calling for the doctor to turn aside from the precepts of the Hippocratic oath and to help the patient deliberately end his or her own life. In some legislatures, such as in the Netherlands, euthanasia has been accepted as part of the medical armamentarium, in others, such as Australia, it remains the subject of controversy and profound disagreement (Editorial, 1997). Those opposed to euthanasia argue from religious and moral grounds, citing the inviolability of human life, and warn of the danger that the acceptance of euthanasia could lead to abuse, whereby lives are sacrificed to interests other than those of the patients (van den Berg, 1978). The shameful endorsement of the eugenics policy by many previously respected colleagues in Nazi Germany 50 years ago (Beumont, 1992) is reason enough to remain genuinely concerned that such distortions are possible.

Even among those who accept that euthanasia may at times be an appropriate response, there is much disagreement as to when it is appropriate. There is little doubt that Sigmund Freud's physician deliberately ended his patient's life by an overdose, in response to his request, and many would applaud the humane action of a wise doctor in his treatment of an old man with a long history of intolerable pain and a mature judgement as to his own good (Ellard, 1989). However, the same clinicians might well be more cautious in condoning the deliberate killing of a patient with intractable depression, schizophrenia or obsessive compulsive disorder (Ogilvie et al., 1994). Because of the controversy which surrounds it, the true extent of euthanasia is unclear. A recent study reports that almost a third of all Australian deaths are preceded by a medical decision explicitly intended to end the patient's life (Kuhse et al., 1997), a rate of unofficial euthanasia apparently higher even than in the Netherlands, where the law officially permits it. However, this study has been severely criticized on methodological grounds.

On 31 October 1990, a Dutch physician gave a lethal potion of 8 gram secobarbital to a 25 year old woman suffering from anorexia nervosa for more than 15 years. In the presence of the physician, a priest, and her parents, she drank it herself, fell asleep, and died about one hour later. The doctor had followed all the official rules concerning euthanasia in the Netherlands (Huyse and van Tilburg, 1993). Nevertheless the physician had to appear before the Court because the patient was a young person with a 'mental illness'. In fact, the Dutch Department of Justice used it as a test case to make official a set of legal rules in similar cases of 'physician-assisted suicide' (Spreeuwenberg and Kastelein, 1992; Vermeulen, 1992). The issue remains highly controversial, not only with respect to basic attitudes about euthanasia, but also because of widely differing opinions about crucial questions, such as: when has an illness like anorexia nervosa become intractable, and the cause of desperate and unbearable suffering? And does the mental state of the anorectic patient allow him/her to make such a decision in all consciousness and full freedom?

THE FAMILY AND OTHER HEALTH PROFESSIONALS

As clinicians, we are aware of the deleterious effects of inconsistency in parents and other relatives on the course of our patients' illnesses, and we exhort them to be united in their response. Lack of unity may arise from basic dysfunction within the marriage, but it is just as likely to be the result of the great stresses that the illness imposes on all members of an afflicted family (Vandereycken, Kog and Vanderlinden, 1989). Indeed, it is extremely difficult for a family to function well when one of its members is obstinately engaged in self-destructive behaviour for motives which the rest find difficult to understand.

The relations between patient, family, and therapeutic team, are highly susceptible to triangulation. Even the most loving and best intended of parents become frustrated by the patient's unwillingness or inability to rectify her behaviour, and such frustration leads to an ambivalent conjunction of desperate concern and angry response. When forced to turn over the care of their child to someone else, their gratitude for the help they receive is mingled with guilt at having failed themselves, and resentment at surrendering control. From the therapist's stance, on the other hand, it is all too easy to trace the patient's psychological difficulties back to her parents' influences, or to condemn the parents' attempts to deal with the illness as excessively coercive. The patient may soon become aware of this divisiveness, and manipulate both parties so as to avoid treatment. If for no other reason than to prevent this development, the role of family therapy that Lackstrom and Woodside describe in their chapter appears crucial to the treatment of younger patients.

A similar divisiveness among the therapists involved in her treatment may also be disastrous for the patient's welfare. And yet there are many reasons why it is difficult to maintain consistency in therapy. Because anorexia nervosa is a multifactorial disorder, optimal management entails a multidisciplinary approach. Psychiatrists, psychologists, physicians, family doctors, nurses, dietitians, family therapists and occupational therapists all bring their own special skills and ideologies to the treatment, and often there are genuine differences in approach. A team functions best when there is no acrimonious dispute about ownership of the patient, when all therapists are able to make their special contribution, but a unity of purpose is maintained, and when there is a clear delineation of the lines of responsibility.

More difficult are the problems that may arise with practitioners outside the core team, such as a consultant physician who wants to pursue further unnecessary physical investigations, or a legal guardian or childcare officer whose legitimate concerns for protecting human rights are manipulated by the patient in her attempts to avoid treatment. As already stated, in New South Wales (Australia) one can make use of the provisions of guardianship legislation rather than the mental health laws if necessary for the treatment of anorexia nervosa patients. The problems that may arise are a function of the interactions between the appointed public guardian, the patient, and the treating team. Unfortunately, because of the intractability of the illness, some treatment regimes have been excessively restrictive and punitive, and these have been publicized widely by the media. The patient's legal guardian is likely to be suspicious of any therapeutic intervention that appears coercive, and this brings into sharp focus the fact that treatment almost always contains an element of coercion. Some patients bluntly refuse treatment, but more frequently they want treatment only on their own terms: treatment without restriction of physical activity, although their state of undernutrition and overwhelming drive to exercise imperil their lives; treatment without alteration of diet, although the energy content of the Vegan foods they will accept is so low that nutritional restoration becomes impossible; even treatment without gaining weight, claiming the right to be as thin as they like and denying that thinness in itself is a health problem. When the treatment team refuses to condone these refusals, the patient may turn to her guardian for help in persuading the therapists that treatment should be undertaken within such limitations. To do so inevitably leads to failure, and hence some patients are made untreatable by those who are seeking to protect them. We recall several instances where the reasoning of the clinicians, and the entreaties of the patients' families, were unable to overcome the legal guardian's rigid defence of her client's rights, with dire consequences for the patient.

Treatment for serious eating disorders may last many years (Hamburg, 1996) and still long-term outcomes remain difficult to predict (Herzog, Deter and Vandereycken, 1992). So, how long should one go on with treatment trials? When does the disorder become chronic or recalcitrant (Yager, 1991)? What should we do for those patients who have chosen a life as an abstainer or a bulimic (Hall, 1982)? And what exactly do we mean by recovery? Perhaps only a minority of patients fully recover from their illness (Windauer et al., 1993).

The use of electroconvulsive therapy has been proposed for intractable anorexia nervosa (Ferguson, 1993). According to an American court, a committed patient cannot be forced to undergo an intrusive psychiatric treatment like electroshock or psychosurgery without a hearing. However, in the case of a committed anorexia nervosa patient, a court ruled that tube feeding was not an intrusive procedure (Hughes, Eckert and McManus 1985).

However, committed or not, anorectic patients may experience tube feeding as a kind of rape (Meyer and Otte, 1970) and for those who have been physically or sexually abused in the past, it is more than likely to be experienced as an abuse re-enactment (Gutwill, 1994b). Moreover, other kinds of medical procedures can also be psychologically traumatic (Shopper, 1995). What in the eyes of most outsiders would look like minor or ordinary procedures might be experienced by the patient as intrusive, humiliating, frightening, disgusting, offensive, or infantilising. For example, putting an eating disorder patient in her underwear on the scales is not necessarily an instance of neutral, objective measurement. For the patient it may be an act of forced exhibition.

A common source of friction between the clinician, the patient, and her family is the implementation of a *behavioural therapy programme*. Even the renowned Hilde Bruch was fiercely critical of behavioural programmes, claiming that they were ultimately countertherapeutic, although unable to suggest alternative ways in which the patient's life-threatening food refusal might be overcome (Bruch, 1987). Despite claims that these are reward programmes rather than punishment programmes, they are inevitably seen as punitive and coercive. Undoubtedly, they do contain such elements, but over the last two decades much has been done to make programmes less offensive and more accommodating of the patient's needs and wishes (Touyz et al., 1984). In this volume, Touyz describes how behavioural interventions have evolved to become more humane but equally effective. It is interesting that the majority of the patients for whom these programmes were prescribed found them helpful, and that their major complaint about being on a programme was that of boredom (Griffiths et al., 1998). It is now not unusual for our patients to ask to be placed on a programme before we suggest it, in order to hasten recovery and shorten hospital stay.

One of the most common beliefs of the patient's relatives is that there must be some *secret reason* behind her illness, and this view is fostered by inexperienced therapists who do not understand the nature of anorexia nervosa and who insist on searching for and treating an underlying psychopathology without paying any attention to the eating disorder itself. Indeed, a pathological secret may well be present, but its relationship to the eating disorder is not necessarily direct (Beumont, Russell and Touyz, 1995). Just as it is important to deal with the addiction and with the factors sustaining the drinking of an alcoholic, so it is important that in treating the anorectic patient, the anorexia nervosa is directly addressed. Unfortunately, some therapists are unwilling to do this. Frustrated by their inability to change the patient's implacable attitudes and rigid behaviour, they abandon the attempt altogether, focus entirely on the presumed underlying psychological problems (albeit that these problems are just as likely to be the result of the illness and its undernutrition) and even go so far as to ban the topics of weight and eating from the therapy sessions. Nor is this tendency confined to psychotherapists. Conventional psychiatrists may focus entirely on the patient's dysthymia, treating her depression in the false belief that the anorexia will take care of itself (Beumont, 1995).

It is optimal that the person directing management is willing and able to deal with all aspects of this complex illness. Handing over the *medical management* to a physician is far short of ideal. The medical complications of anorexia nervosa are not only serious and complex, but they also have features that are specific for the illness, the results of the interaction of the various pathogenetic influences of undernutrition, malnutrition, electrolyte disturbance, deficiencies in neurotransmitters and endocrine dysfunctions (Beumont, Russell and Touyz, 1993). The nature of the nutritional disturbance is unique, a process which starts with energy deficiency and only later leads to protein deficiency and malnutrition, in contrast to the protein-calorie malnutrition of the Third World. It is also different to the malnutrition that results from illnesses such as Crohn's Disease. Although protein depletion occurs in anorectic patients, it may be completely reversed with nutritional restoration because there is no underlying physical pathology (Russell et al., 1994).

In our experience, even highly competent physicians manage the physical manifestations of anorexia nervosa poorly. Some try to correct the undernutrition too rapidly, which may lead to the dramatic exposure of severe electrolyte disturbances and consequent cardiac and other complications (Beumont and Large, 1991). Another common error is failure to understand the essentially compensatory nature of many of the manifestations of the illness, particularly such endocrine changes as the functional hypothyroidism and raised levels of growth hormone (Beumont,

1984). Correcting the hypothyroidism merely acts to block the body's attempt to conserve energy. Or the physician may seek to investigate further, when expert knowledge of the illness would make this unnecessary. Conversely, he may wrongly ascribe features to the illness that are not related to it. We recall the physician who erroneously attributed raised prolactin levels to the endocrine disturbance of undernutrition and missed a hypothalamic tumour. Because patients are frequently obsessional exercisers, the physician may undervalue their extreme bradycardia that in fact results from decreased noradrenergic turnover, and fail to assess properly the risk of increased cardiac demand on a system which is already compromised (Beumont et al., 1996). Perhaps most damaging is the physician's inability to accept that anorexia nervosa is a chronic illness, so that he eventually gives up, allowing the patient to progress with chronic complications such as osteopenia. For all these reasons, it is better that the medical management of the anorectic patient be under the control of a doctor who fully understands all aspects of the illness.

Difficulties in interaction with non-medical members of the therapy team may also be difficult to avoid. Just as the dynamic-focussed therapist may seek to ignore the behavioural manifestations of the illness, so may the behaviouralist psychologist concentrate attention on the modification of the abnormal behaviour, to the exclusion of awareness of the person who is suffering from the illness. Some conflicts based on professional priorities appear inevitable. For instance, our team in Sydney makes much use of professional nutritionists, specifically trained to deal with dieting or eating disorder patients. Their professional objective is to get the patient back to normal eating, that is to eating a balanced and variable diet, composed of appropriate quantities of all food categories and including adequate amounts of fats and proteins as well as of carbohydrates (Beumont and Touyz, 1995). Patients often argue that they are willing to regain weight, but not to eat what they erroneously consider as unhealthy foods. Their families, and their medical and psychological therapists, with their own inadequate knowledge of nutritional matters (Abraham et al., 1981), often condone such resistance and hence deny the patient an opportunity to return to a truly normal eating pattern.

Nurses are at the forefront of the treatment of the anorectic in-patient. They have to implement the treatment regimes decided

by the therapists, and are likely to bear the brunt of the patients'
and their relatives' frustration with the restrictions that need to be
imposed. This places a major responsibility on the director of the
programme: he or she must support the nurses in their difficult
task, but at the same time avoid creating the impression of a
monolithic defence. Every complaint should be listened to atten-
tively, and handled with sense and sensitivity (Beumont, Russell
and Touyz, 1995). A difficulty for the individual nurse is the
patient who confides some secret to her: a story of sexual abuse or
perhaps the intention to self-harm. Here the nurse needs support
and counselling so as to be able to tell the patient that there are
some things she cannot keep confidential because they are too
important, and even, if necessary, refuse to accept hearing something if told to her on the condition of confidentiality. In such
instances, her own right to make appropriate use of the information would be denied.

SUPPLY AND DEMAND

In New South Wales (Beumont, Kopec-Schrader and Lennerts,
1995), and in New Zealand (McKenzie and Joyce, 1992), attempts
have been made to fully describe the extent of in-patient services
for anorexia nervosa patients that are available. Other than these,
there has been little effort to comprehensively describe the
facilities for treating these patients. However, most would agree
that over the last 10–15 years there has been an increased demand
for eating disorder care (Turnbull et al., 1996). In private medicine
there is a growing competition between specialist clinics; it suffices
to read the advertisements in a newspaper or look at the yellow
pages of the phone directory in a big city. In Germany, for
example, the number of specialised centres (with insurance coverage) has increased to the point of oversaturation. In the Netherlands and Norway, the government has stimulated the
improvement of organised care for eating disorders. The rather
conservative policy of the National Health Service in the UK
resulted in a shortage and uneven distribution of specialist centres
(Robinson, 1993). However, making a virtue of need, it has also
led to some interesting experiments with minimally trained therapists and guided self-help (Treasure, Troop and Ward, 1996). Of
course, some professionals may consider this development an

undesirable attempt to subvert their expertise, while others try to incorporate self-help ideas in their therapeutic approach (see, e.g. Johnson and Taylor, 1996). Whatever argument one endorses, the care of eating disorders can no longer be discussed on a purely academic level. It becomes a matter of market forces which differ from one country to another (see chapter by Robinson et al. and Andersen's chapter).

The last decade saw a growing demand for specialised care clashing with economic forces. The average duration of stay for anorectic patients is long, even in competent centres. In Australia, a private health insurance company has recently reported that anorexia nervosa has become one of the most expensive illnesses to treat (Farr, 1997). Increasing limitations of health care coverage in the USA have led to serious restrictions of third-party payment for both outpatient and inpatient care of psychiatric conditions to the point that an American policy of managed care is being looked upon as a strait-jacket for psychotherapists (Wooley, 1993). No doubt, American patients with a psychiatric condition like an eating disorder face considerably reduced treatment possibilities. In the case of anorexia nervosa this has resulted in shorter hospital stays (Kaye, Enright and Lesser, 1988; Silber, 1994), implying that these patients are often discharged while still underweight which, in turn, is linked to a serious risk of relapse (Baran, Weltzin and Kaye, 1995). Fortunately, in the first US court cases on this matter disputes over insurance coverage of costs for inpatient treatment of anorexia nervosa were resolved in favour of the patients (Andersen, 1996). Nevertheless, the direction into which this managed care system is developing seems to involve rather complex triangular interactions between patient/family, health care providers and insurance companies (Zerbe, 1996). Referring to eating disorders, for example, it has been suggested: 'By helping patients become their own advocates, and offering concrete suggestions for asserting the right to adequate health care, patients can learn to assume some measure of control over their situations' (Kaye, Kaplan and Zucker, 1996, p. 801; see also Kaye, 1995). But what if patients are not willing to ask for the health care they need, as is often the case in acute anorexia nervosa? Should the family take the role of advocate in this matter? And how will clinicians cope with this additional burden? In Australia, clinicians acted decisively to influence the Federal Government to make special provisions for extended duration of psychotherapy for patients with anorexia nervosa, as well as with some other psychiatric illnesses, but this has not affected the serious shortfall in hospital placements for these patients.

PROFESSIONALS AT RISK

Stress and burnout are problems for mental health professionals. Not only do they affect their occupational performance but also their job satisfaction and ultimately their own health (Carson and Fagin, 1996). It has been suggested that therapists of eating-disordered patients are more at risk to develop burnout (Rubel, 1986), although this has not been demonstrated.

In a study of American women medical students, about 16 per cent were found to show disordered eating habits (Hamburg and Herzog, 1985). The significance of this data is difficult to gauge in the absence of information about other student groups. One might expect that female dietitians would be more at risk for developing an eating disorder (Morgan and Mayberry, 1983; Kinzl et al., 1997), but the few comparative studies have produced rather equivocal results (Howat et al., 1993; Johnston and Christopher, 1991; Reinstein et al., 1992). Anyway, the interpretation of the findings will always be controversial because the choice of a profession can be influenced by pre-existing problems or some form of predisposition.

Sansone, Fine and Chew (1988) studied the reactions of newly hired nurses after a 13-month period. Compared to their colleagues on other units, the nurses on the in-patient eating disorders unit showed no increased risk of eating disorder symptoms, body weight changes, or mood disturbances. In a survey by Shisslak, Gray and Crago (1989), 28 per cent of a heterogeneous group of health care professionals (the vast majority females), who spend an average of eleven hours per week working in the area of eating disorders, reported to be moderately to greatly affected by their work. They perceived themselves as more aware of food, physical condition, appearance and feelings about their body. Only 30 per cent of this subgroup was classified as normal eaters; the rest – about 20 per cent of the original sample – admitted they had experienced or still suffered from anorectic or bulimic symptoms. It is probably this personal experience that explains their being sensitised to these issues, since the length of professional experience in the field was not significantly related to the perception of being affected by the work. This might have implications for the selection and training of professionals working with eating-disordered patients. Some attention should be paid to this issue in the supervision of health care workers.

As described by some experts in the field (Buhl, 1993; Sargent, 1992; Yager and Edelstein, 1987), the knowledge base and skills required for the treatment of eating disorders are extensive. The risk of iatrogenesis and therapist errors is considerable (Garner, 1985; Thompson and Sherman, 1989). Because of the complexity of the disorders and the many interpersonal difficulties to be expected within the treatment process, trainees need to be closely supervised (Hamburg and Herzog, 1990; Lenihan and Kirk, 1992). Furthermore, the reason for choosing to work in this area should be addressed honestly. For some it might be an attempt to escape from their own history of an eating disorder (Brown, 1991), and that may pose additional problems for both therapist and patient.

EPILOGUE

Colahan (1995) described her experience working as a research therapist on a series of eating disorder treatment trials at the Maudsley Hospital in London. She learnt to make creative use of what appeared to be therapeutic restrictions. Paradoxical as it may seem, she found that having her clinical freedom curtailed taught her to become more flexible: 'Working under constraints of a control trial, I was forced constantly to reassess my work, never become complacent or stuck in a rigid unchanging way of working, and to think around issues that ordinarily I would not necessarily have encountered, such as limited time therapy, weight charts, keeping difficult patients in therapy and out of hospital, complying with supervisors' quirks and dealing with researchers' demands' (Colahan, 1995, p. 93). We would be pleased indeed if the reading of this book were to induce a similar learning experience. However, even more important, we hope that our readers will agree that, as therapists, 'we must learn the virtue of patience [until our patients], freed from the shackles of anorexia or bulimia nervosa can [learn to be] their own valuable and unique selves, at which point we ... should quietly withdraw and leave them to it'

(Beumont, Russell and Touyz, 1995). Perhaps the essential precondition for being a good therapist for these seriously ill, difficult but fascinating patients is humility.

REFERENCES

Abraham, S.F., Beumont, P.J.V., Booth, A., Rouse, L. and Rogers, J. (1981) 'Nutritional Knowledge Questionnaire, Part Two'. *Medical Journal of Australia*, 14: 39–40.

Andersen, A.E. (1996) 'Third party payment for inpatient treatment of anorexia nervosa'. *Eating Disorders Review*, 7(6): 1–5.

Beumont, P.J.V. (1992) 'Phenomenology and the history of psychiatry'. *Australian and New Zealand Journal of Psychiatry*, 26: 532–45.

——(1984) 'Endocrine function in Magersucht disorders'. In Pirke, K.M. and Ploog, D. (eds) *The Psychobiology of Anorexia Nervosa* (pp. 114–23), Berlin: Springer-Verlag.

——(1995) 'The clinical presentation of anorexia and bulimia nervosa'. In Brownell, K.D. and Fairburn, C.G. (eds) *Eating Disorders and Obesity: A Comprehensive Handbook* (pp. 151–5), New York: Guilford Press.

Beumont, P.J.V., Abraham, S.F., Argall, W.J., George, G.C.W. and Glaun, D.E. (1978) 'The onset of anorexia nervosa'. *Australian and New Zealand Journal of Psychiatry*, 12: 145–9.

Beumont, P.J.V., Barin, E., Lowinger, K. and Touyz, S.W. (1996) 'Cardiac function in dieting disorder patients'. Paper presented at the *Australian Society for Psychiatric Research Meeting*, Newcastle.

Beumont, P.J.V., Kopec-Schrader, E. and Lennerts, W. (1995) 'The treatment of eating disorder patients at a NSW teaching hospital: A comparison with state-wide data'. *Australian and New Zealand Journal of Psychiatry*, 29: 96–103.

Beumont, P.J.V. and Large, M. (1991) 'Hypophosphatemia delirium and cardiac arrhythmia and in anorexia nervosa'. *Medical Journal of Australia*, 155: 519–21.

Beumont, P.J.V., Russell, J.D. and Touyz, S.W. (1993) 'The treatment of anorexia nervosa'. *Lancet*, 341: 1635–40.

Beumont, P.J.V., Russell, J. and Touyz, S.W. (1995). 'Psychological concerns in the maintenance of dieting disorders'. In Szmukler, G., Dare, C. and Treasure, J. (eds) *Handbook of Eating Disorders: Theory, Treatment and Research* (pp. 221–41), London: John Wiley.

Beumont, P.J.V. and Touyz, S.W. (1995) The nutritional management of anorexia and bulimia nervosa. In Brownell, K.D. and Fairburn, C.G.

(eds) *Eating Disorders and Obesity: A Comprehensive Handbook* (pp. 306–12), New York: Guilford Press.

Bhanji, S. (1979) 'Anorexia nervosa: Physicians' and psychiatrists' opinions and practices'. *Journal of Psychosomatic Research*, 23: 7–11.

Brotman, A.W., Stern, T.A. and Herzog, D.B. (1984) 'Emotional reactions of house officers to patients with anorexia nervosa, diabetes, and obesity'. *International Journal of Eating Disorders*, 3(4): 71–7.

Brown, C. (1993) 'Feminist contracting: Power and empowerment in therapy'. In Brown, C. and Jasper, K. (eds) *Consuming passions. Feminist approaches to weight preoccupation and eating disorders* (pp. 176–94), Toronto: Second Story Press.

Bruch, H. (1987) 'Four decades of anorexia nervosa'. In Garner, D. and Garfinkel, P. (eds) *Handbook of Psychotherapy in Anorexia Nervosa and Bulimia* (pp. 7–18), New York: Guilford Press.

Buhl, C. (1993) 'A multiprofessional educational programme on eating disorders for psychiatric health services in Norway'. *European Eating Disorders Review*, 1: 90–9.

Burke, N. and Cohler, B.J. (1992) 'Psychodynamic psychotherapy of eating disorders'. In Brandell, J.R. (ed.) *Countertransference in psychotherapy with children and adolescents* (pp. 163–90), New York: Jason Aronson.

Burket, R.C. and Schramm, L.L. (1995) 'Therapists' attitudes about treating patients with eating disorders'. *Southern Medical Journal*, 88: 813–18.

Chisslak, C.M., Gray, N. and Crago, M. (1989) 'Health care professionals' reactions to working with eating disorder patients'. *International Journal of Eating Disorders*, 8: 689–94.

Cohen, S.I. (1978) 'Hostile interaction in a general hospital ward leading to disturbed behavior and bulimia in anorexia nervosa: Its successful management'. *Postgraduate Medical Journal*, 54: 361–4.

Cohler, B.J. (1977) 'The significance of the therapist's feelings in the treatment of anorexia nervosa'. In Feinstein, S.C. and Giovacchini, P. (eds) *Adolescent psychiatry. Volume V* (pp. 352–86), New York: Jason Aronson.

Colahan, M. (1995) 'Being a therapist in eating disorder treatment trials: Constraints and creativity'. *Journal of Family Therapy*, 17: 79–96.

Dial, T.H., Grimes, P.E., Leibenluft, E. and Pincus, H.A. (1994) 'Sex differences in psychiatrists' practice patterns and incomes'. *American Journal of Psychiatry*, 151: 96–101.

Dickerson, V.C. and Zimmerman, J.L. (1995) 'A constructionist exercise in anti-pathologizing'. *Journal of Systemic Therapies*, 14: 33–45.

Dresser, R. (1984a) 'Feeding the hunger artists: Legal issues in treating anorexia nervosa'. *Wisconsin Law Review*, 2: 297–374.

——(1984b) 'Legal and policy considerations in treatment of anorexia nervosa patients'. *International Journal of Eating Disorders*, 3(4): 43–51.

Dryden, W. (1985) 'Death by starvation: Whose decision? An interview with Fay Fransella'. In Dryden, W. (ed.) *Therapists' dilemmas* (pp. 127–37), London: Harper and Row.

Editorial (1997) 'Honesty at life's end'. *Sydney Herald*, 15 February.

Ellard, J. (1989) *Some Rules for Killing People*. Sydney: Angus and Robertson.

Farr, M. (1997) 'Anorexia care costs more than cancer'. *The Daily Telegraph* (Sydney), 7 April.

Ferguson, J.M. (1993) 'The use of electroconvulsive therapy in patients with intractable anorexia nervosa'. *International Journal of Eating Disorders*, 13: 195–201.

Fleming, J. and Szmukler, G.I. (1992) 'Attitudes of medical professionals towards patients with eating disorders'. *Australian and New Zealand Journal of Psychiatry*, 26: 436–43.

Fost, N. (1984) 'Food for thought: Dresser on anorexia nervosa'. *Wisconsin Law Review*, 2: 375–84.

Frankenburg, F.R. (1984) 'Female therapists in the management of anorexia nervosa'. *International Journal of Eating Disorders*, 3(4): 25–33.

Franko, D.L. and Rolfe, S. (1996) 'Countertransference in the treatment of patients with eating disorders'. *Psychiatry*, 59: 108–16.

Garner, D.M. (1985) 'Iatrogenesis in anorexia nervosa and bulimia nervosa'. *International Journal of Eating Disorders*, 4: 701–26.

Ghadirian, A.M. and Leichner, P. (1990) 'Psychiatric residents' educational experiences and attitudes toward eating disorders'. *Canadian Journal of Psychiatry*, 35: 254–6.

Goldner, E. (1989) 'Treatment refusal in anorexia nervosa'. *International Journal of Eating Disorders*, 8: 297–306.

Griffiths, R., Gross, G., Russell, J., Thornton, C., Beumont P.J.V., Schotte, D. and Touyz, S.W. (1998) 'Perceptions of bed rest by anorexic patients'. *International Journal of Eating Disorders*, 23: 443–7.

Gutwill, S. (1994a) 'Transference and countertransference issues: The impact of social pressures on body image and consciousness'. In Bloom, C., Gitter, A., Gutwill, S., Kogel, L. and Zaphiropoulos, L. *Eating problems. A feminist psychoanalytic treatment model* (pp. 144–71), New York: Basic Books.

——(1994b) 'Transference and countertransference issues: The diet mentality versus attuned eating'. In Bloom, C., Gitter, A., Gutwill, S., Kogel, L. and Zaphiropoulos, L. *Eating problems. A feminist psychoanalytic treatment model* (pp. 172–83) New York: Basic Books.

Hamburg, P. (1996) 'How long is long-term therapy for anorexia nervosa?' In Werne, J. (ed.) *Treating eating disorders* (pp. 71–99), San Francisco: Jossey-Bass.

Hamburg, P. and Herzog, D.B. (1985) 'Studying reports of women medical students on their eating disorders'. *Journal of Medical Education*, 60: 644–6.

Hébert, P.H. and Weingarten, M.A. (1991) 'The ethics of forced feeding in anorexia nervosa'. *Canadian Medical Association Journal*, 144: 141–4.

Herzog, W., Deter, H.C. and Vandereycken, W. (eds) (1992) *The course of eating disorders: Long-term follow-up studies of anorexia and bulimia nervosa*, Berlin-New York: Springer-Verlag.

Hughes, J.R., Eckert, E.D. and McManus, K.M. (1985) 'Tube feeding as a psychiatric procedure' [letter to the editor]. *American Journal of Psychiatry*, 142: 1127–8.

Jarman, M., Smith, J.A. and Walsh, S. (1997) 'The psychological battle for control: A qualitative study of health-care professionals' understandings of the treatment of anorexia nervosa'. *Journal of Community and Applied Social Psychology*, 7: 137–52.

Johnston, C.S. and Christopher, F.S. (1991) 'Anorexic-like behaviors in dietetic majors and other student populations'. *Journal of Nutrition Education*, 23: 148–53.

Kaye, W.H., Enright, A.B. and Lesser, S. (1988) 'Characteristics of eating disorder programs and common problems with third-party providers'. *International Journal of Eating Disorders*, 7: 573–9.

Kleinman, I. (1986) 'Force-feeding: The physician's dilemma'. *Canadian Journal of Psychiatry*, 31: 313–16.

Kluge, E.H. (1991) 'The ethics of forced feeding in anorexia nervosa: A response to Hébert and Weingarten' *Canadian Medical Association Journal*, 144: 1121–4.

Köpp, W. (1994) 'Can women with eating disorders benefit from a male therapist?' In Dolan, B. and Gitzinger, I. (eds) *Why women? Gender issues and eating disorders* (pp. 65–71), London: Athlone.

Kuhse, H., Singer, P., Baum, P., Clark, M. and Richard, M. (1997) 'End-of-life decisions in Australian medical practice'. *Medical Journal of Australia*, 166: 191–6.

Lanceley, C. and Travers, R. (1993) 'Anorexia nervosa: Forced feeding and the law' [letter]. *British Journal of Psychiatry* 162: 835.

Lehmkuhl, G. and Schmidt, M.H. (1986) 'Wie freiwillig kann die Behandlung von jugendlichen Patienten mit Anorexia nervosa sein?' [To what extent can the treatment of young anorexia nervosa patients be voluntary?]. *Psychiatrische Praxis*, 13: 236–41.

Levine, M.P. (1994) 'Beauty myth and the beast: What men can do and be to help prevent eating disorders'. *Eating Disorders*, 2: 101–13.

McKenzie, J.M. and Joyce, P.R. (1992) 'Hospitalization for anorexia nervosa'. *International Journal of Eating Disorders*, 11: 235–41.

Meyer, A. and Otte, H. (1970) 'The semantic differential as a measure of the patients' image of their therapist'. *Psychotherapy and Psychosomatics*, 18: 56–60.

Mitchell, P., Parker, G. and Dwyer, D. (1988) 'The law and a physically-ill patient with anorexia nervosa: Liberty versus paternalism'. *Medical Journal of Australia*, 148: 41–4.

Morgan, G.J. and Mayberry, J.F. (1983) 'Common gastrointestinal diseases and anorexia nervosa in dietitians'. *Public Health*, 97: 166–70.

Murray, S.H., Touyz, S.W. and Beumont, P.J.V. (1996) 'Awareness and perceived influence of body ideals in the media: A comparison of eating disorder patients and the general community'. *Eating Disorders: The Journal of Treatment and Prevention*, 4: 33–46.

Ogilvie, A.D. and Potts, S.G. (1994) Assisted suicide for depression: The slippery slope in action? *British Medical Journal*, 309: 492–3.

O'Neill, J., Crowther, T. and Sampson, G. (1994) 'Anorexia nervosa: Palliative care of terminal psychiatric disease'. *American Journal of Hospice and Palliative Care*, 11: 36–9.

Piran, N. and Jasper, K. (1993) 'Countertransference experiences'. In Brown, C. and Jasper, K. (eds) *Consuming passions. Feminist approaches to weight preoccupation and eating disorders* (pp. 161–75), Toronto: Second Story Press.

Rabinor, J.R. (1995) 'Overcoming body shame: My client, myself'. In Sussman, M.B. (ed.) *A perilous calling: The hazards of psychotherapy practice* (pp. 89–99), New York: John Wiley.

Ramsay, R. and Treasure, J. (1996) 'Treating anorexia nervosa: Psychiatrists have mixed views on use of terminal care for anorexia nervosa' [letter]. *British Medical Journal*, 312: 182.

Reinstein, N., Koszweski, W.M., Chamberlin, B. and Smithjohn, C. (1992) 'Prevalence of eating disorders among dietetics students. Does nutrition education make a difference?' *Journal of the American Dietetic Association*, 92: 949–53.

Rubel, J.B. (1986) 'Burn-out and eating disorders therapists'. In Larocca,

F.E.F. (ed.) *Eating disorders: Effective care and treatment* (pp. 233–46), St. Louis: Ishiyaku EuroAmerica.

Russell, J. (1995) 'Treating anorexia nervosa: Clinical concerns, personal views'. *British Medical Journal*, 311: 584 (with anonymous letters on p. 635).

Russell, J., Allen, B., Mira, M., Stewart, P., Vizzard, J., Arthur, B. and Beumont, P.J.V. (1994) 'Protein repletion and treatment in anorexia nervosa'. *American Journal of Clinical Nutrition*, 59: 98–102.

Sansone, R.A., Fine, M.A. and Chew, R. (1988) 'A longitudinal analysis of the experiences of nursing staff on an inpatient eating disorders unit'. *International Journal of Eating Disorders*, 7: 125–31.

Sargent, J. (1992) 'Teaching housestaff about eating disorders'. *Pediatric Annals*, 21: 720–7.

Spreeuwenberg, C. and Kastelein, W.R. (1992) 'Hulp bij zelfdoding anorexia nervosa-patiënt' [Help with self-killing of anorexia nervosa patient]. *Medisch Contact*, 17: 541–3.

Steiner-Adair, C. (1991) 'New maps of development, new models of therapy: The psychology of women and the treatment of eating disorders'. In Johnson, C.L. (ed.) *Psychodynamic treatment of anorexia nervosa and bulimia* (pp. 225–44), New York: Guilford Press.

Stockwell, R. and Dolan, B. (1994) 'Women therapists for women patients?' In Dolan, B. and Gitzinger, I. (eds) *Why women? Gender issues and eating disorders* (pp. 57–64), London: Athlone.

Strasser, M. and Giles, G. (1988) 'Ethical considerations'. In Scott, D. (ed.) *Anorexia and bulimia nervosa: Practical approaches* (pp. 204–12), London: Croom Helm.

Thompson, R.A. and Sherman, R.T. (1989) 'Therapist errors in treating eating disorders: Relationship and process'. *Psychotherapy*, 26: 62–8.

Tiller, J., Schmidt, U. and Treasure, J. (1993) 'Compulsory treatment for anorexia nervosa: Compassion or coercion?' *British Journal of Psychiatry*, 162: 679–80.

Tinker, D.E. and Ramer, J.C. (1983) 'Anorexia nervosa: Staff subversion of therapy'. *Journal of Adolescent Health Care*, 4: 35–9.

Touyz, S.W., Beumont, P.J.V., Glaun, D., Philips, T. and Cowie, I. (1984) 'A comparison of lenient and strict operant conditioning programme in refeeding patients with anorexia nervosa'. *British Journal of Psychiatry*, 144: 517–20.

van den Berg, J.H. (1978) *Medical Power and Medical Ethics*, New York: W.W. Norton.

Vandereycken, W. (1987) 'The management of patients with anorexia nervosa and bulimia: Basic principles and general guidelines'. In

Beumont, P.J.V., Burrows, G.D. and Casper, R.C. (eds) *Handbook of eating disorders. Part 1: Anorexia and bulimia nervosa* (pp. 235–53), Amsterdam: Elsevier-North Holland.

——(1993) 'Naughty girls and angry doctors: Eating disorder patients and their therapists'. *International Review of Psychiatry*, 5: 13–18.

Vandereycken, W. and Hoek, H.W. (1993) 'Are eating disorders culture-bound syndromes?' In Halmi, K.A. (ed.) *Psychobiology and treatment of anorexia nervosa and bulimia nervosa* (pp. 19–36), Washington, D.C.: American Psychiatric Press.

Vandereycken, W., Kog, E. and Vanderlinden, J. (1989) *The family approach to eating disorders: Assessment and treatment of anorexia nervosa and bulimia*, New York-London: PMA Publishing.

Vandereycken, W. and Meermann, R. (1984) *Anorexia nervosa: A clinician's guide to treatment*, Berlin-New York: Walter de Gruyter.

Vanderlinden, J., Norré, J. and Vandereycken, W. (1992) *A practical guide to the treatment of bulimia nervosa*, New York: Brunner/Mazel.

Vanderlinden, J. and Vandereycken, W. (1997) *Trauma, dissociation, and impulse dyscontrol in eating disorders*, New York: Brunner/Mazel.

Vogler, R.J.M. (1993) *The medicalization of eating: Social control in an eating disorders clinic*. Greenwich (CT)/London: JAI Press.

Whyte, B.L. and Kaczkowski, H. (1983) 'Anorexia nervosa: A study of psychiatrists' and psychologists' opinions and practices'. *International Journal of Eating Disorders*, 2(3): 87–92.

Windauer, U., Lennerts, W., Talbot, P., Touyz, S.W. and Beumont, P.J.V. (1993) 'How well are "cured" anorexia nervosa patients?' *British Journal of Psychiatry*, 163: 195–200.

Wooley, S.C. (1991) 'Uses of countertransference in the treatment of eating disorders: A gender perspective'. In Johnson, C.L. (ed.) *Psychodynamic treatment of anorexia nervosa and bulimia* (pp. 245–94). New York: Guilford Press.

——(1993) 'Managed care and mental health: The silencing of a profession'. *International Journal of Eating Disorders*, 14: 387–401.

——(1994) 'The female therapist as outlaw'. In Fallon, P., Katzman, M.A. and Wooley, S.C. (eds) *Feminist perspectives on eating disorders* (pp. 318–38), New York-London: Guilford Press.

Yager, J. (1991) 'Patients with chronic, recalcitrant eating disorders'. In Yager, J., Gwirtsman, H.E. and Edelstein, C.K. (eds) *Special problems in managing eating disorders* (pp. 205–31), Washington, D.C.: American Psychiatric Press.

Yager, J. and Edelstein, C.K. (1987) 'Training therapists to work with eating disorders patients'. In Beumont, P.J.V., Burrows, G.D. and Casper, R.C. (eds) *Handbook of eating disorders. Part 1: Anorexia and bulimia nervosa* (pp. 379–92), Amsterdam-New York: Elsevier Science.

Zerbe, D.H. (1986) 'Countertransference, resistance and frame management in the psychotherapy of a 15 year old anorexic and her mother'. *Clinical Social Work Journal*, 14: 213–23.

Zerbe, K. (1993) 'Whose body is it anyway? Understanding and treating psychosomatic aspects of eating disorders'. *Bulletin of the Menninger Clinic*, 57: 161–77.

——(1996) 'Extending the frame: Working with managed care to support treatment for a refractory patient'. In Werne, J. (ed.) *Treating eating disorders* (pp. 335–56), San Francisco: Jossey-Bass.

Zunino, N., Agoos, E. and Davis, W.N. (1991) 'The impact of therapist gender on the treatment of bulimic women'. *International Journal of Eating Disorders*, 10: 253–63.

CHAPTER TWO

Knowable secrets: Transference and countertransference manifestations in eating disordered patients

Kathryn J. Zerbe

I have a confession to make. I am a fourth year medical student with a dark secret: bulimia. I am only able to write this because my name does not appear above this article ... I wonder why our profession still draws a distinction between physical and psychological disorders. I wonder why a disorder effecting an estimated 18 per cent of college women in this country is still such a secret. I wonder how many of my classmates have eating disorders or suffer from depression or anxieties they cannot share ... I keep my secret because I am ashamed. I have internalized the societal view that mental illness is a character flaw, and I feel I should be able to control my appetite, lose weight, cease obsessing about my appearance.... My condition remains my secret, shared only with my closest friends. And, when I am asked during residency interviews to name my greatest flaw, I will lie. Anonymous (1995, p. 1395)

Continuing self inquiry, reflecting the therapist's own continuing self-analysis, fosters empathy or counterresonance which makes it possible to bear the often painful and explosive sentiments and wishes from which the analysand seeks flight and from which, in a complimentary manner, the therapist might otherwise take flight.' Burke and Cohler (1992, p. 189)

Secrets are beguiling. As these controvertible perspectives attest, holding onto a secret takes an enormous toll; but the flight from self-exposure and personal knowledge is a deeply ingrained human experience. One of the burdens and rewards of the therapist are the personal confidences that we are entrusted with over the course of treatment. To know what another holds most dear is a powerfully gripping and sacrosanct experience. However, therapists often find themselves responding to the powerful, personal knowledge garnered in the therapeutic process (Burke and Cohler, 1992; Zerbe, 1991, 1993, 1995a) by concealing, restraining, curbing, or otherwise interdicting the flow of disclosure. Helping to make the patient's secrets less shameful, and hence more manageable, by judicious unveiling and listening, is difficult work. As in organization life where one's stature is frequently touted by the hierarchy of confidences one is privy to, so does the influence and potency of the therapeutic relationship intensify when 'painful and explosive sentiments' come to life. In essence, it can be said that an important transferential relationship has been allowed to flower, precipitating a concomitant host of countertransferential reactions on the part of the therapist. Fortunately, over the past forty years there has been a tremendous growth in the psychodynamic literature to help clinicians understand these transference and countertransference reactions (Aktar, 1995; Hunter; 1994; Gabbard, 1989a+b; Gabbard and Wilkinson, 1994).This enables clinicians to have multiple resources available for self-education and to realize they are not alone in their struggles to understand, contain, and eventually interpret and master their responses for the patient's growth and change.

First, however, the therapist must receive validation that these responses are not a sign of treatment gone awry but grist for the therapeutic mill. Participating in workshops, conferences, small group discussions and supervision, and reviewing a significant body of literature on the topics supports the notions that these conundrums are more the norm than an anomaly. Indeed, one of the major contributions of psychodynamic theory in the treatment of eating disorders is that it informs clinicians about the ubiquity of their personal responses and offers strategies about how we might deal with these most vexing problems and arresting secrets (Zerbe, 1987, 1996; Burke and Cohler, 1992).

In this chapter I intend to review the most commonly encountered transference and countertransference paradigms of eating disordered patients and describe a number of tools to help therapists manage their countertransference reactions. The intent is to attenuate the self-vilifying internal criticism and personal vulnerability clinicians experience when treating complicated, recalcitrant eating disordered patients. The therapist is then more likely to be less discouraged and more persistent in working with a significant percentage of these patients who have not responded to the common repertoire of behavioral and psychopharmacological techniques. These patients require a deeper understanding of the meaning of the eating disorder in their lives. For them, anorexia and bulimia have become a way of life. The eating disorder is paradoxically a repugnant secret and a secret entrée into the inner workings of the self.

One of the most important rationales for including a chapter on the management of transference and countertransference reactions in a book about the 'burdens of the therapist' is, indeed, to help the clinician feel less discouraged when dealing with those 30–40 per cent of patients who do not easily respond to treatment, despite improved diagnosis and new treatments (Smith and Lafranboise, 1995; Clinton, 1996; Zerbe, 1993; Zerbe, Marsh, and Coyne, 1992). At least 5–8 per cent of these patients will eventually die, a remarkable mortality rate for a psychiatric illness. This figure is conservative as some of the long-term European studies point to an even greater degree of lethality, particularly when one includes the higher frequency of suicide, and under reported medical events (e.g. fatal arrythmias, gastrointestinal rupture) that are not included in the mortality statistics of large populations. That is, the eating disorders, occurring 9 out of 10 times in females, are a major and often unrecognized women's mental health problem. Small wonder many clinicians refuse to take these patients into their practices, aware as they are of the extraordinary demands and sense of urgency these patients beget.

THE CLINICIAN'S CAULDRON

Two examples from a typical clinical practice serve to illustrate the problem. In the first scenario, the therapist has worked with the patient for over 18 months. After initial good collaboration and a sense that the treatment was moving forward, the patient now begins to defy the injunctions of the therapist. Despite the therapist's use of state-of-the-art cognitive and behavioral techniques, the patient persists in engaging in extreme binge/purge behaviors that have required hospitalization on two occasions. Frequently, the patient talks of wishing she were dead but has not threatened suicide. The therapist finds himself frustrated, worried, and disconsolate. Despite a modicum of success with other patients, he agonizes that his professional training has been to no avail. He thinks about this patient throughout the day and evening to the exclusion of other aspects of his work, his family life, and his hobbies. Does his angst reflect a transference/countertransference enactment that, if understood more fully, would help inform ensuing intervention strategies? Has the patient been able to successfully project onto the therapist her own internal anguish and frustration? If the therapist is unable to protect his own boundaries and sense of personal space, he will be rendered ineffectual with the patient. The tenacity with which he thinks about the patient and the degree to which he empathizes with her pain are signals of his resonance with her; without the capacity for self-inquiry or self-awareness, these notable professional attributes may be jeopardized in a therapeutic stalemate.

Another patient, a 19-year-old male anorectic, begins to gain weight and to stabilize his dietary regime on an outpatient basis. As the patient improves with respect to his eating disorder and begins to look and to feel more 'alive', he expresses sexual feelings to his individual psychotherapist, a psychiatrist in her 30s. He begins to place demands that the treater transgress the usual boundaries of the therapeutic relationship and 'teach' the patient how to please a woman. The therapist finds herself seductively entranced by her patient, and begins to have sexual fantasies about him. An experienced treater, she realizes that her thoughts are part of an intensely eroticized countertransference reaction that she has not previously experienced with other male patients. When this conscious recognition of the intensity and depth of her feelings does not help them to subside, she begins to berate herself for their intransigence and her 'lack of professionalism.' Finally, she seeks out supervision after she begins to experience headaches and stomach pain during the patient's session. Aware that these psychophysiological symptoms are signals of a perturbation in her capacity to bear and work through distressing affects, she turns to the supportive contact of interpretative supervision to safeguard the therapy.

EASING THE THERAPIST'S BURDEN: CONTAINMENT OF ANXIETIES
AND ACQUIRING PERSONAL KNOWLEDGE

What follows is a description of the most commonly encountered transference reactions and countertransference responses that arise when working with eating disordered patients. In addition to discussing the typical affective reactions and enactments encountered with these patients, I pay particular attention to those less encountered psychosomatic or psychophysiological expressions that occur during the treatment (McDougall, 1989, 1995; Kramer and Aktar, 1992; Roose and Glick, 1995; Siegal, 1996; Zerbe, 1993b). Lastly, I suggest some practical ways that clinicians may deal with the multitude of reactions that are stirred in the psychotherapies of such complex and engaging patients.

In this respect, I ascribe to Little's (1985) dictum that the most ill patients inevitably engender the most intense responses from the therapist but also teach us the most about the work and ourselves. Psychotic transference anxieties are met with parallel psychotic countertransference anxieties. Those patients who challenge us by their refractory symptomatology or attempt to defeat us may initially bring out the worse in us. Getting some distance from the heat of the moment helps us to regain a more solid footing in the treatment as the clinician becomes a container of the patient's most horrific projections (Epstein, 1979, Grotstein and Rinsley, 1994; Ogden, 1982; Zerbe, 1988). With forbearance and tincture of time, this intervention of containment may prove lifesaving to the patient as well as professionally rewarding for the therapist.

What avenues of support or emotional sustenance are available to the therapist to lighten the burdens of day-to-day work that may often be quite taxing? Acquiring personal knowledge – learning something new – helps the therapist demonstrably (Landford and Poteat, 1968; Scharff, 1994). When we are upset, angry, confused, irritated, or sexually aroused, we may begin by posing the query to ourselves about what role the patient is placing us in and what is being demanded of us (Bloom et al., 1994; Davies and Frawley, 1992; Scharff, 1994; Zerbe, 1988, 1993, 1995b). This temporary trial identification allows the therapist to gain optimal distance from the role suction of the patient while experiencing first hand the array of transferential figures (or cast of characters) from the patient's past. A sense of one's own competence and mastery as a therapist grows as one experiences the impact of the patient's projections but is less compelled to emotionally react to them.

Transference reactions occur on a continuum reflective of the relative health or illness of the patient. Individuals with severe eating disorders, especially those with borderline features, tend to develop intense negative transferences to the treater. The fear that they will become controlled or overpowered oscillates with their desire to be emotionally held and soothed. Because the patients also have great yearning for the therapist's empathy and compassion, many will experience a nascent 'love' during the treatment, only to intensify when inevitable disappointments and feelings of rejection are stirred by the treater's neutrality and inability to fulfill the patient's infantile needs. When boundaries are maintained and feelings stirred by the patient are scrutinized by the therapist's silent reflection, the patient grows in the capacity to tolerate frustration. Ego functions expand (Gabbard and Lester, 1995; Gill, 1994; Zerbe, 1995a and b, 1996). 'Being real' is not discouraged but limitations on the extent of personal revelation, physical contact, expression of affect, values, and beliefs safeguard the psychotherapeutic process.

The therapist acts in accordance with the needs of the patient and not to unconsciously gratify one's own unmet personal desires or longings. In the forefront is always the ethical principle of 'tailoring the treatment to the patient' (Horwitz et al., 1996) and creating an ambiance of safety, respect, and belief in the patient's capacity to grow beyond the needs for the therapist alone (Davis, 1991; Wooley, 1991, 1994; Zerbe, 1991, 1992, 1993a and b, 1995b).

A. PREOEDIPAL DETERMINANTS

Eating disordered patients have distinctive inhibitions in experiencing pleasure in their body. Physiologically, poor nutrition, emaciation, and the medical complications of anorexia and bulimia augment the psychological inhibitions to feeling alive and vibrant. Severe aggression is reflected in the patient's poor self-esteem and may unconsciously represent an attack on the primary caretaker. That is, many patients experience their mother, in particular, as requiring them to submit to her and controlling their body (Zerbe, 1993). They have enormous difficulty separating and becoming autonomous human beings (Kernberg, 1995; Zerbe, 1993, 1995) and will attempt to blur boundaries with the therapist based upon their personal histories of enmeshment.

In the transference, envy of the therapist's nurturant qualities and attempts to negate them by devaluation occur. Overtly attacking the treatment by failing to take prescribed medication, engaging in self-destructive behaviors, including manipulating dietary advice, and refusing to acknowledge the medical effects of their actions (e.g. denial), they launch an unconscious assault on themselves. Gender identity is concomitantly attacked when the patient experiences the self as a 'victim' of the therapist 'perceived as the sadistic mother' (Kernberg, 1995, p. 41).

When the anorectic patient starves herself, she attempts to assert her autonomy while masochistically rebelling against her primary caretaker, usually the mother. This dynamic is concretely replayed in the transference relationship as the patient refuses to abide by the dietary or psychopharmacological recommendations of the treater, attempts to sabotage the therapeutic contract by not maintaining a safe weight, erratically comes to appointments, or religiously arrives on time to each scheduled hour only to repeatedly attempt to defeat the treater by comments such as, 'I've tried what you are telling me before and it just doesn't work.' I have frequently consulted on cases of severely medically ill anorectic patients who shout at the bedside, 'I don't want you taking over my body!' (Zerbe, 1993a and b). This quasipsychotic maternal transference reflects their projection onto me of a sadistic, hated maternal caretaker they harbor inside themselves. By the same token, their verbal eruptions reflect their striving to become autonomous human beings, in control of their own body as they experience me, at that moment, as an abusive perpetrator out to control them rather than to help them learn to control themselves (Zerbe, 1993b).

Initially, the tendency I have encountered is to try to defensively explain my therapeutic rationale or to become angry with the patient. A more useful intervention is to contain or gently reflect back to the patient the role one is being placed into and outline the goal of treatment as the eventual autonomous control of the self (Scharff, 1994). The therapist might visually conceptualize the task at hand as one of temporarily taking on the identity of a beautiful Indian basket or piece of pottery. One best supports the patient by 'holding' or containing the raw inner contents that are projected outward, sometimes experienced as 'doing nothing' in the treatment for days or even months at a time (Gabbard, 1989a and b). This particular tact is, however, an active and therapeutic useful device in dealing with intense transference and counter-transference reactions because the therapist proves durable in the face of the patient's attack. By staying alive and avoiding retalia-tion, the therapist begins to be viewed by the patient as the mother who can tolerate separation and growth in spite of nonpareil rage and devaluation.

In some cases, prolonged 'hatred' of the therapist may reflect a traumatic past. Although physical abuse and incest have received the greatest degree of attention in the literature in the past decade, the definition of what constitutes trauma is now widening in its scope. Case histories of patients are being verified by relatives in multigenerational, systemic family systems work (Vanderlinden et al., 1992; Fallon et al., 1994). This body of literature substantiates how the patient may be depersonified or misused in childhood (Coen, 1992; Rinsley, 1980). The patient believes life must be lived for others , not one's self. These patients are exquisitely attuned to signals in the therapy about what the treater wants from them and will repeatedly test the resolve of the clinician to permit the patient to flourish and set her own goals and agenda.

With respect to transference issues, it is understandable that such a patient brings a high degree of distrust and anxiety to the clinical encounter, if the past includes physical abuse, sexual assault, or the experience of growing up in a narcissistically callous and intrusive relationship with either parent. The patient has, in fact, not been treated as a human being with needs and desires of one's own but rather as a 'thing' for the gratification of others. *Genuine* pleasure becomes anathema. Turning to the misuse of food is a concrete expression of the paradoxical attempt to internalize goodness and warmth by 'greedy incorporation' (Kern-berg, 1995), only to expel these dangerous contents moments later with aggressive furor. Thus, many bulimic patients tend to 'vomit back' interventions of the therapist as a way of acquiring self-definition, simultaneously avoiding pleasure or fulfillment. They belie their wishes to take what good the therapist has to offer while quickly ridding themselves of the forced feeding, lest they recapitulate earlier, symbiotic experiences with a parent who cannot affirm the child.

For example, one memorable patient who displayed this narcissistic-masochistic dynamic (Cooper, 1988) was the only child of an acclaimed writer and an agoraphobic, highly self-involved mother. After the couple divorced, their daughter was left to fend for herself. She lived with her mother whose dearth of maternal supplies was experienced as abandonment on the part of the patient. Medication trials, cognitive behavioral therapy, dietary interventions, and the structure of an inpatient hospitalization did little to curtail her bingeing and purging frequency. She shouted at me in therapy when I made even the most banal clarification, explosively chiding me for 'not listening.' On the other hand, she would leave the session only to tell unit personnel and her peers how much I had failed her for not giving her more 'to chew on' in the sessions. Her intense transference hatred stirred feelings of deep aggression and despair in me as they reflected an unconscious fantasy that I could omnipotently give her, even without the use of words, that which she most desperately needed if I only chose to do so. It seemed safer for her to reject pleasure – and the therapist – than face being 'misused' by the object of her desire again. She thereby maintained a precarious selfhood based on her control of me, recreated in the transference as a cruel, damaging abandoning mother.

Like many bulimic patients, this young woman attempted to spoil her therapy and the therapist's supplies, based on the actual traumatic experiences of her past. For good reason, she believed that maternal figures could never mollify her anxious, dysphoric inner states. Such patients tend to be pros at collecting injustices, to seeking out figures to whom they can maintain a painful, powerful masochistic relationship (Glick and Meyers, 1988) Not surprisingly, this patient became embroiled with female peers who would destructively urge her to act out with respect to her eating disorder and defy structure. She would seek out relationships with men who would respond to her provocative seductions and neediness, only to leave her when she was unable to meet their demands for support and succor. This particular patient, like other eating disordered patients commonly seen in practice, manifested 'narcissistic–masochistic' character traits whereby she attempted to 'achieve self-definition through the experience of unpleasure' (Cooper, 1988, p. 130). Self-accusatory at the hint of any physical relief, she viewed the world at large as withholding and was quite guilty about 'doing better than my mother' as her treatment progressed.

B. OEDIPAL CONFLICTS AND GENDER ISSUES

Eating disordered patients also struggle with an array of oedipal issues that manifest themselves in the transference. When the treater is male, a female patient on the road to recovery will often find herself 'falling in love' for the first time. This erotized transference reflects growth in the patient and in the therapeutic alliance; however, on the continuum of transferential feelings, the patient may implore the therapist to sexually act out. Especially in those patients who have had a history of boundary violations within their own families of origin, there may be an attempt to master early trauma in the therapeutic relationship by an illicit affair with the therapist. This identification with the aggressor proves a particularly seductive invitation for treaters at mid-life who may yearn for new excitement and romance as a way of dealing with the vicissitudes of aging (Gabbard, 1989c; Gabbard and Lester, 1995; Ogden, 1989; Siegel, 1996; Zerbe, 1995a and b).

Male therapists may find that such erotic transferences may be manipulative and aggressive, reflecting as they do a sense of distrust and prohibition vis-à-vis the father. Female therapists may observe oedipal concerns manifested in an attack on femininity and a flight from legitimate competition. In my experience, anorectic and bulimic patients exhibiting oedipal conflicts become more curious about the therapist's life, particularly relationships with male and female peers. Struggling mightily with their own superegos, they worry that the therapist will shame them for having their own aspirations for mature companionship and pro-fessional competence (Their search is not to have the therapist 'tell all' about one's real life, but to provide a safe haven for the patient's phase specific curiously and learning.)

Countertransferentially speaking, the therapist may feel a sense of pride as the patient makes progress through this new stage even as a sense of mourning of an earlier, more dependent time in the treatment simultaneously occurs. Aware that interest in others and in life outside of the eating disorder alone signals psychological growth, the therapist may constructively intervene by 'communicative matching' (Masterson, 1981). This technique of asking questions about new interests and hobbies mirrors the patient's need to have an interested person support individuation and redress the early deficit left by maternal withdrawal in the face of autonomy.

This intervention style (informed by observing and silently interpreting the major transference/countertransference paradigms) has ramifications for the maturing 'sexual self' of the patient (Zerbe, 1995a). Recall how narcissistically vulnerable mothers have difficulties allowing their daughters to compete with them and to take their rightful role as sexual beings. These primary caretakers they may have unwittingly prohibited their daughter's desire to temporarily 'be the apple of their father's eye'. Subtle, unconscious messages that men ought to be feared (McDougall, 1989) may also have transpired in the mother-daughter dyad. Feeling repelled by one's body or sexual identity may also have been engendered by (1) the mother's unconscious projections of her own homoerotic desires onto the child, or (2) the illusion of 'cohabiting' or 'possessing' the child's body by over meticulous physical care, intrusiveness, or disrespect for age-appropriate modesty. The result is a disparagement of one's body and sexuality (McDougall, 1995).

The eating disorder may thus be understood as but one potential manifestation and 'psychological solution' for a demeaned and nugatory self-image. In the transference, these eating disordered patients seek female treaters whom they can model themselves after and with whom they can successfully compete. Male therapists who are warm and compassionate but able to maintain good boundaries usher these patients into the 'other than mother world.' From the skilled male therapist, the patient learns that relationships with men can promote growth.

Such oedipal transference issues invariably suggest that the patient has moved to a plane where trust and a stable therapeutic alliance permit that one can explore one's feelings, including sexual ones, safely. The patient will attempt to test the treater's consistency and affirmation of development of self. This may take the form of 'trying to one up' the therapist as the patient engages in dating and other activities typical of adolescence and womanhood. Direct questions about the therapist's life, including personal facts about one's mate, children, or pets, exemplifies improvement in object relatedness. To be curious about one's self and others portends movement to a wider world than one inhabited by one's eating disorder (or mother) alone.

COMMON COUNTERTRANSFERENCE REACTIONS.

A. AGGRESSION AND ANGER

Throughout the treatment it is *expectable* that the therapist will experience a range of countertransference feelings. The novice must be periodically reminded that experiencing them neither connotes failure nor lack of professionalism; yet, managing them successfully and usefully can be challenging to even the most experienced and wise psychotherapist. It is prudent to remember that one can learn much about the patient and the trajectory of treatment issues from assessing one's countertransference; such acknowledgment connotes movement in the depth of the therapeutic work and the hidden potentialities of the patient to deal with secret shame and hidden corridors of the self.

Look for parallels in what the patient is alluding to in the transference in beginning to insightfully explore elements of countertransference. When working with an interdisciplinary team or supervising trainees, I find myself restating the maxim: Countertransference feelings impede treatment only when acted upon or taken to extremes. I find that this is a very good reminder to myself because treaters at all levels of professional experience are never devoid of countertransference blind spots. In fact, we are probably most at risk for committing a boundary violation or reacting to our countertransferentially-based affects when we naively believe we are beyond doing so. Thus, when one feels bored, exhausted, or even hateful toward the patient, it is best to be content with 'doing nothing' (Gabbard, 1989a), that is, containing, or silently processing the channels of the treatment. This further enables the patient to develop a capacity to self-soothe and to have a sense of object constancy. It also permits the therapist to have the 'private space' (Modell, 1993) to reflect on what is transpiring in the dyad at a deeper level to move the work forward.

In the patient's past, it is likely that anger was met by withdrawal or retaliation with anger; the therapist who can silently contain and process these emotions helps that individual establish memories or engrams of others who can survive intense, negative feelings. During such stormy periods in the treatment, it is best to avoid making interpretations which can be perceived by the patient as attacks (Epstein, 1979). Later one can return to the material and interpret it; in the words of Pine (1985) 'strike while the iron is cold.'

Because therapists are human, we will all be, on occasion, countertherapeutic and react with aversion or malice in response to a patient. These visceral reactions protect the therapist's self-esteem from the patient's hatred, slow movement, or castigation. As outlined by Maltsberger and Buie (1974), those defensive postures that may reflect countertransference are: (1) Repression: the attempt to place the patient's difficulties out of awareness by daydreaming and fantasizing, boredom, forgetting aspects of the patient's history, appointments, etc.; (2) Turning against the self: Because therapists consciously want to help patients, we tend to be self-punishing and masochistically submissive when the patient thwarts intervention, (3) Reaction formation: Instead of feeling expectable hostility or anguish when the patient does not get well, the therapist engages in rescue fantasies and unrealistic involvement in the patient's life (Akhtar, 1995).

Eating disordered patients have personal histories replete with anguish and struggle. They will bring their own tendencies to avoid addressing their pain by repression and denial (Brisman, 1996; Clinton, 1996; Fallon et al., 1994; Kerney-Cooke, 1991; Werne, 1996; Zerbe, 1993c; Zerbe, Marsh and Coyne, 1993) to treatment hours. Because of the shame and stigma associated with their 'dark secret' (anonymous, 1995, p. 1395), they feel 'desperate, panicked, and prone to binge,' especially after hearing others inadvertently disparage those with emotional illness, anorexia, or obesity.

Parents, friends, and even therapists collude with the patient by neither addressing the specific symptoms, frequency and rituals of the disorder nor permitting the patient a psychological space or companionship to reveal what is innermost on their minds. Of course, the toll of personal secrets kept hidden have been most thoroughly explored in the sexually abused patient. But all of us have the need to share what are profoundly burdensome skeletons from the closet of one's past. Emotional abandonment (Bowlby,1979) transpires when those loved ones distance us by turning away from our pain, most notably manifested in the inexpressible grief we feel in the losses we are not permitted to mourn. These bereavements can take the form of abandonment, death, or separations with others (Bowlby, 1969, 1973, 1979, 1980) or loss of the sense of one's self as an effective and worthwhile person.

Therapists must pay attention to our own tendency to refrain from listening to and dealing with the emotional pain of the eating disordered patient. As helpful as the host of cognitive-behavioral, dietary, and pharmacological treatments may be for a given patient, their implementation may also be a reflection of the countertransference difficulties experienced in tuning into the anguish of another human being. As Bowlby's (1980) research on effects to children of the suicide or murder of a parent has demonstrated, messages given *not to speak* about events or experiences of great consequence only augment the sense of loss and mystery resulting in depression, cognitive inhibitions, compli-cated bereavement, and anxiety. Paradoxically, the individual knows all the while what she 'is not supposed to know or to feel', but stifles that knowledge to protect others in the environment. How much might we be able to lessen the burden of our eating disordered patients and ourselves by opening up the treatment to include those most grievous and unacceptable thoughts, memories, fantasies, and incidents? Confronting the transference/counter-transference paradigm of deception in silence may diminish the tendency to sabotage one's growth in the eating disorder (Bloom, et al., 1994) and provide new avenues for 'the development of self, voice, and mind' (Belensky et al., 1986).

B. THE NEED TO CHANGE THE PATIENT

The excessive need to change the patient or 'furor therapeuticus' on the part of the therapist reflects underlying despair in the patient and the projection onto the therapist of omnipotence. Nevertheless, treaters will on occasion try to 'fill up' the patient by a reparenting motif of giving more and more. Instead of attempting to give the patient those real life experiences that the patient wished to have as a child but can never regain in adulthood, the treatment is best served by helping the patient to mourn. A maxim by Giovacchini (1980) trenchantly makes this point: 'Mother's milk to an adult is never satisfying.'

Sometimes patients believe that the therapist could omnipotently provide for the patient, but chooses not to. This motif becomes part of a transference paradigm that is debilitating to the therapeutic alliance. Such patients tend to be quite masochistic, and in addition to their eating disorder may engage in other self-defeating behaviors such as self-cutting, substance abuse, sexual promiscuity, and suicidal acting out. Relentlessly attacking toward the therapist, they either attempt to get rid of their experience of inner badness by projecting it onto the therapist in vitriolic attacks or by getting others to render punishment (Ogden, 1982, 1989; Glick and Meyers, 1988).

Likely based on an early sense that caretakers were unavailable, the patient will now feel soothed only when others respond destructively. However, note that excessive limit setting and restrictiveness in the therapeutic contract may also reflect countertransference anger or demoralization. When the therapist is placed in the role of the 'bad object' for a lengthy period, one tends to react viscerally and punitively. Paradoxically, the therapist who is comfortable with one's own aggression, as well as accepting of one's strengths and foibles, counters the patient's tendencies to destroy the therapeutic alliance by greed and envy. One 'stays alive' for the patient (Winnicott, 1968) and thereby fosters a 'real' interpersonal relationship. The patient comes to know that the therapist is neither killed off by her own aggression nor robbed of all goodness.

C. FEELINGS OF ADMIRATION AND LOVE; MOURNING

As the patient progresses in treatment, positive countertransferences reactions are also bound to flourish. While it is unwise to place excessive burdens on the patient to improve to fulfill unconscious needs of the therapist, it is legitimate to feel a sense of pride and accomplishment for legitimate progress in the work. Concomitantly, as the patient makes way through the various phases of separation-individuation and consolidates an identity outside of the eating disorder alone, the eating disorder as a pivotal part of one's identity must also be mourned.

For the first time, the patient may begin to speak realistically of termination. Such growth means inevitable loss and mourning for the therapist as well, and the sensitive clinician who has moved with the patient through a series of life's milestones will likely experience the same anxieties and achievements as an emotionally healthy and mature parent whose child embarks for college. By avoiding identification with a narcissistic, internalized parent of the patient who permits growth only if it enhances the desires and ambitions of the parent (Rinsley, 1980), the patient's natural urge to grow and to separate is helpfully fostered.

CONCORDANT AND COMPLIMENTARY IDENTIFICATIONS.

Another way the therapist may grapple with countertransference reactions is to sort out concordant from complimentary identifications. In his classic paper, Heinrich Racker (1957) explained that to begin to understand countertransference responses, the therapist must wonder about what is happening in the relationship with the patient and muse about what particular interpersonal scenarios are being replayed.

With respect to concordant identifications, patient and therapist may experience a sense of similarity or alikeness. As Racker puts it, the therapist feels as though 'this part of you is I', or 'this part of me is you', meaning that the therapist has experienced aspects of the patient as kindred or like himself. In contrast, complimentary identifications occur when the therapist identifies with objects or persons in the patient's world. As the patient allows the therapist to see more deeply and clearly into the repertoire of past experience, the therapist resonates with individuals in the patient's life. This process of resonation with the patient's experience of self and others enables the therapist to distill out the most salient and important interpersonal experiences with which the patient may still be struggling.

For example, one patient, a severe diabetic with subclinical bulimia nervosa, lost her father after three years of battling colon cancer. An expectable regression occurred after the father's death. The patient's control over her diabetes and her eating disorder lapsed during the acute stage of mourning (about six months). The patient denied the emotional toll her loss was taking upon her functioning.

During the session, the clinician felt tears well up inside her and her lips quiver and observed that, although she usually was sorrowful after hearing about a loss another had sustained, she was unusually rueful with this particular patient. With time, the therapist began to reminisce about her own family members and fantasize about losses she herself had sustained. Self-analysis revealed that a concordant identification had occurred between patient and therapist. The therapist was resonating with the patient's previously split off, subterfuged reactions to her father's death. As the therapist was able to make the experience of loss more conscious and bearable for the patient, following the awareness of her own concordant identificatory process, the patient was able to own her own feelings about her father, and her bulimia and diabetes came under better control.

A second example demonstrated the utility of identifying and working through a complementary identification. This patient went through a stormy period of separation from her primary treater after six years of intensive therapy for anorexia nervosa. After the patient began to experiment with dating, finished three semesters of college successfully, and could more openly state political and philosophical opinions, albeit with some hostility, the therapist's staying power and empathy for the patient was tested anew. No longer was the therapist viewed by the patient as the helpful, understanding mentor who could 'listen better than anyone else' (Hunter, 1994). Even though the patient blamed the therapist for not understanding the trials she was facing in growing up, outside of the hours the patient continued to make progress. Meanwhile, the therapist began to dread the patient's arrival to the sessions; fully expecting fresh disparagements and fault finding, for the first time in the entire treatment, the therapist found herself empathizing with the patient's mother! Years before, this was the very mother the therapist had felt silently critical of when the patient accused her of 'not allowing me to grow up and be myself'. Now the therapist wondered how difficult it might have been for the patient's mother to psychologically sustain and nurture the patient during those times of normal developmental surges. This complementary identification with the patient's

mother was utilized in the therapy to address the unconscious
conflict the patient may have had with separation that she partially
projected onto the mother. That is, the therapist made use of her
countertransference response of defeat and frustration – resonating as if she were the patient's mother – to help the patient
become more aware of the implicit internal struggle she had had
with separation and autonomy. The therapist could now point out
the struggle the patient had in accepting good things from her
mother, as she was now doing with the therapist, to propel
integration of mature, ambivalently held object relations.

PSYCHOSOMATIC REACTIONS IN THE THERAPIST

Eating disordered patients have a sadomasochistic relationship to
their bodies and manifest a mind/body dissociation that results in
numerous physiological and psychophysiological difficulties. As a
group, they have a high referral rate to other medical specialists,
not simply for the complications of their eating disorder but
because of their inability to put into words the intense feelings
with which they struggle (Zerbe, 1992; 1993c; 1996). The traumatic
events of their early lives have handicapped them with respect to
using symbolic language. Rather, they partake of the language of
the body to communicate how they have managed to survive early
trauma (McDougall, 1989; 1995).

Anorectic and bulimic patients may be said to live within an
autistic capsule where actions may speak louder than words
(Tustin, 1987; Hunter, 1994). Hence, early verbal interpretation of
feeling states fall on deaf ears because their deficit lies within the
preverbal world of primitive feelings. In my opinion, some therapists attempt to make emotional contact with their eating disordered patients with physical touch because these preverbal
experiences have been tapped. Physical interventions in an otherwise verbal psychotherapy may reflect countertransference anxiety
and demoralization because the patient's grief, despair, and suffering yet cannot be reached in words.

The work of Tustin (1981, 1987, 1990) can be applied to
anorectics and bulimics to understand this preverbal world. Tustin
describes, with respect to the early state of autism, individuals
who become preoccupied with all aspects of their body as a
'protective shell' which encapsulates rage and annihilation. The

eating disorder is one failed solution to 'combat...and cover...a sense of brokenheartedness' (Tustin, 1990, p. 156) the therapist inevitably identifies when working with such overtly gifted but recalcitrant patients.

The countertransference engendered preoccupation to touch or hold the patient is better dealt with by referral to or participation in experiential therapies (Hornyak and Baker, 1989) in conjunction with a more verbally expressive process. Helping the eating disordered to realize that their bodily preoccupations are in effect attempts to feel physically secure in the world where they have felt 'smothered by what they felt to be an engulfing mother who needed them as a solace for her loneliness' (Tustin, 1990p. 159) comes after months of slow, uncovering work. Tustin comments:

> But we cannot hurry them to show their underlying sense of breakdown. This will come only when the patient is ready to reexperience it. In the meantime, we need to be compassionate but realistic about what is happening. Sentimentality is death to psychic development. (Tustin, 1990, p. 157)

Gradually the patient begins to share her pain rather than acting on it by using (1) nonverbal, experiential therapies such as massage, psychodrama, art, and music, while (2) cognitively developing a secondary process language for the feelings. Along the way one may be surprised by the physiological sensations and reactions that occur on the therapist's part during the sessions with such primitively organized patients. It is not uncommon for therapists to discuss how particular patients seem to conjure up questions about one's own body image or body integrity. Moreover, therapists report feeling their heart palpitate, stomach rumble, head hurt, and the like when these preverbal levels are tapped.

In actuality, even the most well integrated human being may develop somatic difficulties at times of stress or psychological vulnerability; these are not necessarily difficulties of our patients alone. However, psychosomatic reactions on the part of the therapist of an eating disordered patient may be one important signifier of a particular type of primitive countertransference response. With time, these reactions will find expression in words but only after the therapist is attuned to the primitive nature with which the patient communicates states of disintegration and painful awareness of body separateness. Individuals who were previously alexithymic, that is, without the ability to experience fantasy or to name feelings, must be *psychologically held* while expanding their frame of reference to 'name the formerly nameless dread' (McDougall, 1995, p. 160). The therapist will then witness fewer psychophysiological reactions of one's own in the treatment hours because the patient will have, to an extent, mastered body separateness. The patient will have less need to violate the therapist's physical space in an attempt to discharge preverbal pain and rage.

Concretely, psychophysiological countertransference reactions may also be manifested by feelings of exhaustion, despair, or ennui in the treatment hours. What I am suggesting is that sensitivity to the patient's somatic symptoms as well as those that occur in the therapist become another mode of communication in the dyad. Growth ensues when attention is paid to the internal and external pressures that may precipitate them, and they can be investigated with compassion, and a sense that an underlying meaning can be found. In this way, self analysis of psychophysiological countertransference reactions are another mode of 'learning from the patient' (Casement, 1985). As in other types of countertransference responses, the therapist need not be afraid of those responses as knowledge of the phenomena bring a sense of mastery and power. Understanding the 'protolanguage' of psychosomatic phenomena allow both treater and patient to move where 'a somatic symptom as the embryo around which to build a protective neurotic wall' can grow and 'in this way the mute somatic communication secondarily acquires symbolic status' (McDougall, 1995, p. 167). The protective cocoon of the eating disorder is shed as the patient emerges with her own psychological wings of vibrancy and meaning.

SUMMARY AND RECOMMENDATIONS

The burden of the therapist and patient can be substantially alleviated by making explicit and working through some commonly occurring transference/countertransference paradigms. This non-inclusive list of guidelines recapitulates the major suggestions of this chapter:

When treating eating disordered patients, having strong feelings is the rule rather than the exception. Pay attention to the range of feelings encountered in the process, but do not blame or chastise yourself for having them.

Allowing the patient's negative transference feelings to come to the surface builds the therapeutic relationship. The ability of the therapist to be the 'bad object' is a sign of forward movement in a patient who has heretofore maintained silence and false compliance within her family of origin and in prior psychotherapeutic relationships.

Many patients who may now be considered to be refractory to pharmacologic, cognitive behavioral, and psychodynamic techniques may, given time and patience, improve. Be content with listening closely and silently reflecting which sanctions the patient's inner world. Remember that the eating disorder has served the purpose of maintaining, however destructive, a sense of identity and meaning. It will not be relinquished easily.

Speculate about how one's own gender may be influencing the state of the transference and countertransference feelings elicited (Wooley, 1991; Zerbe, 1991, 1995a). Because male and female therapists will discover that aspects of the maternal and paternal transference will both be played out over time, it is best not to rigidly adhere to gender role stereotypes but to be open to the multiplicity of evolving transferential paradigms and experiences.

Pay particular attention to boundary issues. As the patient moves ahead, the therapist will invariably be tested to be 'more real' (Davis, 1991). While one does not wish to convey a lack of concern or understanding for the patient's wishes, capitulating with unreasonable demands for physical contact or acquiescing to internal pressures to gratify may place the therapist and patient on the slippery slope (Gabbard, 1994) of undermining the treatment. What appears to be a deviation from standard practice on the patient's behalf may be an attempt to fulfill an unmet personal need of the treater and an indication of countertransference difficulties.

Psychophysiological reactions – including preoccupations with one's own body image, and a host of physical aches and pains – are frequently encountered countertransference responses with eating disordered patients. These somatic reactions usually reflect the patient's inability to put intense states or difficulties into words meshed with the therapist's desire to enter into the preverbal world of the patient. Psychophysiological reactions will lessen as the patient has greater access to verbal modes of expression, e.g. putting feelings into words, writing in journals, etc.

Seek supervision or consultation frequently. These avenues of support are invaluable with respect to enhancing one's professional development, bolstering the therapist's sense of professional efficacy (particularly during long periods where little movement seems to be occurring), and maintaining appropriate and therapeutic boundaries.

In essence, the therapist who can acknowledge one's doubts, failings, and countertransference quagmires to a consultant is a most benevolent and helpful role model for the patient who harbors so many dark secrets, including the need to be the 'perfect patient.' A sense of resiliency, hopefulness, and acceptance of human fallibility convey the notion that life is worth living even during the most turbulent or painful times, ultimately potentiating the resourcefulness and tenacity of both parties in the dyad.

REFERENCES

Aktar, S. (1995) *Quest for answers: A primer of understanding and treating severe personality disorders*, Northvale, NJ: Aronson.

Anonymous. (1995) 'My secret'. *Journal of the American Medical Association*, 274: 7 and 1395.

Belensky, M.F., Clinchy, B.M., Goldberger, N.R. and Tarule, J.M. (1986) *Women's ways of knowing: The development of self, voice, and mind*, New York: Basic Books.

Bloom, C., Gitter, A., Gutwill, S. Kogel, L. and Zaphiropoulos, L. (1994) *Eating problems: A feminist psychoanalytic treatment model*, New York: Basic Books.

Bowlby, J. (1969) *Attachment and loss: Vol. I. Attachment.* New York: Basic Books.

——(1973) *Attachment and loss: Vol. II. Separation: Anxiety and anger*, New York: Basic Books.

——(1979) *The making and breaking of affection bonds*, London: Tavistock.

——(1980) *Attachment and loss: Vol. III. Loss: Sadness and depression*, London: Hogarth Press.

Brisman, J. (1996) 'Psychodynamic psychotherapy and action-oriented technique: An integrated approach'. In Werne, J. (ed.) *Treating eating disorders* (pp. 31–70), San Francisco: Jossey-Bass.

Burke, N. and Cohler, B.J. (1992) 'Psychodynamic psychotherapy of eating disorders'. In Brandell, J.R. (ed.) *Countertransference in psychotherapy with children and adolescents* (pp. 163–90), Northvale, NJ: Aronson.

Casement, P. (1985) *On learning from the patient*, London: Tavistock.

Clinton, D.N. (1996) 'Why do eating disorder patients drop out?' *Psychotherapy and Psychosomatics*, 65: 29–35.

Coen, S.J. (1992) *The misuse of persons: Analyzing pathological dependency*, Hillsdale, NJ: Analytic Press.

Cooper, A.M. (1988) 'The narcissistic-masochistic character'. In Glick, A.A. and Meyers, D.I. (eds) *Masochism: Current psychoanalytic perspectives* (pp. 117–38), Hillsdale, NJ: Analytic Press.

Davies, J.M. and Frawley, M.G. (1992) 'Dissociative processes and transference-countertransference paradigms in the psychoanalytically oriented treatment of adult survivors of childhood sexual abuse'. *Psychoanalytic Dialogues*, 2: 5–36.

Davis, W.N. (1991) 'Reflections on boundaries in the psychotherapeutic relationship'. In Johnson, C.L. (ed.) *Psychodynamic treatment of anorexia nervosa and bulimia* (pp. 68–85), New York: Guilford Press.

Epstein, L. (1979) 'Countertransference with borderline patients'. In Epstein, L. and Feiner, A.H. (eds) *Countertransference* (pp. 357–405), New York: Aronson.

Fallon, P., Katzman, M.A. and Wooley, S.C. (eds) (1994) *Feminist perspectives on eating disorders.* New York: Guilford Press.

Gabbard, G.O. (1989a). 'On "doing nothing" in the psychoanalytic treatment of the refractory borderline patient'. *International Journal of Psycho-Analysis*, 70: 527–34.

——(1989b) 'Patients who hate'. *Psychiatry*, 52: 96–106.

(ed.) (1989c) *Sexual exploitation in professional relationships*, Washington, DC: American Psychiatric Press.

Gabbard, G.O. and Lester, E.P. (1995) *Boundaries and boundary violations in psychoanalysis,* New York: Basic Books.

Gabbard, G.O. and Wilkinson, S.M. (1994) *Management of countertransference with borderline patients,* Washington, DC: American Psychiatric Press.

Gill, M. (1994) *Psychoanalysis in transition: A personal view*, Hillsdale, NJ: Analytic Press.

Giovacchini, P. (1978) 'The psychoanalytic treatment of the alienated patient'. In Masterson, J. (ed.) *New perspectives on psychotherapy of the borderline adult* (pp. 3–39), New York: Brunner/Mazel.

Glick, R.A. and Meyers, D.I. (eds) (1988) *Masochism: Current psychoanalytic perspectives*, Hillsdale, NJ: Analytic Press.

Hornyak, L.M. Baker, E.K. (eds) (1989) *Experiential therapies for eating disorders*, New York: Guilford Press.

Horwitz, L., Gabbard, G.O., Allen, J., Frieswyk, S.H., Colson, D.B., Newsom, G.E. and Coyne, L. (1996) *Borderline personality disorder: Tailoring the psychotherapy to the patient*, Washington, DC: American Psychiatric Press.

Hunter, V. (1994) *Psychoanalysts talk*, New York: Guilford Press.

Kearney-Cooke, A.(1991) 'The role of the therapist in the treatment of eating disorders: A feminist psychodynamic approach'. In Johnson, C.L. (ed.) *Psychodynamic treatment of anorexia nervosa and bulimia* (pp. 295–318), New York: Guilford Press.

Kernberg, O.F. (1995) 'Technical approach to eating disorders in patients with borderline personality organization'. In Winder, J. (ed.) *The annual of psychoanalysis, Vol. XXIII* (pp. 33–48), Hillsdale, NJ: Analytic Press.

Kramer, S. and Aktar, S. (1992) *When the body speaks: Psychological meanings in kinetic clues*, Northvale, NJ: Aronson.

Landford, T.A. and Topeat, W.H. (eds) (1968) *Intellect and hope: Essays in the thought of Michael Polanyi*, Durham, NC: Duke University Press.

Little, M.I. (1985) *Psychotic anxieties and containment: A personal record of an analysis with Winnicott*, Northvale, NJ: Aronson.

Maltsberger, J.T. and Buie, D.H. (1975) 'Countertransference hate in the treatment of suicidal patients'. *Archives of General Psychiatry*, 30:625–33.

Masterson, J.F. (1981) *The narcissistic and borderline disorders*, New York: Brunner/Mazel.

McDougall, J. (1989) *Treaters of the body: A psychoanalytic approach to psychosomatic illness*, New York: W. W. Norton.

——(1995) *The many faces of eros: A psychoanalytic exploration of human sexuality*, New York: W.W. Norton.

Modell, A. (1993) *Private self*, Boston: Harvard University Press.

Ogden, T.H. (1982) *Projective identification and psychotherapeutic technique*, New York: Aronson.

——(1989) *The primitive edge of experience*, Northvale, NJ: Aronson.

Pine, F. (1985) *Developmental theory and clinical process*, New Haven: Yale University Press.

Racher, H. (1957) 'The meaning and uses of countertransference'. *Psychoanalytic Quarterly*, 26: 303–57.

Rinsley, D.B. (1980) *Treatment of the severely disturbed adolescent.* New York: Aronson.

Roose, S.P. and Glicke, R.A. (1995) *Anxiety as symptom and signal,* Hillsdale, NJ: Analytic Press.

Scharf, J.S. (ed.) (1994) *The autonomous self: The work of John D. Sutherland,* Northvale, NJ: Aronson.

Siegel, E.V. (1996) *Transformations: Countertransference during the psychoanalytic treatment of incest, real and imagined,* New York: Analytic Press.

Smith, J.E. and Lafranboise, D.E. (1995) 'Anorexia nervosa and bulimia nervosa'. *Current Opinion in Psychiatry,* 8: 419–23.

Tustin, F. (1981) *Autistic states in children,* London-Boston: Routledge.

——(1987) *Austistic barriers in neurotic patients,* London: Karnac Books.

——(1990) *The protective shell in children and adults,* London: Karnac Books.

Ward, A., Ramsay, R. and Treasure, J. (1995) 'Eating disorders: Not such a slim specialty?' *Psychiatric Bulletin,* 19:723–34.

Vanderlinden, J., Norré, J. and Vandereycken, W. (1992) *A practical guide to the treatment of bulimia nervosa,* New York: Brunner/Mazel.

Werne, J. (ed.) (1996) *Treating eating disorders,* San Francisco: Jossey-Bass.

Winnicott, D.W. (1965) *The maturational processes and the facilitating environment: Studies in the theory of emotional development,* New York: International Universities Press.

Wooley, S.C. (1991) 'Uses of countertransference in the treatment of eating disorders: A gender perspective'. In Johnson, C.L. (ed.) *Psychodynamic treatment of anorexia nervosa and bulimia* (pp. 245–94), New York: Guilford Press.

——(1994) 'The female therapist as outlaw'. In Fallon, P., Katzman, M.A. and Wooley, S.C. (eds) *Feminist perspectives on eating disorders* (pp. 318–38), New York: Guilford Press.

Zerbe, K.J. (1988) 'Walking on the razor's edge: The use of consultation in the treatment of a self-mutilating patient'. *Bulletin of the Menninger Clinic,* 52: 492–503.

——(1991) 'Management of countertransference with eating disordered patients'. *Psychodynamic Letter,* 1(9): 4–6.

——(1992) 'Eating disorders in the 1990s: Clinical challenges and treatment implications'. *Bulletin of the Menninger Clinic,* 56: 167–87.

——(1993a) 'Selves that starve and suffocate: The continuum of eating disorders and dissociative phenomena'. *Bulletin of the Menninger Clinic*, 57: 319–27.

——(1993b) 'Whose body is it anyway? Understanding and treatment psychosomatic aspects of eating disorders'. *Bulletin of the Menninger Clinic*, 57: 161–77.

——(1993c) *The body betrayed: Women, eating disorders, and treatment*, Washington, DC: American Psychiatric Press.

——(1995a) 'Integrating feminist and psychodynamic principles in the treatment of an eating disordered patient: Implications for using countertransference responses'. *Bulletin of the Menninger Clinic*, 59:160–76.

——(1995b) 'The emerging sexual self of the patient with. an eating disorder: Implications for treatment'. *Eating Disorders: The Journal of Treatment and Prevention*, 3: 197–215.

——(1996) 'Extending the frame: Working with managed care to support treatment for a refractory patient'. In Werne, J. (ed.) *Treating eating disorders* (pp. 335–56). San Francisco: Jossey-Bass.

Zerbe, K.J., Marsh, S.R. and Coyne, L. (1993) 'Comorbidity in an inpatient eating disorders population: Clinical characteristics and treatment implications'. *The Psychiatric Hospital*, 24 (1/2): 3–8.

CHAPTER THREE

Gender of the therapist: Daring to ask the questions

Melanie A. Katzman and Glenn Waller

If insanity is a disease requiring medical treatment, ladies cannot legally or properly undertake [that] treatment. (Bucknill, 1857; cited in Crimlik and Welch, 1996)

Except as occasional consultants, the less men doctors have to do with female lunatics the better. (Lowe, 1883; cited in Subotsky, 1991)

The [eating-disordered] patient may fear identification with a female therapist, who may be seen as modeling a deviant sex role – a successful, competent female authority figure. (Bilker, 1993, pp. 418–19)

OVERVIEW

This book is largely about the personal, ethical and legal dilemmas that stimulate the clinician to make complex choices over *how* to work with eating-disordered clients. However, some choices must take place at a different level – *whether* one should work with this group. In particular, there is a debate as to the suitability of huge numbers of potential therapists for work with eating disorders. Within that debate, there are therapists who some see as having a perceived handicap, one which is not amenable to any simple remedy – they are male.

In this chapter, it is our intention to discuss why the therapist's gender may be so important when working with the (largely) female eating-disordered population. It should become apparent that we do not see the topic of suitability based on therapist gender as a simple dichotomy. Nor do we harbour a bias towards one gender. Therefore, don't expect simple 'yes/no' answers. However, through our discussion we hope that the reader will be encouraged to dare to ask the questions that must be made explicit so that we will come to acknowledge the importance of therapist gender and learn to use it constructively.

THE GENDER GAP

The overwhelming majority of adolescent and adult eating disorder sufferers are female (e.g. Barry and Lippman, 1990; Rand and Kuldau, 1992), although the imbalance is not as great amongst children (e.g. Bryant-Waugh, 1993). The reasons for this marked gender bias are not fully understood, but it is clear that sociocultural factors play an important role (e.g. Fallon, Katzman and Wooley, 1994; Hsu, 1989; Waller and Shaw, 1994). Women's social roles typically involve many contradictions, and it is likely that eating disorders partly reflect an attempt to resolve the emotional and control issues that result from attempts to resolve this tension (Katzman and Lee, 1997; Wooley and Kearney-Cooke, 1986; Steiner-Adair, 1992).

It has been posited that therapist gender and the match (or lack thereof) between therapist and client gender is important in any disorder (e.g. Person, 1986; Persons, Persons and Newmark, 1974). This argument has given rise to a number of extreme opinions. A century has done little to resolve those opinions (as demonstrated by the quotes given above), and has yielded very little in the way of concrete evidence.

Unfortunately, this debate often amasses venom, even in the supposedly dispassionate scientific literature. As the issue becomes polarised, any discussion tends to lose clarity and direction. The vitriol has its roots in the potential financial, political and social consequences of the issue. What if studies were to conclude that one gender is more appropriate to work with a particular clinical group? Are we really prepared to finance training and clinical work based on that conclusion? Will male consultants and professors in that field be prepared to see their power base removed or compromised if females are shown to be more appropriate therapists? What if the situation were reversed – would women practitioners step aside gracefully? Are we prepared to recalibrate 'political correctness' in order to take on the Orwellian concept of 'all animals are equal, but some are more equal than others'?

As frightening as this scenario may sound, we believe that it

arises from a red herring – a polarisation of discussion into 'male/
female' and 'good/bad' which leaves little room for compromise
(or for good treatment and science). Black and white thinking
from the therapist chair is as ineffective as any cognitive distortion
from the client's seat. Our actions often suggest that we do hold
highly polarised views, and that the motivations behind those
views are not always directed principally towards the well-being
of our clients.

In this chapter, we consider the issue of therapist gender in
working with the eating disorders, specifically addressing historical
perspectives and the evidence to date, as well as issues of power
and boundaries. We will highlight the importance of therapist
gender by drawing on both the wider literature and our personal
experience, so that clinicians will be able to understand how their
own gender influences the process and outcome of therapy.

OUR PERSPECTIVES

Neither of us believe that science is devoid of subjectivity. As
such, we realise that no matter how well-reasoned our arguments
may be, it is important that we introduce ourselves so that the
reader can take account of our perspectives. We are both clinicians
and researchers in the field of eating disorders. We also both
supervise and teach other professionals. While there may be other
points of overlap, there are also notable divergences, including
our different nationalities, theoretical backgrounds and, of course,
genders. Melanie is an American female clinical psychologist who
has practised in the United States, Hong Kong and England.
Trained in cognitive-behavioural and systems theory, she is most
often described as a feminist in her approach. Her perspective is
not anti-male, but does underscore the need to attend to the
impact of gender and society on scientific inquiry and illness
negotiation, and the ways in which power issues affect women
personally and professionally. Glenn is a male clinical psychologist, who trained and practices in England. His work is principally
cognitive-behavioural in nature, but includes consideration of
systemic and relationship issues. He would not be described as a
feminist in his approach, although he would hope not to be
described as anti-female.

HISTORICAL AND POLITICAL BACKGROUND

Although women are greater consumers of mental health care than men, many authors make the point that men are disproportionately the providers and power players within the mental health professions (e.g. American Psychiatric Association, 1993; Chesler, 1989; Crimlik and Welch, 1996; Katzman, 1995; Showalter, 1987; Ussher, 1991). Given the number of men in a position to 'define' illness, perhaps it is not surprising that the treatment of eating disorders had a slow start. Subotsky (1991) outlined a number of ways in which services need to be developed to be more responsive to the needs of women across the lifespan. An obvious issue underpinning the *development* of services is the *recognition* of potential problems besetting an individual.

The eating disorders have a particularly intriguing history in this respect. There is evidence that eating disorders have existed for many centuries (e.g. Vandereycken and Van Deth, 1994), and yet they have only achieved widespread recognition in the past few decades. Despite clinical observations and writings in the late 19th century, it was not until the work of Bruch (1962) that anorexia became widely recognised as a clinical phenomenon. It has been suggested that the very gender-specific nature of eating disorders is a factor underlying their obscurity (e.g. Ussher, 1991). First, anorexia has been seen as a product of an inherently 'inadequate' female anatomy and physiological function (e.g. Freud, 1895). This perceived flaw made the eating disorders into an issue that was not amenable to psychological intervention. Rather, they were taken to be an inevitable part of being female. Second, given that the mental health professions have been dominated by male practitioners and researchers, there is an inevitable history of assumptions that these 'women's problems' are both incomprehensible and relatively trivial. Dolan and Gitzinger (1994) and Wolf (1991) argue that it is highly unlikely that the eating disorders would have received so little attention and funding if they had a similar prevalence among males.

In the late 20th century the existence of eating disorders and their serious social, medical, and psychological consequences are beyond question. While few would argue that these problems require treatment, discussion of who is appropriate to provide care has been surprisingly absent from plenary podiums and paper presentations. Meanwhile, outside of the field of the eating disorders, views on the therapist's gender have run parallel to the development of the talking therapies.

THERAPIST GENDER IN GENERAL PSYCHOLOGICAL AND PSYCHIATRIC PRACTICE

The phenomenology of therapy has been studied intensively. While there has been a strong focus on the characteristics of the client and of the therapy itself, the research literature on the role of therapist variables is comparatively small (see Beutler, Crago and Arizmendi, 1986, for an extensive review that includes the role of gender). The lack of such research may reflect the fact that the therapist's characteristics are the least amenable to manipulation in clinical research. The process of choosing a therapist is also difficult – should the client or the therapist have the empowered view? The mechanism for deciding who makes the best therapist is unclear. For example, the client and the therapist may disagree over whether a variable such as the gender of the therapist should take precedence when choosing a referral. Should one prioritize the research literature (which may not address the individual client's particular circumstances), the client's preferences (which may be driven by a desire to make therapy painless, rather than effective), or the therapist's views (which may be determined by his or her own gender and socialisation)?

The existing studies suggest that therapist gender has at most a modest influence upon the process and outcome of therapy, but that any such effect seems to be a product of gender matching or mutual acceptance of each others' perspectives rather than a result of males or females being more effective *per se* (Beutler et al., 1986). For example, Persons et al. (1974) found that female clients perceived female therapists as having particularly helpful characteristics. However, that study examined the impact of relatively unskilled therapists, and may reflect a greater level of natural female-female empathy rather than representing the capacities of trained therapists. These findings are complex and suggest that the impact of gender is not universal enough to translate into clear differences in therapeutic outcome across different clinical problems. Yet it seems critical to understand the factors that influence the generalizability of results, rather than simply arguing that gender does or does not make a difference to therapeutic outcome. Beutler et al. (1986) highlight the difficulties of studying the role of therapist gender, given confounding variables such as experience, environment and diagnosis.

Perhaps the eating disorders are different from many other disorders, given their 'gendered' nature (Fallon et al., 1994). Is it possible that outcome is more clearly linked to the sex of the therapist in this diagnostic group? Unfortunately, while it might appear natural to study the potential role of male and female therapists in the eating disorders, here again there is far more opinion than research to date.

THERAPIST GENDER IN WORKING WITH THE EATING DISORDERS

OPINIONS

Ask any professional working in the field of the eating disorders about therapist gender and this population and most likely you will get a passionate response (e.g. Zimmer, 1995). There is no shortage of views in this area, and many of these views have the apparent strength of being based on clinical impressions. Unfortunately, the conclusions are not always consistent. A number of authors have suggested that women have more to offer than men when treating women with eating disorders, arguing that women are more likely to have developmental, biological and socialisation experiences that will make them able to empathise with female eating-disordered clients. For example, Dolan and Noordenbos (1995) reported on a survey of experts' views of the relevance of gender in treating the eating disorders. One of the most striking findings was that female therapists are much more likely to have known people with eating problems outside of the work context.

Working from the perspective of such socialisation experiences, Stockwell and Dolan (1994) conclude that female therapists have a distinct advantage over males. They attribute this advantage to female therapists' experience of many of the aspects of womanhood that can promulgate eating problems (e.g. the biological experience of being a woman, overconcern about weight and shape, sexuality, roles as a woman). In a related vein, Zunino, Agoos and Davis (1991) concluded that a similar variety of factors

make women therapists more likely to be able to work produc-
tively with their female clients (e.g. importance of the client's
concern with body image, overinvolvement with mother, ambivalence about gender identity, and need for a role model). In
contrast, other therapists have suggested that the issue of gender
is not a simple one when working with the eating disorders, and
that both male and female therapists need to attend to a range of
issues (e.g. Bilker, 1993; Frankenburg, 1984; Köpp, 1994; Wooley,
1994). The nature of those issues is generally agreed upon by these
authors. They include emotional issues, supervision, and client
choice. Each of these is addressed below.

   It is critically important to understand one's own and the client's
emotional issues. Some therapeutic orientations and trainings
appear to treat these issues as relatively trivial in the eating
disorders. This charge has sometimes been levelled at behavioural
and cognitive therapies that focus on the role of food-related
beliefs without focusing on relational variables. While this may be
an unfair assessment, manualized programs (which are gaining in
popularity) do tend to treat therapists as interchangable parts,
seldom examining differential effects of gender or other characteristics. Other therapies seem to recognise the role of interpersonally
generated reactions, while at the same time encouraging one to
dissociate from the emotional tone of the therapeutic encounter.
This attitude is reflected in the use of technical terms (such as
'transference' and 'countertransference') to describe what might
otherwise be seen as normal emotions on the part of the therapist
and the client (e.g. Masson, 1992; Wooley, 1991).

   It is our experience that therapists and trainees often dislike
their clients or develop very strong positive feelings for them.
These feelings may be gender-related reactions, albeit idiosyncratic ones (e.g. Wooley, 1994), and may or may not get communicated directly to the client. For example, there may be sexual
attraction, difficulty in empathising, or anger at the client's desire
to retain control. Any of these emotional states may be experienced by a male or a female therapist, but the routes to those
feelings may vary according to the therapist's gender and socialisation experiences (e.g. Ernst and Gowling, 1994). In addition, the
freedom to discuss those reactions and the facility to recognise
them may vary depending on the supervisor's style and gender –
providing there is a supervisor, of course.

The issue of *supervision* is clearly important (particularly given the 'transference' and 'countertransference' issues raised above). It has been suggested that male therapists should have a female supervisor and vice versa (e.g. Köpp, 1994). Adopting this relatively balanced approach would allow the therapist to benefit from understanding his or her own emotions, thoughts and behaviours in a way that transcends socialised roles. In reality, however, time and economic resources do not always allow for such a balance. This solution also begs the further question of how do you deal with male therapists seeing male eating-disordered clients: Is a male supervisor needed then, or is a female still an important part of the treatment team?

Finally, wherever possible, the client should have a *choice* over the gender of their therapist. The many issues of control that underpin the eating disorders mean that the therapeutic alliance requires particularly careful handling. It is our clinical impression that it is often the client's perception that she has this choice that contributes greatly to her willingness to form a therapeutic alliance, rather than the decision *per se*.

Superordinate to the above considerations, it is clear that therapist gender cannot be treated as an isolated variable. For example, cultural background is a critical factor in understanding the eating disorders (e.g. Katzman and Lee, 1997). Lee (1996) has noted that culture and nationality have an understandable impact upon the alliance forged by the therapist and client, and that gender will interact with these conditions. For example, success in family versus individual treatment may depend upon the creation of multiple alliances, which will need to be managed differently (and potentially more extremely) depending upon the culture of the family and the society at large.

Writing on health care in Hong Kong, Pearson (1985; Pearson and Leung, 1995) argues that one cannot provide information 'western style' and assume that people will understand it. As Swartz (1985) has indicated, the conversation between patient and provider defines the illness negotiation and varies across cultures. However, in eastern and western environs, when the professionals are men, women seem more often to produce descriptions of distress based on somatic complaints rather than 'wasting his time' with everyday problems (Pearson, 1985). Similarly, Bilker (1993) has concluded that one cannot generalise conclusions about the role of therapist gender across ages of client, nor socio-economic class. It may be more important for the therapist to recognise gender and cultural issues and to utilise them in therapy, rather than simply assuming that they are immutable. That perspective will involve challenging assumptions, rather than accepting them.

EVIDENCE

Existing outcome studies have examined a wide range of client and therapy variables that predict the efficacy of eating disorders treatment (e.g. Fairburn et al., 1995; Garner et al., 1993). However, as in the general treatment literature, the roles of therapist gender and therapist-client gender match have barely been considered.

In a study of group therapy for bulimia, Lacey (1984) compared the groups that were led by either two female therapists or one male and one female therapist. In a review of the group therapy literature, McKisack and Waller (1997) found no cases where a group was run by male therapists alone, suggesting that Lacey's comparison was an appropriate one. He showed that the therapists' gender did not moderate the level of symptom reduction. However, it is also important to consider the process of therapy. Despite the equivalence of outcomes, the patients in a group run by female therapists alone rated the group as more helpful and relevant to them than the patients in the group with a male co-therapist. Lacey's (1984) study appeared to offer great promise, raising more questions than it could possibly answer. Would the same efficacy patterns be found in one-to-one therapy, with different individual therapists, and when using different forms of psychotherapy? Would other therapist characteristics (e.g. age, experience, type of training) interact with any effect of gender? Unfortunately, this study also seems to have been the last of its kind. For more than a decade, the direct study of therapist gender appears to have been in hibernation.

Awakening this issue from its slumbers, Waller and Katzman (1997) asked experienced clinicians to assess what aspects of a clinical case would make them more likely to recommend either a male or a female therapist for a female client with an eating disorder. We found that relatively few aspects of the situation made clinicians consistently recommend a therapist of a specific gender, although a history of sexual abuse, body image disturbance, and a desire to see a particular gender of therapist figured prominently in the decision. However, one could not simply consider the client's characteristics. A female therapist was more likely to be recommended if the therapist responding was a non-medical practitioner (e.g. a psychologist) or a female. While the participants' age and number of years qualified were also associated with recommending a female therapist, the number of years that the respondent had been working with eating-disordered women (an index of degree of expertise) did not influence the decision about whether the client should see a female or a male therapist.

SUMMARY

It is clear that there is little evidence that the outcome of therapy for female patients with eating disorders is related to therapist gender, although the limited research suggests that therapist gender does influence the patient's perception of the process of treatment. Further research is needed into the role of therapist gender in both outcome and process of therapy. However, the opinion that exists to date (e.g. Bilker, 1993; Frankenburg, 1984; Köpp, 1994; Stockwell and Dolan, 1994; Zunino et al., 1991) suggests that the relevance of therapist gender is likely to be greater when the client has particular characteristics, rather than a simple sorting based on chromosomal composition.

WHO HOLDS OPINIONS, AND WHO HOLDS THE POWER?

In many ways, the study of gender forces us to examine power differentials in the treatment setting, and may offer us a framework to share power with our clients and with each other. Frequently, when considering questions of male/female therapists, the issue (sometimes overt but often covert) is how one deals with the almost automatic compliance with hierarchical roles. One of the few exceptions to this compliance is where the client is a much older woman, in which case a young male therapist may struggle with different role prescriptions. Embedded within these discussions is the interchangable use of gender (male) and hierarchical supremacy. Katzman and Lee (1997) have argued that we may too often confuse gender and power concerns. Female therapists may act much like males if their positions are genuinely perceived as equal. Especially when treating problems such as eating disorders, where issues of control are so paramount, the identification, negotiation and experimentation with power in the treatment situation is vital (Sesan and Katzman, 1997).

The discussion of gender, competition, power and self-disclosure have most frequently appeared in the feminist literature of our field. However gender – and certainly power – is not merely a feminist concern. By housing these questions (no matter how increasingly popular) in a marginalized literature, the issues are kept out of the mainstream. There is a potential cost to this stance. The majority of male therapists working with women with eating disorders will at some time have questioned their own efficacy when treating particular issues, such as body image concerns or budding sexuality (e.g. Zimmer, 1995). Failure to integrate these discussions into general theory is to disempower men, who run the risk of having their fears silenced.

Similarly, when examining societal questions of power, we should not ignore the 'society of our field'. As a community of experts, how do we handle questions of inclusion, professional exposure, and promotion from a gendered perspective? Many of the questions that we raise in this chapter about therapist/client issues hold in the supervisor/therapist relationship as well. For example, female and male senior practitioners and professors run the risk of misusing the power that is inherent in their position, while students' dependence and eagerness to please may make them vulnerable to abuses.

Robin Sesan (1994) questioned whether inpatient treatment can ever adequately challenge control and self-determination issues for eating-disordered women unless we examine the hierarchical structures of hospital teams. More often than not, men head the group and are less visible, while female staff are both accessible and attendant to emotional (rather than administrative) needs. Raymond et al. (1994) also underscore the need to examine the dynamic and modelling *between* professionals. Writing on a collab-orative approach to medications, they highlight the need to examine the choices of male/female pharmacologists and the interaction of therapist discipline and power issues. As with any workgroup, relationships between team members always need to be processed, and to the extent that those relationships fall along gender lines they need to be tackled as such.

As should be becoming evident, a fully articulated discussion of gender issues inevitably leads one to questions of power and boundaries, and then to personal character and contact inside and outside of sessions. It has become increasingly clear over recent years that, to put it charitably, a number of therapists see the therapeutic boundaries as rather more flexible than one might expect. This issue is at its most dramatic in the finding that a number of therapists admit to having had sexual contact with their current and ex-clients (Jehu, 1994). The finding that this is common across professions does not make it acceptable. As a profession, if we do not tackle boundary violations and sexual abuse by therapists, we run the risk of replicating the social ills that we struggle to treat.

The problem of sexual contact between clinician and client does not appear to be localised. Sexual contact with clients is reported by approximately 4–6 per cent of therapists in the UK and the USA, and is found across the helping professions (Garrett, 1994; Garrett and Davis, 1994). Wincze et al. (1996) asked clinicians in the USA and Australia whether their clients reported having had a sexual experience with a previous therapist. Similar proportions of clients reported such experiences in each country. A number of therapists perceive sexual contact with clients as potentially bene-ficial for the client (Garrett, 1994). Masson (1992) points out that such contact is not a new phenomenon, and explores the historical, psychological and ethical roots of the problem. The great majority of cases of such contact involve an older male therapist and a younger female client – a pattern that seems particularly relevant when treating anorexia and bulimia nervosa, where the vast majority of help-seekers are young women. However, this pattern of sexual abuse in therapy is not simple. There is also evidence that female therapists engage in sexual contact with their clients (albeit in much smaller numbers), and it has been suggested that female therapists are disproportionately likely to develop sexual relationships with same-sex clients (Mogul, 1992).

In a number of countries, these violations constitute a breach of civil and/or criminal law. This issue has been particularly prominent in the USA (Bibsing, Jorgenson and Sutherland, 1995), where *Zipkin vs Freeman* (1968) was a landmark civil case. The male therapist formed a sexual relationship with his female client, who went on to sue him for negligent behaviour. The court held that Dr. Freeman had negligently mishandled the transference, and that this was 'analogous to ... medical negligence'. Since then, therapist-client sexual contact has been criminalized in 15 states of the USA, with other states considering similar legislation (Bibsing et al., 1995). Given the preliminary nature of this literature and the potential legal ramifications, perhaps one should be most worried that there is underreporting of such acts by therapists.

With specific reference to the eating disorders, we have each worked with female clients who have reported sexual experiences with previous therapists or similar professionals. These have ranged from consensual relationships many years after therapy to sexual assault during therapy sessions. Again, our experiences suggest that the majority of such cases involve male therapists, although this is not a perfect association.

Susan Wooley (1994) described a potential backlash of attempts to quell abuse, such that behaviour deemed deviant for some may in fact reflect 'normal female relating' by others. She asserted that many women feel like 'outlaws' if they hug their clients (and might not share this publicly), yet in some cases *not* to touch would be cruel. Interestingly, when we as authors discussed this issue with each other, Glenn saw touch during therapy as a violation of his male, English culture. In contrast, Melanie admitted that she asked first, but often did hug clients to say goodbye at the conclusion of therapy. It has been Melanie's experience that this act was very validating of the intimate work that had taken place, although it was not an everyday practice for her. Of course, who decides to 'allow' a hug is itself an assertion of power – an issue in supervision as well as in treatment.

It would be unfair to focus only on dramatic cases of boundary violations without paying some attention to the less charged but equally problematic situation of therapists who develop friendships with their clients outside of the therapeutic setting. This seems to happen in a number of cases. Although we have no statistics on this issue, the proportion of female therapists developing friendships with their clients seems to be greater than the proportion of female therapists developing sexual relationships with them. We have each seen cases where this has happened. In the most benign instance, this can be an innocuous friendship that fades over time. Conversely, a highly dependent relationship can ensue, with no satisfactory resolution. The ethical position of such friendships may be less clear than for sexual relationships, although professional bodies discourage them. The therapist should be responsible for considering the motivations behind such contact, who will benefit and if it can be avoided. It is hard to imagine a case of contact with a past client that should not first be discussed with a supervisor.

What can one do about the issue of therapist-client contact? It is clear that having had personal therapy does not seem to provide 'inoculation', since over 40 per cent of Garrett and Davis's (1994) sample of abusing therapists had had such therapy (either before or during the period when the abuse took place). Perhaps it is most important that we focus on the issues of training and supervision. Training is a time when there is a particular opportunity (and perhaps obligation) to encourage appropriate consideration of boundary and relational issues in therapy. It would be interesting to consider whether the gender differences with respect to one's willingness to discuss emotional issues (so often observed in the sociological literature; see Tannen, 1994) also pertain to budding clinicians. If so, creative ways of training to compensate for such differences should be explored.

However, while initial training may be necessary, it is unlikely to be sufficient. We would encourage all clinicians to seek out supervision and to maintain collegial conversation focused on their emotional relationships with their clients. Strasburger, Jorgenson and Sutherland (1992) support this stance, and also recommend that employers should provide in-house educational programs on the topic of sexual exploitation by mental health professionals. Supervisors should dare to ask their colleagues questions such as: 'When the patient talks about her appearance, are you able to remain objective or do you find yourself getting attracted or tempted?'; 'Do you find yourself becoming competitive with your client?'; 'Do you ever find yourself wishing that there were a way to see your client outside of the therapeutic context?'; and 'Do you ever feel sorry that you met this person first as a client?'. Unfortunately, the time and expense of such supervision after training makes it a recommendation with inherent non-compliance. Perhaps greater consideration should be given to these issues at professional meetings and as part of post-qualification professional development. Rather than simply 'locking away' professionals who have ventured past reasonable boundaries, we should begin to integrate the knowledge that potentially follows the self-reflection of recovery. If we as a profession believe in the individual's capacity for cure, then perhaps we should be developing our own treatment and prevention programmes based on previous transgressions.

A DIALOGUE BETWEEN THE AUTHORS

So far, we have considered the bearing that psychological and sociocultural theories might have on work with the (largely) female eating-disordered population. As collaborators, we found that we had relatively little disagreement 'in theory'. However, as we explored the translation of abstract principles into clinical practice, it was a different matter. We discovered that we had some very different ways of working, and guessed that many of our contemporaries might have equally idiosyncratic ways of working with some of the issues raised thus far. These divergences might not emerge in the context of an academic report or a conference discussion, but instead come to life when one talks about the specifics of their behaviour in the consulting room. Therefore, we decided that the most appropriate way of proceeding would be to compare and contrast our clinical experiences in the form of a dialogue. We invite you to join in this dialogue, in order to consider your own opinions about these issues.

GW: As a male clinician, I am aware of a number of issues that are critical in working with a largely female population. Early in my career, I found it important to recognise that I did not have a good instinctive empathic grasp of why anyone should binge, purge or restrict. Therefore, I found myself adopting a more 'scientific' approach to understanding these disorders. It took me a while to learn that the most important source of information in these cases was sitting there in front of me all the time. I still believe that there is much virtue in the scientific approach, but I have also come to learn the value of simply adopting the perspective of the person with the problem. This empathy does not seem to be as much a part of the masculine socialisation process (which is *not* to say that it is found in all females but in no males), but I would suggest that it should be a target for all of us.

MK: Unlike Glenn, I had little doubt about why women were at war with their bodies. Although I always said 'no' to that often asked question 'did I have an eating disorder', I honestly could say that as a women I have not escaped the personal turmoil around body satisfaction and appearance concerns. As I became more seasoned, my struggle was not over how to value the perspective of my client (I felt I did that fairly naturally). Rather, it was to trust what I knew about being female and living in my body, and to explore ways that I could employ that awareness effectively in the therapy room – basically, to follow Belenky's doctrine 'to know what we know' (Belenky et al., 1988).

GW: There are social conventions that govern male-female relationships, and I have learned that I must always remind myself that those conventions apply to the therapeutic setting as well as in the outside world. It seems to me that there is a danger in ignoring the issues of power and sexuality that are inherent in these settings. I know that it is easy to feel flattered during therapy (by the client or by myself). Given such feelings, there is inevitably a danger of intimacy developing in the therapeutic relationship, regardless of one's professed orientation (I sometimes think that the strongest difference between orientations is not whether this intimacy develops, but whether the therapist is prepared to recognise it).

MK: I agree with Glenn that we must attend to when intimacy develops and how it is managed (and what to do if it doesn't). However, when working with a female client group, I am usually less focused on abuse of sexual intimacy. Instead, I struggle with what constitutes judicious self-disclosure. Many of the women I treat (especially those who are younger than me) want to ask personal questions. These range from what I eat for lunch to how I juggle a family and a career. On the one hand, it is flattering to be seen as a potential role model and I respect the importance of sharing related experiences. On the other hand, I would like to believe that I can be clear about what is appropriate.

GW: It is not difficult to see how male therapists fall into unacceptable relationships with their female clients, since the 'scientific' basis to practice means that one may not easily identify the point where one's actions are guided by inappropriate motivations. I can see this possibility in many of the therapeutic relationships that I have had with clients, particularly at the stage where they are developing trust in me. The best strategy that I have found is a multi-faceted one. If the client should make any attempts at intimacy, discuss them with her (with an emphasis on the feelings being a part of the therapeutic process rather than anything to be taken at face value) and with your supervisor. If you feel a desire for such intimacy, discuss it with your supervisor (forcing you to face your own fantasies). Finally, always remind yourself that few men are *that* attractive to such a large swathe of their female acquaintances, and that the conditions here are ripe for an abuse of power.

MK: I think that Glenn's suggestions around careful monitoring are critical whenever you are in doubt.

GW: I have also learned that a lot of women with an eating disorder enter therapy with expectations of their own, even if they were not aware of them until they enter the room. An understanding of the client's perspective is perhaps obscured by a belief that therapists set the agenda in therapy – a conceit that may be born of our training and of our perception of clients as having no ability to solve their problems without us.

MK: It's funny how you think you have similar views, and then you write a chapter together! I would never assume that I set the goals for care independently of my client. Not all people I see are comfortable setting their own course, but I see the client's development of personal aspirations as critical. I am attentive to how we share power, when the client gives it away, and when it is claimed indirectly through weight control. An ongoing struggle for me is not to fall into the position of believing that I have the answers.

GW: As far as gender goes, I have often had clients have emotional reactions to me being male. These reactions range from mild surprise at a man working with women with eating problems to outright hostility or sullen withdrawal. My recommendation is that male therapists should always address the issue of their gender as part of therapy with eating-disordered women, and that this should be seen as part of forming the therapeutic relationship. When should one tackle the issue? During the first session, unless there is a pressing reason to delay. Addressing the issue of one's gender should include explaining that you see it as a potential issue for the client, acknowledging your inability to be what she may have expected, and striking a deal (perhaps along the lines of 'Can we see how you feel by the end of the assessment, and then decide whether to ask one of my female colleagues to see you instead?'). The deal confers some feeling of power on the client, and thus allows her to decide whether she will discuss information with you (without feeling that she will reduce her chances of gaining from therapy if she keeps quiet). While I do not recommend that the client should be given no real choice over the gender of therapist, I find that very few of my clients maintain their level of wariness once they have got to know me (which I attribute to my putting the issue on the agenda, rather than to my magnetic personality).

MK: While few clients overtly comment on my gender as an issue, the trappings of my position often create unspoken anxieties (as might my comfort with a weight beyond low average). I find that women's competition with other women remains an undiscussed Achilles heel in human relationships. The therapy room is no different. Like Glenn, I label the potential competitive feelings at the outset – not that I assume I will necessarily be envied for anything unique to me, but I do believe comparison is inevitable. How I am 'sized up' will matter, and I try to keep this an open agenda item. When working with groups, I expand this question to all participants, who will inevitably be competing (hopefully first by weight and then for recovery).

GW: Finally, I must stress the importance of supervision. Over the years, I have had supervision from both male and female colleagues, and I have found each to be valuable. However, I have been struck by the ease with which female colleagues reflect on the clinical material that I discuss with them. I have also found it easier to discuss many of my own perceived vulnerabilities with female colleagues. Perhaps this ease is a result of my feeling that they would be more accepting of my inadequacies while being less tolerant of my delusions of adequacy. I see clinical supervision as a highly desirable part of clinical work, regardless of one's theoretical orientation. Perhaps this is just a product of my own experiences, but I would recommend that male therapist should have a female supervisor. I suspect that there is a good case for a female therapist having a male supervisor, since I feel that the balance between an empathic and a scientific approach is the key to ensuring that the client gets the best deal from the therapist, regardless of gender.

MK: I have a hard time with Glenn's division along gender lines, such that females are empathic and males are scientific. I have been surprised by feedback from some people I supervise, which characterises me as very objective and bordering on the too distant at times. In contrast, others have described me as emotionally available. In the most optimistic scenario, I hope to model flexibility and not 'either/or' operating styles. Similarly, I have had male supervisors who (perhaps secure in their positions) have demonstrated wonderful openness. I would endorse supervisors of the opposite gender, but more for the reasons we discussed earlier than for scientific/empathy balance alone.

SUMMARY

As our conversation above reveals, even as collaborators on the same chapter we do not fully agree on the ways of addressing power and gender issues in treatment. While we don't expect any reader to share all of our views, we do hope that we have stimulated you to pursue some new discussions, internal as well as collegial. In sharing our personal views, we realise that some of the differences we note may be attributable to our genders. However, we suspect that other qualities contribute to our perspectives, such as our histories, culture and training. We do not believe that a single right solution exists. However, we do feel strongly that the pursuit of answers to these questions should remain an overt and active part of clinical practice and training.

CONCLUSIONS: MAKING OUR GENDER A TOOL RATHER THAN AN OBSTACLE

In this chapter, we have addressed an apparently simple question: Who is most appropriate to work with the largely female eating-disordered population? It should be clear that the answer is far less simple. It would be very easy to conclude by saying that further clinical research is needed into this area. However, such a conclusion must be tempered by an acknowledgement that there are issues of practicality and power involved, which have made the question so hard to ask for so long and which make it relatively unlikely that such research will happen or be implemented. Given that the power issues include valuing and funding the necessary clinical and research work, it becomes relatively unlikely that such research will be implemented easily.

Perhaps the most important step forward would be to acknowledge that gender is not exclusively a feminist issue, and that in fact 'gender' may just be a code word for examining boundaries, power and relationships in the therapeutic milieu. Kaplan (1985) has argued that framing the issue of male and female treatment providers as a dichotomous choice is too simplistic. Rather, we should be asking 'what therapeutic conditions are most likely to facilitate women's emotional growth, and how might these best be established in therapy' (p. 111). We would go a step further and ask why only examine the gender conditions that are most conducive to recovery in predominantly female disorders such as anorexia and bulimia nervosa? Why not also examine the role of gender of therapist in predominantly male problems, thus beginning a line of enquiry that might be beneficial to the mental health of all concerned?

Choice over who is the ideal clinician needs to be guided by our client's needs, rather than by dogma of any kind. We would do well to discuss the issue of therapist gender with our clients, both as a form of assessing the match and as a gateway to issues around sexuality and socialization. Supervision can serve as a forum to consider how our gender influences our interactions with the individual, while professional meetings can keep the conversation current and our awareness high by putting gender of therapist on their agenda. All training courses should include discussion of case studies where boundaries were violated or gender issues were not respected. The question for all of us should be: 'What stops me from doing that?', so that we can learn to promote better practice.

We also need to consider what skills are trainable throughout our careers as clinicians, and what different contributions male and female therapists might make when teaching their students. In the United States, mandatory courses in reporting child abuse are prerequisites for maintaining licensure. Perhaps we should consider a continuing education requirement focusing on relationships with clients.

In closing, we should not forget that the authors are both from 'western' cultures, and that this factor may have led us to make some assumptions that are not generalizable to other cultures. As such, it will be very valuable to hear reflections on this topic from clinicians (and clients) whose cultural assumptions are very different. We will hope to see this theme emerging from a broader literature on the role of therapist variables in the treatment of the eating disorders.

The issue of therapist gender encourages us to examine power in a number of ways – not the least of which is the power of choice. By considering gender in making referrals and by entertaining the recommendation that all potential clients should be given the option of a male or female therapist, we are instituting a recognition of the client's collaborative efforts. Rather than shying away from gender issues because they are so vaguely defined at present, future work on gender's component parts (boundaries, power, empathy, socialization) will provide us with a less dichotomized debate, which might even be richer than the sum of its parts.

REFERENCES

American Psychiatric Association (1993) 'Women in academic psychiatry and research'. *American Journal of Psychiatry*, 150: 849–51.

Barry, A. and Lippman, B.B. (1990) 'Anorexia in males'. *Postgraduate Medicine*, 87: 161–5.

Belenky, M.F., Clinchy, B.M., Goldberger, N.R. and Tarule, J.M. (1988) *Women's ways of knowing: The development of self, voice, and mind,* New York: Basic Books.

Beutler, L.E., Crago, M. and Arizmendi, T.G. (1986) 'Therapist variables in psychotherapy process and outcome'. In Garfield, S.L. and Bergin, A.E. (eds) *Handbook of psychotherapy and behavior change* (pp. 557–610), New York: John Wiley.

Bibsing, S.B., Jorgenson, L.M. and Sutherland, P.K. (1995) *Sexual abuse by professionals: A legal guide,* Charlottesville: Michie Butterworth.

Bilker, L. (1993) 'Male or female therapists for eating-disordered adolescents: Guidelines suggested by research and practice'. *Adolescence*, 28: 393–422.

Bruch, H. (1962) 'Perceptual and conceptual disturbances in anorexia nervosa'. *Psychosomatic Medicine*, 24: 287–94.

Bryant-Waugh, R. (1993) 'Epidemiology'. In Lask, B. and Bryant-Waugh, R. (eds) *Childhood onset anorexia nervosa and related eating disorders* (pp. 55–68), Hove: Lawrence Erlbaum.

Chesler, P. (1989) *Women and madness,* New York: Harcourt Brace Janovich.

Crimlik, H. and Welch, S. (1996) 'Women and psychiatry'. *British Journal of Psychiatry*, 169: 6–9.

Dolan, B. and Gitzinger, I. (eds) (1994) *Why women? Gender issues and eating disorders,* London: Athlone.

Dolan, B. and Noordenbos, G. (1995) *Therapist gender and eating disorders.* Paper presented at the Second London International Conference on Eating Disorders.

Ernst, S. and Gowling, D. (1994) 'Psychotherapy and gender'. In Clarkson, P. and Pokorny, M. (eds) *The handbook of psychotherapy* (pp. 86–99), London: Routledge.

Fairburn, C.G., Norman, P.A., Welch, S.L., O'Connor, M.E., Doll, H.A. and Peveler, R.C. (1995) 'A prospective study of outcome in bulimia nervosa and the long-term effects of three psychological treatments'. *Archives of General Psychiatry*, 52: 304–12.

Fallon, P., Katzman, M.A. and Wooley, S.C. (eds)(1994) *Feminist perspectives on eating disorders,* New York: Guilford Press.

Frankenburg, F.R. (1984) 'Female therapists in the management of anorexia nervosa'. *International Journal of Eating Disorders,* 3: 25–33.

Freud, S. (1895) *The standard edition of the complete works of Sigmund Freud. Volume 1: Pre-psychoanalytic publications and unpublished drafts,* London: Hogarth Press (1966 reprint).

Garner, D.M., Rockert, W., Davis, R., Garner, M.V., Olmsted, M.P. and Eagle, M. (1993) 'Comparison of cognitive-behavioral and supportive-expressive therapy for bulimia nervosa'. *American Journal of Psychiatry*, 150: 37–46.

Garrett, T. (1994) 'Epidemiology in the USA'. In Jehu, D. (ed.) *Patients as victims: Sexual abuse in psychotherapy and counselling* (pp. 27–35), Chichester: Wiley.

Garrett, T. and Davis, J. (1994) 'Epidemiology in the U.K.' In Jehu, D. (ed.) *Patients as victims: Sexual abuse in psychotherapy and counselling* (pp. 37–57), Chichester: Wiley.

Hsu, L.K.G. (1989) 'The gender gap in eating disorders: Why are the eating disorders more common among women?' *Clinical Psychology Review*, 9: 393–407.

Jehu, D. (ed.) (1994) *Patients as victims: Sexual abuse in psychotherapy and counselling,* Chichester: Wiley.

Kaplan, A.G. (1985) 'Female or male therapists for women patients: New foundations'. *Psychiatry*, 48: 111–21.

Katzman, M.A. (1995) 'Managed care: A feminist reappraisal'. *The Renfrew Perspective,* 1 (1): 1–9.

Katzman, M.A. and Lee, S. (1997) 'Beyond body image: The integration of feminist and transcultural theories in the understanding of self-starvation'. *International Journal of Eating Disorders* (in press).

Köpp, W. (1994) 'Can women with eating disorders benefit from a male therapist?' In Dolan, B. and Gitzinger, I. (eds) *Why women? Gender issues and eating disorders* (pp. 65–71), London: Athlone.

Lacey, J.H. (1984) 'Moderation of bulimia'. *Journal of Psychosomatic Research*, 28: 397–402.

Lee, S. (1996) 'Reconsidering the status of anorexia nervosa as a western culture-bound syndrome'. *Social Science and Medicine*, 42: 21–34.

Masson, J. (1992) *Against therapy* (2nd edition), London: Fontana.

McKisack, C. and Waller, G. (1997) 'Factors influencing the outcome of group psychotherapy for bulimia nervosa'. *International Journal of Eating Disorders* (in press).

Mogul, K.M. (1992) 'Ethics complaints against female psychiatrists'. *American Journal of Psychiatry*, 149: 651–3.

Pearson, V. (1985) 'Discussion'. *Hong Kong Psychological Bulletin*, 14: 28–31.

Pearson, V. and Leung, B.K.P. (eds)(1995) *Women in Hong Kong*, Hong Kong: Oxford University Press.

Person, E.S. (1986) 'Women in therapy: Therapist gender as a variable'. In Meyers, H.C. (ed.) *Between analyst and patient: Dimensions in countertransference and transference*, Hillsdale: Analytic Press.

Persons, R.W., Persons, M.K. and Newmark, I. (1974) 'Perceived helpful therapists' characteristics, client improvements, and sex of therapist and client'. *Psychotherapy: Theory, Research and Practice*, 11: 63–5.

Rand, C.S.W. and Kuldau, J.M. (1992) 'Epidemiology of bulimia and symptoms in a general population: Sex, age, race and socioeconomic factors'. *International Journal of Eating Disorders*, 11: 37–44.

Raymond, N., Mitchell, J., Fallon, P. and Katzman, M.A. (1994) 'A collaborative approach to the use of medication'. In Fallon, P., Katzman, M.A. and Wooley, S.C. (eds) *Feminist perspectives on eating disorders*, New York: Guilford.

Sesan, R. (1994) 'Feminist inpatient treatment for eating disorders: An oxymoron?' In Fallon, P., Katzman, M.A. and Wooley, S.C. (eds) *Feminist perspectives on eating disorders*, New York: Guilford.

Sesan, R. and Katzman, M.A. (1997) 'Empowerment and the eating-disordered client: Differentiation within feminist therapy'. In Seu, B. and Heenan, C. (eds) *Feminisms and psychotherapies*, New York: Sage.

Showalter, E. (1987) *The female malady*, London: Virago.

Steiner-Adair, C. (1986) 'The body politic: Normal female adolescent development and development of eating disorders'. *Journal of the American Academy of Psychoanalysis*, 1: 95–114.

Stockwell, R. and Dolan, B. (1994) 'Women therapists for women patients?' In Dolan, B. and Gitzinger, I. (eds) *Why women? Gender issues and eating disorders* (pp. 57–64), London: Athlone.

Strasburger, L.H., Jorgenson, L. and Sutherland, P. (1992) 'The prevention of psychotherapist sexual misconduct: Avoiding the slippery slope'. *American Journal of Psychotherapy*, 46: 544–55.

Subotsky, F. (1991) 'Issues for women in the development of mental health'. *British Journal of Psychiatry*, 158 (suppl. 10): 17–21.

Swartz, L. (1985) 'Anorexia nervosa as a culture bound syndrome'. *Social Science and Medicine*, 20: 725–31.

Tannen, D. (1994) *Gender and discourse*, New York: Oxford University Press.

Ussher, J. (1991) *Women's madness: Misogyny or mental illness?* London: Harvester Wheatsheaf.

Vandereycken, W. and Van Deth, R. (1994) *From fasting saints to anorexic girls: The history of self-starvation*, London: Athlone.

Waller, G. and Katzman, M.A. (1997) 'Female or male therapists for women with eating disorders? A pilot study of experts' opinions'. *International Journal of Eating Disorders* (in press).

Waller, G. and Shaw, J. (1994) 'The media influence on eating problems'. In Dolan, B. and Gitzinger, I. (eds) *Why women? Gender issues and eating disorders,* London: Athlone.

Wincze, J.P., Richards, J., Parsons, J. and Bailey, S. (1996) 'A comparative survey of therapist sexual misconduct between an American state and an Australian state'. *Professional Psychology: Research and Practice*, 27: 289–94.

Wolf, N. (1991) *The beauty myth*, New York: William Morrow.

Wooley, S.C. (1991) 'Uses of countertransference in the treatment of eating disorders: A gender perspective'. In Johnson, C. (ed.) *Psychodynamic treatment of anorexia nervosa and bulimia*, New York: Guilford.

Wooley, S.C. (1994) 'The female therapist as outlaw'. In Fallon, P., Katzman, M.A. and Wooley, S.C. (eds) *Feminist perspectives on eating disorders*, New York: Guilford.

Wooley, S.C. and Kearney-Cooke, A. (1986) 'Intensive treatment of bulimia and body image disturbance'. In Brownell, K. and Foreyt, J. (eds) *Handbook of eating disorders*, New York: Basic Books.

Zunino, N., Agoos, E. and Davis, W.N. (1991) 'The impact of therapist gender on the treatment of bulimic women'. *International Journal of Eating Disorders*, 10: 253–63.

Zimmer, S. (1995) 'Living in the gender gap'. *Renfrew Perspective*, 1 (2): 6–7.

CHAPTER FOUR

Personal experiences of a male therapist

Joseph McVoy

As you view the title of this chapter, you will most likely set your expectations as to what is to come. This is isomorphic to the woman client who, at first exposure, begins to form her expectations of the therapist and her relationship with the therapist. Although there are many factors involved in the first stage of this relationship, gender is one of the most potent for both client and clinician. Used therapeutically it can significantly aid the treatment process. Unfortunately, male therapists are not often fully aware of the impact that their gender has on their patients or of the influence that their history with women has on shaping the 'therapy dance' that they enter with female clients.

In this chapter I will explore the complex issues that this relationship raises, and its potential for harm. I will also present how a male therapist can evaluate his own gender programming and, as a result, improve his personal understanding of his women clients. Hopefully, this will lead to a richer and more effective therapeutic relationship. The need for increased awareness by male therapists is great. Most of us know of unhealthy and sexually abusive relationships between male therapists and women clients. If you ask your own clients, as I have, about their experiences with male therapists you may be surprised at some of the personal accounts that you hear. For instance, clients consistently say that one of the most telling and bothersome differences between male and female therapists is their office. 'Sterile, cold, too office-like' are often the words used to describe male therapist's offices. In contrast women therapists consistently have offices described as being 'warm filled with plants, personal objects, and furnished like a home.' As we will see, these differences are also reflected in personal style and the approach to treatment. Most importantly, it reminds us that we are being observed. How we are seen on a personal level in the first five minutes can profoundly influence the therapeutic relationship.

Just as the ambiance of our offices seems to set the emotional climate for therapy, the structure of this chapter sets the expectation for my presentation. This piece is personal and its assumption is that personal exploration, and not empirical research, offers the best method for understanding the male therapist and his client. What I will present is drawn from the assumption that much of what I have inculcated in becoming a male can limit my work with eating-disordered women. Consequently, my task has been to change the gender paradigm from which I operate. Therefore, I have attempted to encounter the world from different basic assumptions. This chapter reflects this change by drawing from feminist research the belief that personal accounts are valid not despite their subjectivity but precisely because of it.

I discovered over the years that it was very uncomfortable for me to give up the sanctuary of the empirical research article which reflects my masculine training. I was robbed of the safety of being the 'objective' expert. Gone is the Review of Literature to demonstrate my competence. Missing is the research protocol and empirical data analysis that 'proved' my correctness. The discomfort arises, I believe, from the loss of my gender organized world. A world eloquently described in Carol Gilligan's book, *In a Different Voice* (1982). I was similar to the archetypal boy in her book, who seeks agreement 'impersonally through systems of logic and law 'unlike the archetypal girl who does so 'personally through communication in relationship.'

Typically, I have functioned most comfortably in a quantitative environment of rules and structure. So, whether it is an article, a relationship, or performing therapy, I have a greater sense of comfort when I know the rules. Of course the best way to be secure with rules is to be able to dictate them. Being at the top of the hierarchy and in power provides the greatest comfort of all. This is what I learned as a male child. I am the oldest of two sons and the father of two sons. I had a rigidly traditional father. Despite attempting to be totally opposite from my father, and being partially successful, I remained at my core a traditional male.

I inherited at birth a world where males were in control. As the oldest I was expected to continue the tradition. Without sisters I was deprived of a comfortable intimacy with females and so learned control instead of communication. This can be useful for traditional fathers and kings, but not for understanding the world as women often do as 'a network of connection, a web of relationships that is sustained by a process of communication' (Gilligan, 1982, p. 32). Entering this qualitative world of relationship without control proved to be very frightening. To do so meant giving up the role of king/therapist which I believed made me special.

Ironically it may be that we are asking our patients to make a similarly painful paradigm shift by giving up the identity that has given them their illusion of control and power, their emaciation. Further many of them may also organize and understand their world by overvaluing logic and goal attainment rather than trusting their intuition and the value of relationships. In other words these patients have adopted the same stereotypic male cognitive organization as I. If so, the male therapist and female client may be vulnerable to a frustrating struggle for power and control with each other. While the therapist's sense of being special lies in his ability to help the client achieve the goal of weight gain that he established, her's lies in maintaining her existing weight or achieving further loss. This could be conceived of as two competitors who are arm wrestling. In reality, however, the interaction is more complex and potentially confusing because of the patient's concurrent need to please the male therapist, his more powerful position and often the presence of unrecognized gender tension arising from each party's family of origin belief systems.

Metaphorically the male therapist could be seen as the Wizard of Oz attempting to show only his power and control to his patients while hiding much of himself behind a curtain. But this Dorothy will not be intimidated into performing his prescribed treatment – obtaining the witches broom. To avoid this stalemate a therapist must first understand his investment in control, winning and pride that may underlie his logical rationale of treatment goals. Only then can he integrate his legitimate responsibility to assist recovery from the symptoms with an increased understanding of the importance of his relational role with the client. In that role the male therapist can greatly reduce struggles for power in treatment. Instead of being limited to being the great and wonderful wizard he is free to be the sensitive patent medicine man who understands Dorothy's fears and uses his skills to support her in getting home. To discover and understand the aspects of my life script that limited my ability to relate successfully with eating disorder clients. This required an examination of my personal history and underlying beliefs and the adoption of a new personal paradigm for my understanding of interpersonal relationships. Searching for the core meaning free of the contamination of learned assumptions is similar to the process of ethnographic research which was developed to objectify the study of other cultures. For me it was used as a framework to explore my family and society's shaping of my belief system.

A PERSONAL ETHNOGRAPHY

In retrospect I know that I entered the specialty of eating disorders treatment ignorant of my gender-based beliefs. Beliefs that could be deleterious to the treatment of anorexic and bulimic women. Even though I had explored my family of origin through genogram work, little had been done to teach me about the gender system that distorts from within the family system. It was a fellow graduate student and not my training which provided my first awareness of my ignorance. She pushed me to understand why I shouldn't call women 'girls' and why women see their bodies and themselves so differently from males.

She shared an article by Gloria Steinem, 'In Praise of Women's Bodies,' that astounded me. In discussing why women were trained to be so self-conscious about their bodies the author mentioned the different worlds of gymnasium showers. Males were sharing an open shower room. Females were hiding their bodies in enclosed shower stalls. I had always assumed that my world was universal. We all had open shower stalls! I was so surprised by my ignorance that I asked women colleagues for weeks, 'when you were in school where did you take showers?' Like the cultural ethnographer I was beginning to shed my presumptions and attempting to learn about others' reality through questioning. What I learned was that my experience of reality was invalid for women.

The concept of transference may seem to be an intellectual attempt to objectify the subjective aspects of ourselves and the therapy process. It is, however, an acknowledgment of the importance of resolving and understanding in the therapy process the system of personal interaction between therapist and client that I am discussing. Hilde Bruch (1974), in *Learning Psychotherapy*, a guide for residents in training, summarizes the transference phenomena: 'The doctor-patient relationship involves many irrational aspects, unexplained carryovers from childhood experiences and attachments and that their clarification is an important step in resolving conflict.'

For our purposes this concept needs to be transformed into a gender/societal based model. In this wider view the 'irrational aspects' and 'unexplained carryovers' would be seen as the result of how we assess our worth, interpret our world and control our relationships based on the often fallacious beliefs about male/female relationships that we learn. It is very difficult to recognize and objectively interpret our underlying belief system. Consequently one needs a method to assist in this process of self-exploration.

Ideally a male can utilize a female colleague to provide peer supervision of his work. If that is not practical he needs to construct his own map. This requires an examination of:

- Our family of origin.
- View of the roles of men and women.
- Our relational/sexual development.
- Current relationships with women friends, wives, daughters.

MY FAMILY

In reconstructing our present behavior from our family experiences a thorough genogram is strongly recommended. It is beneficial if you can get a colleague familiar with doing genograms to help you with this process. The key is to focus on family rules about male/female roles and your interaction with the women in your family.

A study of my genogram revealed that my family's history and its expectations of males did little to prepare me for working with eating-disordered women. My father's father was a traditional Patriarch who had four daughters and three sons. He provided little emotional support and was preoccupied with his work on the railroad. My mother had five sisters. They adored their father but he too was absent most of the time. None of the daughters had a career outside of the home and saw their roles as homemakers who supported their husbands. None of the men knew how to be emotionally close to women.

My father was a womanizing alcoholic salesman who traveled constantly by car throughout the South. I learned from him that being a male meant idealizing women but ignoring their needs. In his absence I grew up in a world of women. My mother, grandmother and aunts met my needs and did not teach me to meet theirs. My world of men was primarily one of the absence of men. On the rare occasions when my father would spend time with me, it usually was with his friends at Trader Jon's, a popular and somewhat notorious waterfront bar that featured strip tease. In that bar my father and his friends shared the intimacy of beer soaked hours where women were the subjects of sexual jokes, treated as sexual objects and conquests. In my parents' relationship I saw little intimacy and less of shared interactions, and, I learned that males had to be in control and get their way.

Our memories are an important guide to our family learning about gender without the formal structure of a family genogram. As a male therapist you will find clues to your relationships with women clients in these memories. Here is one of mine: I'm nine years old and on my annual summer trip traveling with my father on one of his sales trips. We ride eight hours a day from town to town as he visits customers. We talk little but I enjoy the excitement of seeing real cities like New Orleans, Dallas and Miami. The main thing I remember was going to the movies. This was the 1950's and the downtown hotel was where everyone stayed. Following dinner I would be taken to a nearby movie theater and left by my father. He never went with me. Night would be creeping in and when I left the movie it would be dark. I mainly remember the anxiety of waiting by the ticket takers box for my father to come and take me back to our hotel. But my anxiety would increase in a confusing way when we would reach the hotel and my father would introduce me to women who had been waiting at the bar for him to return. I have blurred memories of those faces. Women with alcohol washed breath who were more important than me. They were clearly not companions or friends but dangerously exciting sirens. Throughout his life this was his pattern.

My mother reinforced this male learning. We spent many hours alone together. She would pass the time playing endless games of solitaire and drinking sweet sherry while sitting on her bed. I would create great battling armies out of match sticks while sitting near her on the floor. In all of that time I never heard her complain about her needs not being met or talk about her own plans and goals. It was understood that her role was to support her husband and care for her son. Sadly she did this by allowing my father to ignore her and me to discount her. And sadly she did not teach me to respect her.

She also failed to teach me about touch. We never did. Nor did she show me how to express love and praise. I finally broke the family rule by telling her that I loved her when I was 35. I had realized in examining my family of origin in graduate school that we had never shared this word. So from her I learned to take care of women but not how to care for them, and how to manipulate them but not how to communicate with them. Of course my father failed me equally by not teaching me about the importance of women and how to share intimacy and respect with a woman. Both of my parents were doing the best that they could do given what they knew. Yet it is sad to realize how much pain I had to experience as a husband, father and therapist to women because there had been no one who could teach me this as a boy.

It is nostalgic to look at our past and for some of us it is painful. One's family memories do not have to be sad or painful, however, to reveal patterns that block our ability to relate openly with our women patients. It is helpful to examine your childhood among men and women no matter how functional or dysfunctional the past appears. To not do so will prevent you from being fully aware and effective in your work. There are important questions that should be explored by all of us. How was I taught to resolve conflict with women? How well did I learn to listen to and meet the needs of women? How comfortable am I with emotional intimacy with women? What stereotypes about women shaped my view of them? In my case I was taught to feel threatened if I did not get my way and I did not learn to hear or compromise. I learned to please women and take care of them, but not to listen to them or to meet needs that I did not understand or approve of.

Intimacy was covert and a source of anxiety not comfort. Once I looked at these emerging patterns I became increasingly aware of how they might affect my clinical work.

Unfortunately, some of the characteristics that I discovered in myself explain very well my first work with eating-disordered women. I would join well with them and earn their trust. As we reached a point where they would not comply to my view of what they needed, I became the 'controlling father.' I would at times skillfully create a coalition with parents to force treatment. The strength of this could be seen in my willingness to take decisive action with seriously ill anorexic clients. The problem with my focus on results was that I often ignored the woman's feelings and needs. I fought so hard to win the nutritional war that I failed to recognize that I was reinforcing the cultural messages that had taught her not to listen to her voice, feelings or needs. Often the result was the illusion of success as measured in pounds gained that was followed by rapid regression. My goal orientation in my early career ignored the relational aspects of therapy. Like my father, I organized the relationship to get my way with little true awareness of the other's needs and feelings.

In this way I was typical of many male therapists according to eating-disordered women. They were asked to list the characteristics of male therapists that they had seen which detracted from their treatment. They were asked to be specific to identify characteristics not generally seen with female therapists. Overwhelmingly their first concern was that male therapists showed an inability to listen. Today I still expect clients to engage in behavioral changes necessary for recovery, but now I listen more closely to the woman's own goals and fears. I then adjust my expectations of them to reflect what I have learned from them as we work together.

SOCIAL-SEXUAL DEVELOPMENT

Anorexic and bulimic women are often caught up in the web of sexuality as a precipitator, initiator or maintainer of their illness. The physical loss of weight often results in the loss of secondary sexual characteristics. Starvation suppresses libido. Frequently it is an act of sexual abuse that triggers the disorder. Many of the women are severely sexualized and have episodes of sexual compliance that damage them. Most have developed their disorders partly because of the appearance standard that has controlled and crippled women for generations. 'It's better to look good than to feel good' has tragic meaning for them. In short, their sexuality, sexual development and physical appearance are central to their illness. As males our presence creates a potential for reinforcing their stereotypical beliefs and for increased insecurity and misunderstanding that may not be as strong a factor with a woman therapist.

I have found that no area is more difficult to openly examine than the one of sexuality between the therapist and the client. To explore this issue can be very uncomfortable. It requires acknowledging our sexual self and that we can react to our patients in a sexual way. To pretend to ourselves and to others that we are not aware that our patients have breasts, hips and thighs or that we don't notice some client's physical attractiveness is potentially dangerous. It contributes to our being less aware of our internal process and more likely to give mixed messages to our client.

A former client of mine recounted to me that her first therapist was a male. He hugged her upon meeting her in the first session and always hugged her at the end of every session. She had experienced sexual abuse as a child but had become adept at hiding her feelings. She would not complain, enduring each hug with a smile. She would dread going to each session and be distracted throughout the session awaiting the closing hug. Finally she felt she could not endure it any more and pretended to be well to escape future touch that she disliked. At the last session she ran out without being hugged.

This male at best had little understanding of boundaries and basic rules for male therapists working with females. Most male therapists know the legal and ethical limits to our relationships with clients, but since that therapist did not, maybe these should be mentioned. Touch of all women clients should be very limited. I believe that there should be no touching of women clients in the closed therapy room. I will give an occasion, supportive pat on the shoulder in the waiting room as a client leaves, after I have discussed her comfort level with touch and know her history. I will hug clients only when we are terminating treatment and only if I am sure that she will be comfortable with it. This is also done in the waiting room with a female staff person present. I will never meet with a client in a location away from my office for therapy or social reasons. This includes rides in my car. Phone calls are limited to emergencies and I will not do 'phone therapy.' All of this is to not only meet the ethical standards of our professional organizations but also because it is always potentially harmful for our clients.

I believe that male therapists that have resolved their issues of sexuality and intimacy and who are comfortable with touch as an important expression of caring and support are also the ones who are less likely to violate these bounds. A male colleague who has been working for years with eating-disordered women once shared with me that he would take his clients out to lunch as 'a therapy task.' When I questioned this he acknowledged that he also did this because he enjoyed it and that he used his clients to meet his emotional needs. This doctor was in a devitalized marriage and his life was his practice. He also had never looked at how his issues were affecting his clients as we are doing in this chapter.

If you explore your early sexual experiences you will have another mirror that reflects your view of women. Like many males my sexual awakening was the pursuit of the unseen object. I do not recall seeing a woman's body as a child. So I peeked on the rare occasions that I could. At age ten I tried to peek at my aunt through the bathroom keyhole as she dried herself from her shower. I was caught by my grandmother and I was very ashamed, but it was not ever discussed. Nor was sexuality ever discussed with me during my development into puberty. I had also found a copy of the original Marilyn Monroe centerfold and had hidden it in the crawl space under our old southern home. In this pre-puberty time my arousal at seeing this icon of 1950's sexuality was intense curiosity and the excitement of seeing what was forbidden. An excitement that turned to shame when an uncle discovered my secret treasure and disposed of it. Again an event that was never mentioned or discussed. Fortunately that episode ended in grammar school my penchant for having or hiding pornographic material. Unfortunately I was to later learn why my sexual curiosity was never commented on. In the sixth grade I discovered that my father kept a collection of these magazines in the house. A habit that continued for many years. It is difficult to deal with educating young boys about respecting women when their fathers are practicing the same behaviors.

In my early teens this intense excitement became sexual as I experienced puberty and began dating. I was in the eighth grade. Again I had learned little about relationships or intimacy. I did not understand girls or know how to listen to them. I had learned to treat female peers as objects and never realized there was a difference between love, sex and intimacy. My adolescence was a time of becoming sexual without learning to feel comfortable with girls, going steady without learning respect or commitment. As a result I dated Norah from the tenth grade through college and we were married eight years. During our entire relationship I never was able to once understand her or hear her needs any more than I could understand my relationship with Marilyn Monroe or my father could understand his failed relationship with my mother. Fortunately, I had resolved many of these issues in my relationships before becoming a therapist. For male therapists who have not yet resolved them, I suggest they would do well to enter therapy before working with female clients.

CURRENT RELATIONSHIPS

My mother died in April, 1992. I learned of her cancer the summer before while visiting her. This visit had begun like all of my visits home. I would work hard to take care of my mother while I was home. However, I became tense and uncomfortable as the days passed. She would go very few places during my visit and preferred to sit in our kitchen and talk. There she would drink while she talked and repeat stories that I had heard over and over for years. This brought up the anxiety and stress of my childhood and adolescence feeling trapped in this kitchen and I would become increasingly disrespectful and seldom listen. During this last summer I visited her I could not fail to see that she was falling down and that she could not control her right leg at times. I began the process of seeking medical help that quickly led to a diagnosis of lung and brain cancer. This was the beginning of the long year of my mother's painful death and of my finally learning to listen to her. I had already learned to listen to Bonnie, my wife, and my step-daughters. This had been aided by a year long supervision program that I was participating in. I had also made progress with clients. My mother, however, had helped me to develop my life-long pattern of pseudo-listening. I could give the impression of attending to what was said but be tuned out. My father had done this to my mother and I learned from him well. So at this time I realized that I had done nothing to give my mother the respect that I was affording other women.

I am very sad that I discounted so much of what my mother shared and that I was unable to understand that listening was a response to the person and not just to the information being communicated. During the year of her dying I listened to old stories, reminiscences, cries of pain and hallucinations. The problem had been that I thought being a good listener was hearing the content and analyzing it. My response was to critique, supplement, or offer suggestions. This reduces the process to an Internet chat room. Before learning this from my mother I would often listen to my female clients as I had listened to my mother. I would assume I knew what they felt and were going to say. When I would hear often repeated stories of clients which usually related to fears of fat and body hatred, I would not listen to how they were feeling or what they said they needed. I would revert to 'I've heard this before' and glaze over as I had with my mother. Now when I feel this reaction, I remember my mother and focus on the client's need to be heard and let them tell me what they feel is important. I hold in reserve my interpretations, suggestions and assignments. Once I perceive that the client knows that she has been heard, I introduce suggestions and a joint plan of actions.

One can argue that this leads to letting one's guard down and being manipulated. That was my argument for years. This argument presumes a concept of strength versus weakness that trapped me for years as a male therapist. It is, I believe, a fear of loss of control that resembles the fear of our clients. Since I have changed this paradigm I have been manipulated no more than in the past. I have at the same time enjoyed my work more and seen more dramatic change in the female clients that I see. My learning to listen, first from my wife and then from my mother, is an example of seeing a need for change in close relationships, and using this to see a need for similar change in the therapist-client relationship. Generally, our current relationships with our clients will be isomorphic to the relationships in our life outside of therapy.

This journey, my personal ethnography, can be seen as a process of listening to one's learned history and uncovering its meaning. Then we can, like a cultural ethnographer, begin to look for patterns in the stories that will help us systematize this learning into clear patterns that explain our behavior. Only then can we find ways to change ourselves in a way that will make us more effective with women clients.

What I learned from exploring my relationships with women was that as a male I had to experience a paradigm shift to make my gender a compliment to my work and not a determent. This has been an ongoing process of ten years that continues. I approached the task of restructuring my role as a male and as a male professional as one and the same. To accomplish this I developed a process of reconstructing what I call my gender-based relational script. The preparatory step was illustrated in the first part of this chapter. I used information about my family and my own memories to recognize patterns of male interaction with females that shaped my scripted responses to women. I then evaluated how I have enacted these patterns with women clients. Once I understood how these patterns were deleterious to treatment, I changed these patterns with my clients. The same process can be used by other male therapist and can, hopefully, help women colleagues better understand when they are caught up in the same process with a male colleague or supervisor.

These relational scripts are the parts that we assume in interactions with females. They are predictable and occur across all female relationships including our clients. They come from our childhood interpretation of our role that grew from our interpretation of how males and females in our family interacted with each other and interacted with us. These roles are like our internal computer's operating system. When they are based on rigid, stereotypic views of the roles of men and women they can be capable of harming the therapeutic process. When they are based on a healthy view of equality, mutuality, respect and understanding they equip us to work naturally and comfortably with women clients.

Role reconstruction is the process of changing the underlying world view that we hold in our interactions with women and replacing them with more healthy rules. This requires us to see not only our clients and other women in our life differently but to also acknowledge the flawed nature of our way of understanding, processing and relating to women. Most of the scripts that initially influenced my professional role with eating-disordered women are common for many other males but my list is by no means exhaustive. Exploring your own family of origin will reveal yours. You will be surprised how they are played out in your own work. Mine were: the idealized hero, creator, coach, and father.

IDEALIZED HERO

I looked forward to my sessions with Holly, a bright, energetic high school student who had bulimia. She looked up to me in the ways that make fathers, teachers and coaches feel special. She made her adulation overt by her intense eye contact, tone of voice and even sharing a song that she had taped for me. I minimized the power of this adulation and failed to process it myself or with a colleague. After all I was as consistent and demanding of her in treatment as I was with other patients. Even if her behavior did not influence my treatment, I was recreating the relationship that she had assumed with the other males in her life. Holly had worked very hard to be special for them and for me. Although she was a brilliant student and a gifted athlete, she defined her value in terms of her ability to please and be valued by males. Before I knew it I was validating her view. Ironically, as I helped her see how she was overly dependent on a male teacher and how this was similar to how she met her father's emotional needs at great cost to herself, I was relating to her in a similar manner.

A woman colleague pointed this out to me and also expressed her reaction to Holly as being manipulative and having difficulty in relating with women. Initially I rejected her viewpoint despite having seen that Holly had a relationship pattern with other women that was mistrustful and competitive. Holly failed to sustain friendships because women did not value her in the same attending way as men. She would not value their relationship enough to build a close friendship. So, while I talked about fat grams and frequency of vomiting, I was reinforcing the pattern that fed her eating disorder.

At that time I was not aware of my pattern of being infatuated with being idealized, or that it was a long established pattern for males in my family. My grandfather was the manager of a furniture store in a small Alabama town. He lived in a small hotel room, had no activities that interested him and saw us only infrequently. The bright spot in his life appeared to be young women he would champion. He would tell me about one he had helped find a job, another he helped to go to nursing school and another he lent money to. It was always young women and not men. I do not believe that he crossed any boundaries, sexual or otherwise, but feel that he was 'helping' them more from his need to be their hero and was thus treated as special by them. It bothered me then that these young women seemed more important to him than my brother or I. Yet I was proud of him for being caring and giving. I learned that adulation of women was something special that I wanted to have.

My father was even more obsessed with girls, the daughters that he never had. He seemed to be always attending to friends' daughters. When they responded to this with any form of idealization he would emotionally 'adopt' them. Two stayed with us during the summer when I was in the ninth and tenth grades. When I was in high school and again when I was in college two adolescent females lived with my parents for prolonged periods. My father valued these girls and young women over his sons because of his infatuation with females. The girls responded by idealizing 'uncle' Joe. Ultimately these relationships would end painfully, usually after the women had depleted my parents resources and my mother's energy. It was my mother who was left with the actual caretaking role. Although I am less sure that my father was not sexually exploitive, I believe that he, like my grandfather, was addicted to this adulation of young women and did not overtly abuse them. As I watched, I learned a way of relating to females that was particularly unsuitable for my role with women clients.

This tendency still lurks in me. Once I became aware of my pattern I worked on changing it. I am now able to offer another relational model to my clients. I suggest that they see me as a valuable support, while I do not respond in a reinforcing manner if they seek to relate through idealization. Instead, we examine their gender role scripting and discuss this openly. We then use our interaction to illustrate this pattern and to change it. At the same time we examine how they enact the same patterns in their lives and how costly this type of relationship is for them. They learn that they must suppress their feelings and needs when they overidealize males. A task of therapy then is to help them express those feelings to all of the men in their lives, including me. It is not as enjoyable for me to be made aware of how my behaviors frustrate and may even anger these women as it is to be idealized; but it is a more healthy relationship. Changing this interactional pattern has helped me be a more effective and responsible professional and allowed me to better facilitate meaningful change.

Most know the pygmalion myth and its retelling in the musical *My Fair Lady*. It is the archetypal story of man creating woman. This belief that the powerful male is able to transform the average woman into a woman of great success or to restore the damaged or defective woman to a state of grace appears to be universal. For the male therapist this narcissistic sense of his own power can be as addictive as being overidealized. Of course idealization is also inherent in this type of relationship and can be equally harmful to the female client. It also makes clear the issue of power that can not be ignored in any relationship, especially a therapeutic one. We can not escape the presence of power in any relationship. It is neither good nor bad. Historically males have had control of the resources of power in the family as the patriarch and, more recently, in the work place. In the therapy relationship male practitioners assume a greater responsibility than their female counterparts to be aware of this power inequity and to not abuse their position. I believe that any time we use the threat of withdrawal of our support to control our clients, or deprive our clients of credit for their successes to enable us to feel that we are the savior, we are abusing our power. I learned from my personal experience that I have assumed the creator script in both my personal and professional life. Although the men in my family enjoyed being the caretaker and supporter of women, I took this role to new heights in my family.

The males in my family were not Henry Higgins, the male 'god' of *My Fair Lady*. Although they thrived on idealization they were not in the position of power or charismatic enough to serve as a catalysis for women. Further they seemed to be unable to understand the concept that you would want to advance women. My father and grandfather were salesmen who lived in the work world of males and saw women in traditional serving roles. Like the men of my family I expected to be in control in relationships with women, but unlike them I had the ambition to be more successful and this led me to positions where I had more power to promote women. Also I was unlike the males in my family because I was politically and socially liberal, living as a young man during the birth of the modern feminist movement. Consequently, I developed a view of women that was less stereotypical than my father's. I valued a female's competence if not being able to treat her as equal.

Before returning to graduate school and entering the therapy field, I established a small business that was successful and employed a number of young women and men. One was a dedicated and sensitive young woman who had rebelled in her middle class family and ultimately married a member of a motorcycle gang. It was a debilitating life for her and when she was hired as an employee she was profoundly depressed. Seeing her abilities I gave her not only the job but also support and encouragement. Her dedication grew and she transformed herself into a successful and competent store manager. During this transformation she shared her struggles with me. She also idealized me and my contribution to her life. I, too, deluded myself that it was my support not her inherent strength that led to her success. I ultimately married this woman. Being married transformed our relationship. I was no longer her employer and mentor, relationships based on unequal power. Now we wanted our marriage to be based on equality and commonality. Neither of these attributes existed in our relationship and with great pain I ended the marriage several years later. Fortunately I experienced this relationship well before my training as a therapist. I learned the importance of appropriate boundaries from this experience and have never become enmeshed in a destructive relationship like this again. I still find myself, however, capable of believing at times that I can save a woman and transform her life.

Sheri was diagnosed as borderline personality disorder. She was a severe bulimic who also self-mutilated, and several times a week would get very drunk and have anonymous sex. She suffered major depression and was very closed off to me when we began therapy seven years ago. Over the course of a year she struggled with all of her impulsive and addictive behavior. She also shared her abuse history and took control of her life. By the year's end she was alcohol and bulimia free, and had ceased her self-mutilation. She had also begun successful dating relationships. She graduated the following year from college and took a position with a prestigious organization. We had worked well together but, in retrospect, I realize that I believed at that time, that it was my power that 'saved' her and wrought such change. Worse she believed the same.

I'm sure that women therapists are also vulnerable to such professional grandiosity, but I believe that males tend to assume this role more often and the damage done is potentially more harmful. I was reenacting with Sheri her lifelong script of getting her power from the male and restricting her from developing confidence in her own strength. I learned from this and other experiences that it is essential for me to help my clients differentiate their voice and power from their therapist's support. It helps to keep me grounded and to teach them not to seek their definition from others. Now the client and I review her accomplishments from the past and present, and challenge the attribution of her successes to her mentors, ensuring that she ultimately gives herself credit for her accomplishments.

COACH

There is an obvious overlap between the stereotypical view of coach and creator. But the coach role has one defining attribute that I learned and which has greatly handicapped my effectiveness as therapist. The coach demands absolute loyalty and compliance. He sets the training regime and the athlete complies. A role similar to the military commander and many fathers. A role that many males learn from early childhood. 'What Dad says is law' is an unstated rule in many families and one I experienced.

I loved to read during my early childhood the comics in the newspaper. I would get the paper in the morning and explore Little Abner and Dick Tracy when my father was not home. When he was I would have to sit patiently until he read the entire paper before I could see any section. That was his rule and it was not open to debate. This event was repeated in a thousand small ways in our home. If his authority was challenged or questioned, the offender was beaten back with a vengeance. Men are in charge and their authority was not to be challenged! As a male I learned this well and it was reenforced by school coaches and later by those in command in the military. Later I was also to experience similarly despotic women. But this method of domination as leadership was firmly taught as a male attribute long before I was aware that women too could value winning over relationships. As a result of this upbringing there was hiding under my adult view of respect for and equality with women a desperate need for them to obey me and be completely loyal.

Superficially, this gives one the confidence of authority. However, this view makes you vulnerable on two fronts with women clients. For those who challenge your authority you become the critical parent and often recreate their family experience. For those that accept your power and comply you reinforce their own powerlessness and undermine their attempt to find an authentic voice. Particularly damaging is the situation where a compliant woman who appears to be the ideal client suddenly stops complying. I, in the past, would personalize this as an act of disloyalty and project my sense of failure onto her. She had let me down. This could even at times result in discharging her from treatment and referring her to someone else. There are, of course, times when patients are pressured into treatment or clearly have no interest in changing their eating disorder. At such times, I feel that clients are appropriately discharged from treatment and I will still do so. But until I had understood my script I could not differentiate between the two situations. Now when I realize that it is my need to triumph that is threatening our interaction, I restore an equilibrium by asking the client what they feel they can do at this time and start there.

Judy, a 90 pound anorexic woman with severe bulimia, had made many improvements since beginning treatment over the summer. She no longer vomited or took laxatives. She was, however, resistant to any change in her eating and was not gaining weight. She had committed to attend a closed group for six months. Midway through the group she stopped coming without discussing it with me or the group. I personalized her actions and believed that she had let me down. She was not following my orders. Her history with me was to comply in therapy despite her having not done so for previous therapists. I had worked very hard in supporting her and my script's expectation had unfortunately led me to feel betrayed. My unfortunate response was to make continued individual treatment contingent on remaining with the group. In doing so I was punishing her for disloyalty but like the men in my family I was not aware that it was my own disloyalty to our relationship that was controlling our interaction. I had lost sight of the basic fact of hierarchy, power and responsibility. Blurring these lines, so natural for males in my family, also enforced the messages that these women so often received from their fathers: 'If you let me down I will abandon you.'

Fortunately I recognized my need to dominate and 'win' in this crisis with Judy. My body told me. Whenever I am emotionally struggling with a client the tension in my body screams out. After years of ignoring this kinesthetic voice I have learned to use it as my 'transference warning system'. It is invariably correct. Judy and I met and sorted out both of our emotional reactions which were my anger with her and her feeling of being abandoned by me.

Unlike the intoxication of being idealized or feeling like the master creator, the reaction to disloyalty is intense and very negative. It also frequently occurs suddenly and without warning. The longer a client has been seen and the more invested you are to her recovery can be predictors of an increased likelihood that this will occur. Being aware of your vulnerability to assume this role can help reduce its occurrence. Also learning to use your physiological reactions to warn yourself will help to interrupt your script early in its enactment. Since so many of our eating-disordered clients struggle to maintain control at all cost, this characteristic in a male therapist makes him particularly vulnerable to betray their relationship and damage the woman's emerging sense of self trust.

FATHER

The noun, father, conveys a panoply of concepts, definitions and emotions. The simple descriptor of one's biologic male parent has assumed many responsibilities, roles and isomorphic relationships – God the Father, Father Joseph, father figure. The image of a healthy father, supportive, protective, and caring seems to be one that could be adapted well to the male therapist. In this role the therapist could offer a healthy model to help the client feel secure and to be 'reparented' into greater self-esteem. Compared to the role of creator or coach this scripted role seems to offer a model for interaction.

I liked the image of myself 'fathering' but realized that it was just that, an image, and not a reality. To assume this image is to forget the important limitations of the therapeutic relationship. Male therapists aren't fathers and, if they act as if they are, they are setting up in the client emotional expectations that they can't and shouldn't attempt to meet. We are a male therapist. We are paid to assist a woman correct behaviors and patterns that hurt her life. We then cease our involvement in her life. A more healthy model may be that of a teacher who works intensely with a student and then helps them move on to their next challenge. After they move on further interactions are limited and we are replaced by other teachers who will further their progress.

I have had greater difficulty recognizing the occurrence of this role than the other scripts of idealized hero, coach and creator. Early in my role as therapist I made the same mistake with my clients that I had made with my sons. In my attempt to be the father I didn't have I became my father's mirror image. On one hand I was very attending and supportive but I was also still demanding complete control. This was confusing to my sons and baffling to my clients.

Julie, a 21-year-old college student, had an alcoholic father who had ignored her and a mother who was only marginally involved in her life. She had a severely alcoholic brother and an equally dysfunctional sister. Her grandmother had given birth to her son as a result of incest. Julie was the first in her family to go to college. She appeared at the hospital for treatment for her bulimia and major depression. While at the hospital she learned that her father was not her biological father. Her actual father did not know that she existed and, when she met him during treatment, he showed no interest in her.

In treatment Julie made dramatic progress in all areas. As treatment at the hospital neared its end she became anxious about returning to her home. Without being aware of it I assumed a father-like role and supported her moving to the town where our hospital was located. From a family therapy standpoint this may not have been a bad decision and the outcome was positive. But in retrospect I am aware I gave her the expectation that I would provide more emotional and direct support than I felt was appropriate. In my protective stance I was feeling fatherly but I was not willing nor ethically able to assume this role. I have seen female colleagues vulnerable to this script as well by assuming a mother's part. So this role may be less gender-based than the other previously discussed. Many of the eating-disordered clients, however, have distant withholding fathers. To create a mirage of a therapist father-figure with attending expectations can have negative consequences for the client when the expectations are not met.

To help avoid the development of the emotional expectations of my being a father-figure, I stress early in the treatment process the importance of developing a strong woman support network. Many women clients have a distrust of other women and an overvaluation of male friends. I equate recovery with learning to build an increased interdependence with women friends. It is not in the therapist/client relationship but in friendship that the client has to build her relationships. Further I reinforce the fact that it is their efforts, and not mine, that is responsible for their success. I also am careful to let them know that I care for them but that I can not be a part of their life beyond therapy. Finally, I help them attempt to construct a supportive relationship with their father, if possible, and to grieve its loss if a relationship is not possible. When this is the case I never offer myself as a replacement but encourage her to find that support from other male and female mentors.

RESTRUCTURING MY ROLE

Restructuring my role as a male meant also restructuring my role as a therapist. Once I had learned from my family story, women supervisors and the gender based literature, I was able to begin to transform my therapy. Restructuring my role has not, however, changed the core of who I am and it shouldn't. When a male therapist enters the process of reevaluating how he is programmed to interact with women, the important goal is to learn a second language. It is not to repudiate the strengths and richness of his heritage. The same family environment that taught me rules that inhibited my ability to hear and understand the issues women struggle with, also gave me the strengths that have made me a good clinician.

Fifteen years ago, when I first presented my family genogram in clinical supervision, I learned an important lesson. As part of our graduate supervisory process each student presented their family of origin in detail and the group discussed how our family history might affect our clinical world. I presented my family and was prepared to deal with my anger at my father and its possible effect on my work with males. When I had concluded my presentation the supervisor asked one question: 'What are the strengths that you got from your father?' I had no answer, yet this helped seek out strengths in myself and my family. I realized that I had developed a strong sense of self-reliance and a willingness to stand up for my beliefs. I am ethical, creative and a hard worker. Realizing these strengths helped me develop a closer connection to my father before he died the following year.

My strengths as a therapist also grow from my past and are a part of who I am. I have experienced similar feelings of inferiority and insecurity that clients describe and I am able to convey that understanding. I have a strong sense of humor that often seems to help clients through their pain. I am also very spontaneous and have retained a child-like sense of the world that can help clients rediscover such joy in themselves. I am also willing to take the responsibility for facilitating change which can be reassuring and help restore hope for clients and their families. Finally, I am male and that is a strength. I provide a model for a more respectful and supportive male/female relationship. Clients often express surprise that such an interaction is possible. Once they accept that it is, they seem more able to demand similar behavior from other men in their lives.

CONCLUSION

The process that I have outlined as my own personal experience as a male therapist has followed a course that parallels the stages of change that I see in many of the women I work with. I first realized the need to make changes. I learned from my past how I developed my distorted view of male and female relationships. I found in my present life specific behaviors that grew out of these views and needed to be modified. At the same time I also sought out my own strengths both from my past and from my current behaviors.

If I were to look at my work today and compare it with the work that I did five years ago, there would be many similarities as well as many differences. I still value the critical importance of nutritional recovery. The full restoration of the woman's body weight and body fat percentage to her normal range is stressed. The resumption of eating all foods without guilt is emphasized. I promote the reduction of physical activity to realistic levels and insist on complete abstinence from vomiting and laxatives. The clients are assisted in slowly restoring trust and acceptance of their bodies. We jointly explore their family of origin to attempt to understand and, when appropriate, restructure their family inter-actions. All issues of past abuse and trauma are sensitively dealt with.

The greatest change in my work can be seen in several areas where I have placed increased emphasis. I now spend much more effort listening to all of my clients beliefs, feelings and expressed needs. In doing so I have to constantly monitor my tendency to assume and interpret rather than ask. The most concrete example of this can be seen in the way I now structure my group work. After years of experience with inpatient group therapy and traditional outpatient groups I have begun to specialize in long-term closed groups. Last summer I began an intensive outpatient program for females with eating disorders. Four women live together as roommates in a group housing situation. They are trusted to support, nurture and monitor each other without staff interference. The staff meets with the women each day in the morning, afternoon and evening. The professionals establish the parameters and help them stay on task as well assist them in resolving issues that arise and which they can't resolve. It is the group, though, that has the power to change any aspect of treatment emphasis or structure. The only exceptions are the expectations with regard to nutrition, eating and bulimia which are set by staff. The results of this approach have dramatically surpassed the outcome that I experienced while working with more traditionally structured inpatient programs. More import-antly the women retain their progress to a much greater degree over time.

I feel that the key to this success is the different paradigm of empowering and listening rather than that of suspicion and control. It is derived from a second major difference in my work in general. I now encourage clients to embrace a more feminist world view. First and foremost, I encourage them to reconnect to their own needs, feelings and opinions. Next we work on their verbal expression of these. This includes developing an increased valuing of women and reliance on other women. I encourage them to develop more friendships with other women and to attempt to restore relationships with mothers and grandmothers. I discuss the importance of finding women mentors. I suggest that the clients read books that empower women such as *The Beauty Myth* (Wolf, 1991) and *Women Who Run With Wolves* (Estes, 1990).

Finally, I now give greater emphasis to the restructuring of their relationships with males. I teach women clients to take more responsibility for demanding respect from all males and for teaching males to hear their needs. This is not done from a belief that all boyfriends, husbands and fathers are the enemy. Rather the message is that these men are as much the victim of their own gender scripts as are the women. I utilize genograms to teach clients to understand how their father, for instance, was taught to deal with women in the way that he has been treating them. The client is then encouraged to reconstruct her father's view by educating him and interacting assertively with him.

Of course, there are some males that are abusive or so rigid that these attempts are unrealistic. The majority of men in their lives, however, will respond and can make dramatic changes. Most important is that the women learn that they have the power to be heard and the right to expect that they are. The fact that I have been able to change has proven to be a useful motivator for them to take the risk to believe that the males in their life can do so as well.

In 1996 in Washington DC hundreds of thousands of black men came together and marched in The Million Man March. They did so to demonstrate their commitment to being healthy husbands, fathers and friends. The act of marching was a commitment to change in the male role for these men. I believe that the process of my own change is my equivalent to that march. It is my recognition of the responsibility that I have accepted as a male who has chosen to work with eating-disordered women. Many male therapists have been fortunate enough to have absorbed in childhood a view of males and females that I am having to work to obtain. An equal number have learned gender scripts that are more like mine. These scripts reduce their ability to use their strengths as males unencumbered by their distorted views. I offer to them the support of someone who learned from his personal experiences to be a more responsible and more effective therapist. I now have clients stop in the middle of angry denunciations of men with an embarrassed laugh and comment: 'I'm sorry. I forgot that you were a man'. I hope that your clients will reward you with the same apology.

REFERENCES

Bruch, H. (1974) *Learning psychotherapy: Rationale and ground rules*, Cambridge: Harvard University Press.
Estes, C. (1992) *Women who run with wolves*, New York: Ballantine.
Gilligan, C. (1982) *In a different voice*, Cambridge: Harvard University Press.
Wolf, N. (1991) *The beauty myth: How images of beauty are used against women*, New York: Morrow.

CHAPTER FIVE

Families, therapists and family therapy in eating disorders

Jan B. Lackstrom and D. Blake Woodside

While working with eating disorder families is a rewarding and privileged experience, there is no doubt that the experience can also bring out significant challenges outside of the experience and training of most family therapists. Complications seem to appear from nowhere; therapeutic issues lead to clinical complications at best and therapeutic impasses and dropouts at worst. The unique and complex environment of the family of a person with an eating disorder provides family therapists working in this area with a very unusual experience – one where the most critical issue, that of the therapeutic alliance, is tested severely. Working with eating disorder families can lead to feelings of impotence, helplessness and hopelessness, while simultaneously engaging therapists into battles for control, rescue fantasies, or desires to punish. Therapists may find themselves using primitive, unsophisticated techniques as they try to force change by becoming authoritarian, plead for change in a state of desperation or even fire families who don't seem motivated to change. Therapists may come to view their treatment of such families as reduced to using one technique and trick after another in an effort to effect some sort of change – any change! What is it about these families that can make us feel as if it is a burden to engage them in treatment?

In this chapter we will present our approach to practice, and review some of the common problems a family therapist can expect to encounter in some form or another when working with eating-disordered families. We view the burden inherent in treating these families to be made up of equal parts simple extra work, and complex psychological and countertransferential issues. As such, many of the issues that we will review involve a basic understanding of the nature of countertransference, that is the sets of feelings that the patient/family induce in the therapist, which are themselves affected by the therapists past life experiences.

GENERAL PRINCIPLES OF OUR APPROACH

Specific elements of our approach have been described in a variety of sources (Shekter-Wolfson and Woodside, 1990; Woodside and Shekter-Wolfson, 1991; Woodside, Shekter-Wolfson, Brandes and Lackstrom, 1993). Colleagues commonly comment that we 'must be tired of working with those people' or 'how do you stand it?' This attitude reflects a general belief that eating-disordered families are manipulative and resistant to change. In some instances our colleagues see the individual with the eating disorder as a victim of her disturbed family or at the opposite extreme as a scheming manipulator who is purposefully destroying her long suffering family in her search for attention. These views are usually derived from simplistic interpretations of the theories of specific schools of family therapy, such as the Structural (Minuchin et al., 1978) or Milan Strategic (Selvini-Palazzoli, 1978) schools. We tend to view eating-disordered women and their families as caught in a process that they know is not working and yet are unable to change. We have rarely met a patient or a family member who has declared their goal to be the production of misery for other family members. Our experience has been that almost all members of eating-disordered families are making their best efforts to either recover or to help with the process of recovery. This is not to say that their efforts are successful; but rather that they are generally well intended, although often affected by fear, frustration, anger, guilt, despair and misunderstanding.

Given the above, we are not interested in finding out who is to blame for the eating disorder and we convey that clearly and directly to the family as a whole. Rarely is the cause of the illness clear. We are interested in finding out what individual family members think has caused the eating disorder and what is perpetuating it, and view the family as a rich source of information in these areas. The shift from a blaming stance to a more neutral position helps everyone, including the family therapist, recognize the complexity of the influences acting on and within the individual and the family. These families are very often stuck in rather rigid, inflexible patterns of behavior, and a search for blame serves to increase the rigidity of the family system while members seek to defend themselves. On the other hand, the acceptance of total guilt by a family member ('to blame') can render that person unable to fully participate because of their unworthiness or need to compensate.

This does not mean that individuals are not held accountable for their behavior in our treatment. Rather, their behavior is set within a context of well intended if misguided efforts, that is positively connoted. We facilitate an exploration of multiple causes by taking a stance of curiosity where each person's thoughts, beliefs, ideas and feelings are sought out and respected. Differences between family members are seen as differences to be understood rather than right or wrong answers. The approach appears to gradually erode the rigidity of beliefs and behaviors.

We believe that involuntary treatment is ineffective as definitive treatment for eating disorders, and serves only a limited role in the acute management of medical emergencies. We work with whichever family members are willing to attend the session. We avoid the struggle for control that follows when the therapist insists that every family member attend therapy. Typically, within a few sessions we find that most if not all of the family members are attending. If the identified patient does not attend, we will work with her family for a brief period of time, focusing on how to cope with the eating-disordered person as she is in the present while also getting on with their own lives.

We have clear views about safety. We feel unable to continue with family or marital therapy when one or more members of the family are being physically or sexually abused. We do not have expertise in working with families where abuse is current: with families where physical or verbal abuse is occurring, we demand that this behavior cease as a condition of continuing treatment. We are aware that we will lose some families because of the rigidity of this stance; however, we are prepared to sacrifice the family work for safety. We will normally ensure that the victim of the abuse receives appropriate individual treatment in such a case.

COMMON ISSUES THAT ADD TO THE THERAPIST'S BURDEN

ISSUES RELATED TO THE PHYSICAL HEALTH OF THE IDENTIFIED PATIENT

Family therapists often work with families where one member is medically ill. However, it is rare for there to be such dramatic evidence of physical deterioration as is found in eating disorders. Families with an emaciated individual or with a member suffering the severe complications of purging behaviors present a unique set of tasks for the family therapist. Does one simply ignore the physical state of the patient, and risk becoming marginalized by the family's concerns about the obvious fragility of the identified patient? Or does the therapist risk losing a focus on the family dynamics by responding to the physical problems? The therapist is challenged to delicately balance a number of variables. The therapist must attend to the patient's health status, which typically changes for better and worse a number of times throughout treatment. The meaning of health and illness in the family must be considered. Changing health status may be a meta-communication to the family and as such the interaction between health status and family dynamics must be explored and worked through.

For all family therapists having a physician deal with medical complications is probably the least complicated option. This allows the family therapist to focus on the family systems issues. The family therapist without a medical background is encouraged to learn about the basic medical issues that people with eating disorders experience. The risk of this approach is that additional caregivers provide opportunity for confusion and the playing off of one caregiver against the other. Non-physician family therapists run the risk of not paying enough attention to the physical health issues and consequently not flagging dangerous medical conditions. They may also pay too much attention to health concerns for fear of the patient dying. Either stance can derail the family treatment. Physician family therapists run the risk of blurring their roles. While they may be more relaxed dealing with medical issues, this blurring of roles may pull the physician family therapist away from their systemic focus and draw them into a hierarchical authoritarian stance more typical of a medical model of treatment again, derailing family treatment.

> Andrea, age 18, was initially seen with her family in an intensive care unit, just after an episode of respiratory failure that was secondary to an infection she had acquired due to her very low weight. She had three previous failed treatments. Her parents were focused on her physical state and not very interested in thinking about what had happened since her last admission.

It is not useful to pretend that the family's concerns about physical health do not exist or to view their concerns as resistance to facing more meaningful issues. They must be supported in their concerns especially when the patient's health is in an acute state. While the goal of understanding family process may not appear to be met by such a strategy, the family therapist can use these situations to observe the family in a state of crisis and arrive at some tentative conclusions about the family system. The offer of unconditional support during such a period of crisis is often the beginning of the development of a therapeutic alliance with the family that may allow them to examine more difficult issues at a later time. Many families experience the therapist's insistence on focusing on family process at a time of medical crisis as an empathic failure, and feel the therapist is not tuned into their needs. In the above case, the family therapist validated the parents' preoccupation with their daughter's tenuous physical condition, stating openly that an examination of the reasons for the failure of previous treatments would be delayed until later in the treatment process.

There is no doubt that the addition of health concerns related to anorexia and bulimia add a burden to the therapist. The therapist must contend with concerns about the identified patient's ability to participate if she is medically compromised. People do die from complications related to their eating disorders, and this threat can hold the family and therapist hostage. Both the therapist and family must face the risk of the intervention leading to a worsening of the identified patient's condition. However, by avoiding the risk the therapy may come to a halt and the process of change be stopped.

MULTIPLE HELPERS

For a patient with an eating disorder, the family therapist may be one of a vast array of health care providers. Clear communication between various professionals is essential but typically difficult to accomplish. Even when the family therapist is working as a member of a multidisciplinary team, he or she may feel marginalized or ignored by other team members who do not value the importance of a systems/contextual approach. Issues of power and authority on the team do effect the functioning of the professional group including their ability to collaborate.

The family therapist must bear some responsibility for communicating his or her ideas in a clear, understandable language, being careful to frame treatment goals in terms that will be understood as complimentary to the work of the other professionals. It can be tempting for the family therapist to isolate himself or herself from the treatment team if he or she feels his or her work is unappreciated. Consistently advocating for family treatment or a systems approach can become tiresome. Multiple helpers provides a rich setting for splitting and the undermining of the treatment plan.

> Darlene, a severely ill 14-year old anorexic, had been admitted to hospital against her will in a jurisdiction where her parents could consent to treatment on her behalf. She was adamant that she did not require treatment, and the family meeting where this was discussed was characterized by alternating frosty silences, shouts, pleading and threats. In an attempt to minimize splitting, members from several disciplines were present. Towards the end of the meeting, the family therapist, wearily reviewing the nature of the proposed treatment for the third time with the anxious parents, noticed the pediatrician present talking to the patient quietly. As the family therapist wound up his summary, the parents seeming to be reluctantly coming around, the pediatrician announced triumphantly 'we don't have to do this – Darlene has agreed to come to lunch with me tomorrow – I'm sure she will be fine now'.

Compared to working independently working as one of a number of helpers, whether community or institutionally based, is a great deal more work. When the professional relationships are more distant it can be difficult to confront issues that lead to splitting, such as a variation in approach to treatment. Those family therapists who work very closely on structured teams can find it equally difficult because of they must work together intensely everyday and as such hesitate to confront issues that they fear might lead to further problems.

In an effort to avoid splitting the family therapist must put work into forming a team approach where each person is clear about their own and others responsibilities, know what the mechanisms for making treatment decisions are, and have a clear understanding of the process by which information will be shared. While these are time-consuming and occasionally energy-sapping tasks, we feel that the effort is well worthwhile in the longer run.

MULTIPLE RELAPSES AND CHRONICITY

Many family therapists also find the issue of multiple relapses to be a burden. The therapist may take responsibility for the relapse, either by concluding that not enough had been done or that the actual interventions had become toxic to the family. Working with the family of a patient with an eating disorder, especially a chronic eating disorder, can be a humbling experience. The experience of relapse can make the therapist feel hopeless, angry and ineffective. It is difficult, if not impossible, to maintain one's ability to think strategically and therapeutically if one feels the situation is hopeless or if one feels ineffective.

We have found it helpful to take a long view of the process of recovery. We accept that recovery is a step-wise process and that relapses are frequent. Frequent and sufficient peer support can help the family therapist avoid the extremes of despair on the one hand and anger and blame on the other. It is often easier to blame the family in an effort to deal with one's frustrations and sense of ineffectiveness. Appropriate peer support must include individuals trained in a systems approach, who either work with eating disorder families, or have a large body of experience working with other difficult groups.

Over-investment in a family is another side of this same coin, and is frequent when treatment is prolonged or when very large amounts of treatment resources are invested in a given patient/ family. The family therapist can in effect become a member of the family or become a close friend which clearly compromises his or her ability to observe, assess and intervene in as objective a way as is possible. While this issue is not unique to the eating disorder family, we see it as more common because of the desperate nature of the identified patient's condition, and the age and usual potential for higher functioning of the victims.

The Mettzo family has been in treatment two times in conjunction with their daughter Clara's admission for treatment of bulimia into a day treatment program. Although very eager to engage in family therapy Mr and Mrs Mettzo had difficult appreciating Clara's difficulty crossing two cultures – wishing to remain loyal to her Italian heritage but also wanting the freedom of a Canadian girl. The therapist was very attached to the family as it was clear they had many strengths, were very loving and had good intentions. After the second admission Mrs Mettzo would telephone the therapist from time to time to let her know how Clara was doing. When the third admission was discussed the family therapist was looking forward to seeing the Mettzo's again. Although she enjoyed seeing the family no change occurred. It was only after Mrs Mettzo clearly did not follow through on an agreement to stop going into Clara's room to clean up did the therapist realize how she had been avoiding confronting Mrs Mettzo about a number of issues. The family therapist recognized she was treating Mrs Mettzo carefully, as did family members picking up, a belief that Mrs Mettzo was fragile but, more importantly the therapist also recognized that she did not want to engage in a confrontation, for fear of disrupting her pleasant relationship with Mrs Mettzo.

FAMILY ADAPTATION TO CHRONIC ILLNESS

Families are usually quite good at adapting to chronic stressors, such as a long-standing illness in one of the members of the family. Under normal conditions, this is viewed as a positive occurrence that is often seen as buffering the family from some of the effects of the illness. Therapists should not be surprised to see this occur in eating disorders, which, after a few years, seem to the family as if they are never going to go away. And, in fact, we view most of the adaptation that occurs as healthy. Occasionally, a family will adapt in a way that leaves the family therapist feeling unsettled.

Cathy, aged 36, had been married to Adam for about 15 years. She had been ill with anorexia nervosa at the time, although mildly so. Cathy had been in many treatment programs over the years, sometimes with a partial response and sometimes with very little response. While the severity of her illness would wax and wane, she never became ill enough to warrant involuntary treatment, and had no significant periods of remission from her symptoms. Throughout most of this time, she was able to work: at the time of her most recent assessment she had been off work for about two years due to a gradual deterioration in her work performance related to her chronic illness. Her husband described a careful series of adaptations that the couple had made to her illness – marking times when she was a bit better by deliberately being more active, describing the careful discussion that they had in deciding that children would be a bad choice for them – and while her husband acknowledged that he knew that recovery might be possible for her, he clearly stated that 'if this is as good as it gets, then I'm willing to settle for the way things are'. The therapist, in reporting this to the rest of the team, was unsure as how to interpret the remark, given the chronicity of the patient's illness and her failure to respond to treatment.

A very common situation that we have observed is the family having some difficulty in shedding patterns of adaptation when a patient makes a full recovery after many years of illness.

Vanessa had suffered from bulimia for about ten years. Her family had developed a pattern of monitoring her behaviour, for which her mother had primary responsibility. Vanessa's sister was the secondary monitor, with her father being the monitor of last resort. Vanessa had been symptom-free for over a year before the family felt able to confront this situation more directly.

While this sort of reaction is often viewed as evidence of family psychopathology, it may simple be ingrained habit, habit that no-one in the family ever thought would have to change. While people are socialized to accept the occurrence of chronic illness, by observing the aging of their parents and grandparents, few are prepared for the total recovery of a chronically ill individual. And indeed, there are few illnesses where an individual can be ill for many years and make a full recovery – alcoholism and eating disorders being two of those few.

The additional burden for the family therapist working with such chronic illness is the risk of buying into the belief that the situation is hopeless, or cannot change, which leads to nihilism and despair: or feeling despairing at taking a contrary stand, while the family attempts to convince the therapist that he or she is wrong.

POLARIZATION

Family therapists are often at the center of debates about the need for treatment for individuals with an eating disorder. It is common for the individual with the eating disorder and her family to be at odds about the need for treatment. The most common situation is that where the patient is less critically ill and not interested in treatment. Very often the family and the patient end up in a polarized position with each hoping that the family therapist will side with them.

The most dramatic of these situations involves involuntary treatment. While this is an issue in a number of psychiatric illnesses, the eating-disordered patient is often highly articulate and convincing about her opinions about the advisability of such treatment. Except for the most emaciated patient who looks very ill, most eating-disordered patients do not have the obvious changes in mental functioning that may accompany such illnesses as schizophrenia. Very often the family therapist can quickly find himself or herself caught right in the middle – with both the family and the patient attempting to recruit an ally.

> Barb weighed about 22 kg at 1.57m and had been severely anorectic for over a decade. She was brought to hospital by her very concerned family because she had been fainting at home and they feared that her condition was becoming unstable. Barb vigorously denied that anything was wrong, and objected vociferously when her parents began to ask about involuntary treatment. Both Barb and her parents turned to the therapist hoping that the therapist would make the very difficult decision for them.

As outlined earlier, this situation is made more complex when the family therapist is also a physician who has the power to admit a patient against her will. The family therapist must recognize and acknowledge that the situation involves a profound power imbalance. The therapist must acknowledge that the patient may be at risk to have her rights taken away, while avoiding blaming her parents for having initiated such a significant action.

It must be acknowledged that in situations of polarization and especially in situations of involuntary treatment, the patient may refuse to engage in any sort of family treatment and more importantly forbid the therapist from having contact with the family. In general, we advocate respecting the wishes of the patient in this situation, as failing to do so is likely to result in a further reduction in the chance that the patient will eventually form a therapeutic alliance with the therapist and be willing to consider family or any other treatment in the future. Additionally in some jurisdictions it is illegal to speak of a patient with others without their express permission. Perhaps most important clinically is the continued loss of power that the patient would experiences if the therapist continued without her permission. In such situations the dilemma would be discussed with the family in an effort to plan the next step. Most families are prepared to wait a certain amount of time and begin therapy again when the patient feels ready. In other situations the family might be referred to our family psychoeducation group or referred to a family therapist who is not constrained by the patient's wishes. In the case of Barb, a decision was eventually made to admit the patient essentially against her will: and while she cooperated with the involuntary treatment while in hospital, she subsequently refused to have anything to do with medical personnel and eventually died from medical complications of her illness.

The burden for the family therapist in such a situation can be overwhelming. Usually, the issues seem to be stark – life and death – and the family paralyzed and unable to resolve the impasse between themselves and a child who seems bent on self-destruction. It is almost impossible for the family therapist to avoid getting caught up in the systemic panic about the nearly-dead identified patient: and in such a situation advocating for even a limited amount of autonomy on the part of the identified patient may seem ludicrous.

Nonetheless, this is the stance that we advocate. Occasionally, despite everyone's best efforts, an identified patient will die from her illness and this will leave the family therapist who has advocated for respect of the rights of the patient to decide with a significant burden of guilt and a feeling of responsibility. Sadly, a death does not always bring an end to issues of polarization, as it is unfortunately common for family members and (regretfully) other health care practitioners to lay blame on someone – anyone for the tragic loss of the suffering patient. Therapists who advocate an autonomous stance for the identified patient are easy targets for scapegoating: and as is often the case, the best defense against this is by being open about the risks and benefits of the approach we recommend from the very beginning, both with family members and with other involved health-care practitioners.

SOCIAL AND CULTURAL ISSUES

The recognition of social and cultural issues as an important predisposing factor in the etiology of eating disorders makes it essential for family therapists to be sensitive to social and cultural influences in each family. Most family therapists try to place each family within a context: however, it is rare to complete a detailed assessment and focus work in this area. Assessing cultural influences is of particular importance for eating disorder families for several reasons. First, some culturally determined behaviors and ideas may run counter to treatment suggestions and may inadvertently perpetuate the illness. Cultural ideas about role expectations, especially gender-driven roles, may be very relevant to the eating-disordered person. A thorough understanding of the family's cultural context will also help the therapist avoid labeling behaviors and beliefs as 'wrong', when they are simply driven by the cultural background of family members.

The Frank family discovered Christine's bulimia when Mrs Frank was called to the emergency department of the local hospital. Although suspicious for two years, Mrs Frank's concerns for her daughter were dismissed by her husband and daughter as not likely to be real. Mr Frank clearly held all of the overt power in the family as was indicated by his ability to dismiss his wife's concerns and control her actions. Mrs Frank had little personal power. She was responsible for the house and affective issues within the family although her decisions could be and were overruled by her husband.

Both Mr and Mrs Frank were very concerned about appearance. Each believed their personal and family status rested in how they looked to the world. Mrs Frank took great care of her appearance and spent a generous allowance on clothes. She frequently spoke to Christine about taking care of herself early on in an effort to delay the aging process. She also spoke to Christine about being careful with her weight. Both parents were happy when Christine lost her 'babyfat'. They encouraged Christine to do well in high school in preparation for her professional career.

When Christine lost weight and began to groom herself in a more elegant fashion Mr Frank began to take her out to lunch, not to enjoy his daughters company rather to appear to be lunching with a younger woman. He did not realize that Christine would excuse herself to vomit her lunches in the restaurant washroom.

After the emergency room visit Mr Frank could no longer deny the eating problems. He insisted the bingeing and vomiting stop before he had to tell his family. He put his wife in charge of policing Christine. Again Mrs Frank had concerns about policing but backed down especially when her husbands demands for stricter supervision were supported by her own mother who said that Mrs Frank had always been too lenient with Christine. Needless to say, Mrs Frank was unable to police her daughter effectively enough to stop her from bingeing and purging.

Mrs Frank insisted upon treatment when Christine's health became precarious a second time. When asked about the delay in seeking treatment Mrs Frank said she did not want to bother her busy husband and when pushed admitted she was concerned she would be seen as a bad mother by the extended family. Christine was very upset with her mother for policing because it reminded her of what a failure she was. Mr. Frank was frustrated that the family seemed out of control and he could not understand why his family just didn't do what he told them to do.

Families readily answer questions about how they are similar to or different from the culture at large. While most families are able to identify differences and similarities between their own and the local cultures attitudes towards weight, shape, and appearance, they often become 'stuck' when exploring more fundamental issues such as power and control. Working with an awareness of the effects of culture and ethnicity requires yet another body of information that needs to be mastered by the family therapist. The acquisition of this additional information will require the therapist to examine how his or her own cultural and ethnic background has influenced their own attitudes towards the variables described above.

It can be burdensome to feel one is constantly challenging the social and cultural status quo. Challenging what can appear to be universal and fundamental beliefs and truths or ways of behavior can be overwhelming and exhausting. If attempted in a militant consciousness-raising fashion this sort of work can be seen by the family as a kind of forced political correctness, which will increase defensiveness. The purpose of focusing on social and cultural issues is to help the family examine the way their personal context is influencing their choices and to be more able to make conscious and individual decisions about issues such as the importance of weight and shape, the roles of men and women, the distribution and use of power in the family, the influence of multigenerational beliefs and so on. Again, it is important for the family therapist to have a supportive personal and professional peer group to be able to go to for support and consultation in an effort to avoid capitulation or burnout.

SHAME AND BLAME

Eating disorder families appear to be particularly sensitive to issues of blame and shame. Families report concerns about acceptance within the larger family network, their social acquaintances and their communities. Just as families are concerned about their image within the larger system individuals within the family are concerned about their acceptability within the family. This anxiety may have its origin in the context of blaming and shaming behaviors by significant others.

> Mr Andrews attended an eating disorders conference sponsored by the parent-teachers association at his daughters high school. During a break he approached one of the speakers asking what he should do to help his daughter. He had been trying to support his daughter's recovery by encouraging her to move steadily at her own pace, which put him in conflict with his wife who wanted faster results. Recently two of his best friends confronted him, while golfing, stating that he really wasn't doing a good job as a father because he wasn't 'taking charge' of his daughter, by which they meant he should make her eat. Mr Andrews was very embarrassed about this confrontation and questioned the support he had been giving his daughter, his role as a father and his relationship with his wife.

Many families report that they have been blamed for the eating disorder by family, friends or health-care professionals. Families are often embarrassed about seeking treatment. They may try to make the family look perfect or may quickly learn how to be 'good patients' in an effort to please the therapist. This false front can be difficult to challenge as the family colludes to prevent the therapist from knowing them in a genuine way. In some families one person, often the patient or a younger sibling, may threaten to break the rules about family loyalty and presenting the family in the best light possible. In this case the family may quickly attempt to silence that person in an effort to maintain the family rules. However, the 'rule-breaker' may have a perfect way to continue to present the message that there are problems, especially if she is the identified patient – the eating symptoms remain the sign that all is not well. The more perfect or compliant the family become the 'louder' the symptoms may have to be to alert others to family unhappiness and distress.

We generally find that a gradual approach to such families works best. We start with concrete content issues, using these as a forum to establish that our own approach is non-blaming and that the therapist will not abandon or shame the family. This is both a didactic and experiential process. In particularly rigid families it may be necessary to assess and confront, in an empathic manner, the process of censuring and controlling in the family. Each family member must learn that the therapist is not going to abandon them because they are 'bad'. The family as a whole, or an emissary, may test the therapist in a number of ways to see if the therapist is indeed trustworthy. Just as the family as a whole must learn to experience a trusting and accepting relationship with the therapist, they must also learn to provide the same for each other to enable the family to become a place that is safe for the individual to be a separated person while also remaining a member of the family. This is the work of therapy.

The process of unmasking may happen relatively quickly or may take years. It is not uncommon for a secret to be revealed after the family therapist has confidently reported that he or she has a complete knowledge of the family story. Again, it is important for the family therapist to appreciate the power of shame and to remain empathic while also assisting the family to make necessary changes. It is easy to either collude with the false presentation or to become frustrated trying to force disclosure and change too quickly. It is frustrating to be working with a particular hypothesis that changes completely with the new information. It is also important to try to not become aggravated when secrets or new information are revealed. Even worse is to struggle with the family and blame yourself for not being able to formulate your ideas in a meaningful way and then realize you did not have all of the information needed to do your work.

FAMILY PROBLEMS OUTSIDE OF THE FAMILY THERAPY SETTING

FAMILY CONSTELLATION

As mentioned earlier we work with the family members who present themselves and generally find that the all family members will eventually attend. There are some issues related to attendance that the family therapist must give some thought to. For instance, some parents will ask to be seen alone. As a rule this should be discouraged, especially with adult patients. We appreciating that some parents may have difficulty speaking in front of their children; however it seems to us that 'speaking behind someone's back' does more damage to the therapeutic alliance than it helps. Our experience has also shown that within a reasonable amount of time a secret or issue that parents wish to reveal in this fashion becomes clear by itself in some way. As is the case in much of family therapy, the parents usually discover that the secret is not much of a secret at all!

In some situations the parents will draw a strong boundary around themselves and the person with the eating disorder, excluding other family members. Although this maneuver certainly piques our curiosity, we will usually simply explore it and not insist on anyone's attendance. It is rare for such a prohibition to last for long. While a therapist may be concerned that important and significant information is missing, a decision to force the issue will likely result in a disruption of the therapeutic alliance. Working with eating disorder families is a long term process. When patients have returned for a second or third admission those who have been reluctant to include the entire family usually do so. They have come to trust the family therapist and the helping process or are desperate enough to try anything to help. Our experience is that the addition of the excluded siblings reveals additional problems or intensifies the problematic family interactions.

Some families will be separated or divorced with the parents either living with or married to new partners. There may be children from these new relationships or there may be step-brothers and step-sisters. This requires the family therapist to consider who should be present in which meetings. There are no clear indications to direct the family therapist. Ideally everyone will be involved in some kind of family contact. Taking direction, at least initially, from the patient appears to be the most reliable indicator of how to proceed. The family therapist will want to have separate sessions with each 'new' family. It is not unusual to encounter resistance from the new partners or the patient regarding the inclusion of the new partner in family work. As with any resistance this needs to be explored. In some situations biological parents have actively continued to co-parent. In this situation the biological family should be invited together. If the two families have developed a good working relationship the family therapist should include step parents in these meetings.

A more difficult decision is whether to invite biological parents to one meeting when they are caught in a deeply adversarial relationship. This is often a particularly important issue when the patient is younger and custody is in dispute. In a deeply adversarial relationship there is a great danger of the session becoming unmanageable and destructive to those present. Typically the family therapist will want to keep the boundary between the two families clear and separate. The patient will need to negotiate issues with each separate family. In each family meeting the family therapist will want to explore the effects of the separation/divorce, remarriage, siblings and step-siblings, roles and relationships, the similarities and differences between the two families and the nature of the relationship between the two families.

MULTIPLE PROBLEMS

Eating disorder families can also experience problems in addition to the eating disorder. These problems can be identified directly by the family or remain a secret waiting to be uncovered.

The Scarlett family were attending their second round of family therapy in conjunction with Rachelle's second admission to the Day Hospital Programme for treatment of anorexia nervosa. Rachelle's brother David, who lived at the other end of the country and was visiting agreed to participate in the initial family assessment. David spoke directly about his concerns about his father's drinking problem.

This was not identified during the first set of family sessions. Mr and Mrs Scarlett attempted to minimize the issue, but Rachelle's elder sister supported David. The elder sister was able to persist with this issue despite David's return to his home. At first the children and then the parents began to acknowledge the effects of Mr Scarlett's drinking over the years, including how Rachelle became more agitated and symptomatic when her father went on an alcohol binge. In the end Mr Scarlett declined a referral to a rehabilitation programme. This was processed fully with the family. The eldest sister decided to attend Alanon Meetings for additional support.

Although identifiable as individual problems these problems are entwined within the family dynamics which include the eating disorder. Exploration of the effects of the problem in the individual and the family can be pursued. This exploration includes a discussion of appropriate treatment options. For example, a depressed mother could be referred to her family physician for help with her mood while a sibling who is shoplifting might be attended to within the context of the present family therapy. The decision to refer elsewhere depends to a certain degree on the abilities of the family therapist and the mandate of the eating disorder service. Clinically it may be a wise decision to isolate some individual treatment from a family system that is having problems with boundaries.

PARADOXES AND TRIANGULATION

Finally, we wish to comment on two special situations, paradoxes and triangulation. Patients can find themselves caught in a paradox that immobilizes them.

Vanessa, a 28 year old single woman with a 13 year history of severe anorexia and bulimia was admitted to the Day Hospital Programme directly from an alcohol and drug rehabilitation programme. This was Vanessa's first admission to the Day Hospital although she had three admissions to other programmes. In family therapy Mrs Barfoot begged Vanessa to tell her more about how she was doing. At the same time Mr and Mrs Barfoot complained that Vanessa wasn't taking care of herself. They reported that Vanessa was embarrassed to bump into her friends when she wasn't looking well, despite Vanessa's always being neatly dressed and groomed. Mr and Mrs Barfoot denied they had any concerns about Vanessa's appearance except they believed that if she looked better, 'put a little colour on her lips' she would feel better. Vanessa challenged her parent's concern with her appearance and they denied and concerns about her appearance or social position.

Mrs Barfoot revealed that she had a heart condition and at the time of the family therapy was about to undergo further tests to determine a course of treatment. While she made repeated requests of Vanessa to disclose her own health status accurately, including those times when she was doing poorly, so she could prepare herself, she also reported the news of Vanessa doing poorly upset her terribly and in fact challenged her health. Mr Barfoot acknowledged this, reporting that he had to tend to his wife whenever Vanessa disclosed that the eating disorder was bad and she wasn't doing well Mrs Barfoot insisted that 'Vanessa is going to kill me, I have heart problems but it is better to know about the problems'. Mrs Barfoot said she was afraid that Vanessa was going to kill herself with her illness and she herself would never recover. When questioned directly, she did not think the stress would actually kill her, but ... Vanessa found herself caught. She wanted to become more forthright with her family because she needed their help, however, she was not convinced her mother should tolerate the truth about her status. She thought her mother only wanted to hear the good news as was reflected in her parent's need for her to look put together. This left the entire family trying to appear successful and helpful while avoiding the really difficult issues of Mr Barfoot's embezzlement, Mrs Barfoot's affair and anorexia, Vanessa's eating disorder and the family dynamic. It was understandable when Vanessa would describe herself as trapped in the family and doubting whether she could ever relinquish her symptoms.

This sort of bind is not uncommon in eating disorder families and is very stressful to the family therapist. Family therapists are encouraged to work with a family therapy team or to seek peer supervision when working with these sorts of binds. The family therapy team or consultant can provide support for the family therapist and can help unravel the paradox. It is also tempting to try to gather information directly from third parties about the illness of one of the family members: this is generally a mistake, and the family therapist should simply accept whatever is presented as representing reality.

This type of problem can occasionally progress to one where the therapist is triangulated between some members of the family and other health-care providers.

Marlene had severe, chronic anorexia nervosa, which had not improved despite numerous attempts at intensive treatment and a long course of individual outpatient treatment. She had eventually consented to another course of intensive inpatient treatment when she had a respiratory arrest that required her to ventilated. Because of the frailty of her condition, she required a long period of ventilation, during which she could not speak as she was intubated. One of us, who had been involved with the family over the years, was besieged by requests by all the physicians involved to come down on one side or the other as to whether she should be fed, whether she should be allowed to die, whether her breathing tube should be removed, and so on. While the therapist's natural inclination was to follow the wishes of the family, these wishes eventually became a part of their ongoing battle with the staff of the intensive care unit about any number of issues related to Marlene's care.

Fortunately, issues related to external triangulation are rarely so serious and can usually be resolved without difficulty.

CONCLUSIONS

Working with eating disorder families can be rewarding, but is complex and demanding. The physical state of the identified patient provides an unusual set of circumstances to many family therapists, and the chronicity and severity of the illness may be so severe that family therapists are at risk of losing sight of the principles that usually guide their practice. The requirement for the acquisition of new sets of knowledge adds an additional burden to the family therapist newly come to the area.

When working as members of a multidisciplinary team, family therapists are well-placed to function as leaders when the team is attempting to deal with critically ill patients. The family therapist's background in a systems approach will allow him or her to have a good grasp of what is happening on the team and to be helpful in resolving impasses. However, adopting such a role is an additional burden for the family therapist, and maybe more or less uncomfortable depending on the structure of the team.

In summary, it is important to acknowledge that family therapy with eating-disordered people and their families can be burdensome at times and, as such, can challenge the therapist personally and professionally. Experiencing an excessive amount of burden in

one's work is a serious obstacle to the establishment and maintenance of a therapeutic alliance with a family. The therapist can
mitigate the sense of burden in several ways. First, simply acknowledging the complexity of the issues these families bring to treatment
will assist the therapist to be prepared. Second, a willingness to be
able to monitor one's own objectivity and go for supervisory
assistance or consultation will allow the therapist to feel less stuck
and burdened with the entire responsibility for the case.

A willingness to expand one's knowledge base, both in terms of
reading new material and sharing the experiences of others will
further allow the therapist to feel less isolated and thus more
effective. A less isolated therapist will be more able to remain
grounded in basic family therapy values and principles, allowing
him/her to continue to be empathic, accepting, and neutral, and to
focus systematically on the problem at hand.

Finally, the therapist must expect to need to be more than
usually vigilant to his or her own thought, feelings and reactions
to the identified patient and her family. The struggle of these
families touches on many themes that are currently very active for
our society as a whole – the role of women, power inequities, the
importance of appearance – that are relevant outside of the
therapeutic situation.

REFERENCES

Minuchin, S., Rosman, B. and Baker, L. (1978) *Psychosomatic Families: Anorexia Nervosa in Context*, Cambridge (MA): Harvard University Press.

Selvini-Palazzoli, M. (1978) *Self-starvation: From Individual to Family Therapy in the Treatment of Anorexia Nervosa*, New York: Jason Aronson.

Shekter-Wolfson, L. and Woodside, D.B. (1990) 'Family therapy'. In Piran, N. and Kaplan, A.S. (eds) *A Day Hospital Group Treatment Program for Anorexia Nervosa and Bulimia Nervosa* (pp. 79–109), New York: Brunner/Mazel.

Woodside, D.B. and Shekter-Wolfson, L. (eds) (1991) *Family Approaches in Treatment of Eating Disorders*. Washington, D.C.: American Psychiatric Press.

Woodside, D.B., Shekter-Wolfson, L.F., Brandes, J. and Lackstrom, J.B. (1993. *Eating Disorders and Marriage: The Couple in Focus*, New York: Brunner/Mazel.

CHAPTER SIX

Compulsory treatment of anorexia nervosa patients

Rosalyn Griffiths and Janice Russell

INTRODUCTION

Compulsory treatment – treatment imposed by legal means – may be deemed necessary in the management of anorexia nervosa. For bulimia nervosa, the characteristic symptoms of bingeing and purging can usually be corrected with outpatient treatment, and the normal body weight confers cognitive and biological advantages. In general, bulimic patients refer themselves for treatment and are therefore motivated to accept it, so the question of compulsory treatment rarely becomes an issue.

Anorexia nervosa is a serious psychiatric illness commonly seen in adolescents girls and young women. In females aged 15–19 years, the prevalence is about 0.5 per cent making it the third most common chronic medical condition in this age group, while in women aged 20–24 years the figure is about half this rate (Lucas, Beard, O'Fallon and Kurlan, 1991). It has been estimated that in our home state of New South Wales, Australia, there are approximately 400 new cases each year and approximately 7,500 persons are affected at any time (Beumont, Kopec-Schroeder and Lennerts, 1995). The illness often runs a chronic course, few patients recovering in less than four years and a minority remaining permanently ill. Not only is it the cause of much psychological distress and unhappiness for the patient and family, but it is associated with serious physical morbidity, and with a mortality rate of 20 per cent at 20 years (e.g. Theander, 1985), by far the highest of any functional psychiatric illness, and high compared to most chronic medical illnesses. Treatment is difficult, demanding and time consuming. It is further complicated by the patient's denial and a reluctance to agree to treatment, this difficulty not infrequently being compounded by collusion on the part of their families (Beumont, Russell and Touyz, 1993). Untreated, anorexia nervosa can become life-threatening, and in the event of treatment refusal, compulsory treatment may need to be seriously considered.

We will discuss the ethical, medico-legal and psychological issues pertaining to treatment refusal, compulsory treatment, the implementation of compulsory treatment illustrated by a case study, and special treatment strategies in anorexia nervosa. International mental health legislation and outcome of compulsory treatment for mental disorders are briefly reviewed.

WHY DO ANORECTIC PATIENTS REFUSE TREATMENT?

Treatment refusal may occur prior to admission, but in fact noncompliance throughout the whole treatment process is also a major problem. The prime symptom of anorexia nervosa, 'the intense fear of gaining weight', leads the patient to avoid treatment. Even when the patient can be persuaded to agree to have treatment, she still actively resists it because the therapy contract involves regaining weight.

Treatment refusal in anorexia nervosa is an intense form of resistance which becomes more pronounced as the illness progresses (Goldner, 1989; Treasure, Todd and Szmukler, 1995) being determined by the psychological concomitants of the anorectic patient (Goldner, 1989). These concomitants include a strong sense of self-determination, a fear of giving up control, a lack of trust in interpersonal relationships, the need to counteract a strong sense of ineffectiveness, passive aggression, perfectionism, cognitive distortions, and mood disturbance. When the effects of these are compounded by the physiological sequelae of starvation, rational decision making by the patient is seriously impaired (Goldner, 1989; Treasure et al., 1995).

Because the nature of treatment for anorexia nervosa is multimodal and the common goal is 'to refeed the patient', it is inevitable that resistance will declare itself in many contexts, and will be observed by several members of the team at different times during treatment. Therapists conceptualise treatment resistance differently depending on their theoretical and disciplinary orientation. For example, behaviour therapists regard it as 'noncompliance', family therapists descriibe its operation within the family system, cognitive therapists refer to it as 'negative cognitions', psychodynamic therapists regard it as 'an adaptive defense mechanism', developmental therapists see it as 'a manifestation of a developmental arrest' (Goldner, 1989). Staff involved in the routine management of the patient, such as junior nurses who have not had specific training in the area, may see it as simply oppositional.

Sensitized by stress, the anorectic patient is conditioned to experience starvation and exercise as more rewarding than eating (Bergh and Södersten, 1996). Early vigorous nutritional rehabilitation should override conditioning to perverse rewards, and treatment should proceed to full weight restoration despite the patient's reluctance. In practice, however, treatment refusal may result in delayed or incomplete treatment and the anorectic process may become irreversible.

WHEN IS COMPULSORY TREATMENT NECESSARY IN ANOREXIA NERVOSA?

The issue of treatment refusal in anorectic patients was discussed already more than hundred years ago by eminent clinicians such as Gull, Lasègue and Charcot. The fundamental dilemma for clinicians in regard to involuntary treatment for anorexia nervosa has not changed. Although there may be negative effects resulting from its imposition, without it there may be even more adverse and possibly lethal effects for the patient (Goldner, 1989). Thus, the views of clinicians as to whether or not treatment should be imposed, have, for many years, been divided between either 'libertarian' versus 'paternalistic' or 'utilitarian' stances (Mitchell, Parker and Dwyer, 1988). The libertarian view advocates acceptance of the patient's right to refuse treatment so that her need for self-determination is preserved in the hope that she will eventually decide to be treated (Orbach, 1976; Solomon and Morrison, 1972). The paternalistic or utilitarian view advocates that various treatment approaches can be enforced without the patient's full consent and, if necessary, refeeding may have to be conducted involuntarily (Dresser, 1984a; Fichter, 1995; Newman, Russell and Beumont, 1995; Tiller, Schmidt and Treasure, 1993; Vandereycken and Meermann, 1984).

For some clinicians these views may become polarised even

further when legal means of imposing treatment are considered because the clinical decision begs the question of *how ill does the patient have to be?* The clinician's choice is relatively simple when compulsory treatment is deemed necessary to obviate medical danger and to save the patient's life. In other circumstances, however, it is more problematic. The longer the patient has been at low weight, the greater the likelihood that the anorectic process will become firmly entrenched. The patient's capacity to make a conscious decision to recover will be impaired. But when must the therapist forcibly intervene?

Anorexia nervosa is a chronic illness attended by unacceptable rates of morbidity and mortality. Thus, whether or not legal methods are invoked, the course of action depends on the clinician's degree of comfort or discomfort with these views together with the medical imperative (Goldner, 1989). Overall, it is generally agreed that compulsory treatment should be used only as a last resort. The message delivered by Dresser (1984a) is particularly relevant here as he states that 'voluntary treatment remains the formidable, elusive, yet mandatory goal in the treatment of anorexia nervosa' (p. 50).

In the literature, the main reasons given for the necessity of compulsory treatment have been:
1. To save the patient's life in the case of low weight severely emaciated anorectic patients (Dresser, 1984a; Fichter, 1995; Newman et al., 1995). Tiller et al. (1993) suggested cases considered for compulsory intervention have a body mass index (BMI) of 13.5 and below, or have serious physical and psychological complications.
2. To counteract the effects of starvation which distort the patient's ability to make a treatment decision (Dresser, 1984a; Tiller et al., 1993).
3. To ensure that the patient's 'health and safety are safeguarded' (Treasure et al., 1995, p. 285)
4. To 'demonstrate the clinician's devotion to the patient' (Yager, 1995, p. 376).
5. To 'allow normal maturation of secondary sexual features, growth and sexual development' (Treasure et al., 1995, p. 285).

By far the most often stated reasons are the first two. It has been suggested, that, if compulsory treatment is necessary, then clinicians must make sure that other goals in treatment are not compromised, such as, respecting the patient's sense of dignity and ensuring the 'quality of care' (Birley, 1991; Tiller et al., 1993).

The reasons for not implementing compulsory treatment, provided mainly by opponents or skeptics as to its value, have been:

1. That compulsory treatment infringes patient's rights and autonomy (Strasser and Giles, 1988).
2. That the oppositional patient who is forced to gain weight will merely 'eat herself out of hospital' and be more likely to relapse (Bruch, 1973; Fichter, 1995).
3. That there is no evidence that compulsory treatment benefits the patient in the long term (Dresser, 1984b).
4. That compulsory treatment destroys trust in the therapist and team, erodes the therapeutic relationship and undermines the likelihood of other treatment (Dresser, 1984b; Lanceley and Travers, 1993).
5. That a power struggle with the therapist may develop which is counterproductive (Fichter, 1995).
6. That enforced weight gain encourages bingeing and the use of abnormal means of weight control, such as, self-induced vomiting and purging (Dresser, 1984b; Palazzoli, 1978).
7. That involuntary patients are more likely to become depressed and commit suicide when discharged (Palmer, 1980; Theander, 1985).

Despite these objections there has been no definite evidence that compulsory treatment results in a worse outcome for anorexia nervosa. Thus far, support for this view has been only anecdotal.

ETHICAL VIEWS ON COMPULSORY TREATMENT

Some authorities argue that compulsory treatment is unacceptable because it does not support the ethical principle of autonomy (Strasser and Giles, 1988). They also suggest that deciding whether an anorectic patient is incompetent or irrational to make a judgement about treatment is fraught with difficulty. They suggest this may preclude recommending compulsory intervention because it may violate patient autonomy. However, in some clinical situations the other ethical principles of treatment – beneficence, nonmaleficence, justice and utility – can be fulfilled while the patient's autonomy may have to be put aside temporarily (Russell, 1995). This is defensible if the patient is seen to be the hostage of her illness and if any autonomy claimed is not in her best interest since it may permit her the dubious choices of dying of anorexia nervosa or remaining chronically ill.

Despite Gull's (1874) edict that the clinician must never give up on the anorectic patient, we must ask ourselves whether some patients are truly incurable (Russell, 1995), in which case a palliative care or hospice model (O'Neill, Crowther and Sampson, 1994) might be more appropriate. Although there may have been an increase in patients actively seeking this option, it is far more common for patients, driven by denial, to engage in so much fruitless conflict and bargaining that it forces the therapist to adopt such limited treatment goals that, in fact, entail little more than palliative care. Some patients will often accept or even demand calcium and hormonal replacement, antidepressants, hypnotics, antipsychotic agents, psychotherapy and any amount of relaxation and assertiveness training while resolutely refusing to submit to any sort of treatment regime which might result in weight gain and complaining of physical and psychological symptoms referable to emaciation. More frustrating are patients who are similarly resolute about not gaining sufficient weight to reverse the pathology and refuse all other interventions apart from attending appointments and communicating their distress.

There have even been anecdotal reports of patients making a decision to start eating when their overt or covert request for palliative care has been accepted. This phenomenon has also been reported in patients seeking euthanasia (see Chapter 1 in this volume). In our experience, there is usually so much denial or so little insight in patients with anorexia nervosa that the issue of palliation or euthanasia becomes irrelevant. Therefore, when these options are requested serious consideration must be given to the possibility of major depression. In such cases, aggressive treatment to the point of full resolution of signs and symptoms is warranted together with a simultaneous effort directed towards weight restoration.

The clinician also needs to be aware of other ethical questions which are not easily resolved. For example, in accepting the patient's request for palliation or euthanasia is the clinician colluding with her pathological nihilism, or that of her family, or the funding authority? Can a patient whose judgement is seriously impaired by psychiatric illness be allowed to make a decision concerning her medical welfare which does not concur with the clinician's? Could it be that the patient's reluctance to take responsibility for her own needs, or faulty perception that others would be better off without her, underlie her request for palliation or euthanasia? If the decision to enforce treatment is made, to what lengths does the clinician resort to ensure that the patient achieves the treatment objectives? What alternatives does the clinician have when the patient rejects lenient and flexible approaches to treatment?

Our views might be considered to be 'paternalistic' but from our experience, we find that compulsory treatment can be implemented successfully and shaped with due processes in mind so that the patient's rights are not violated. We tend towards the view expressed by Dresser (1984a), who stated that 'the refusing anorexia nervosa patient presents a case in which the discord between individual freedom and optimal health care is less extreme than in other instances of treatment refusal' (p. 44), and by Birley (1991, p. 1) 'that compulsory treatment is not a threat but a right'. In doing so, we hold no rescue fantasies, only the belief that our patients have a right to life and we have a responsibility to provide the best care possible.

Indeed, in the current medico-legal climate, the 'libertarian' versus 'paternalistic' views may have been overarticulated since we have entered a phase in which quality of care, accountability, professional competencies, and consumerism dominate. At the same time, the treatment of anorexia nervosa can also be very humbling. For every patient who subsequently thanks the clinician for having enforced treatment, which at the time was experienced as unacceptably restrictive, another remains recalcitrant and blames her repressive management, while yet another recovers using her own devices when clinicians have given up on her.

HOW SHOULD COMPULSORY TREATMENT BE IMPLEMENTED?

The situation with a gravely physically ill patient requiring emergency treatment presents no dilemma for the clinician (Newman, Russell and Beumont, 1995). However, the situation is very different with a gravely ill anorectic patient who presents to a clinician and proceeds to refuse hospital admission and treatment which may entail life-saving intervention, such as, parenteral and enteral nutrition. How does the clinician deal with this situation which inevitably leads to compulsory treatment? We will expand our advice to clinicians which we have discussed elsewhere (Griffiths, Beumont, Touyz, Russell and Moore, 1997).

1. The decision to admit a patient to hospital and to impose compulsory treatment should only be made after due consideration to the risks and benefits to the patient (Goldner, 1989). Obviously legal support will be needed and in New South Wales (NSW), Australia, where the authors practice, there are three alternative forms of legislation available (discussed later in this Chapter). The legislation most commonly used in NSW is Guardianship. Cases are reviewed by a Guardianship Board which has the power to order emergency admission as well as medical treatment throughout all phases of care. In this way, as with other forms of legislation, the ethical burden of decision making by the clinician is shared in the forum provided by external review (Miller, 1991).

2. Implementation of compulsory treatment requires that all parties be painstakingly consulted. Recommendations must be obtained from the patient, her family and the entire treating team and it is essential that those involved are given support and respect for their views during and after implementation.

3. The family must be fully informed of the reasons for implementation of treatment against the patient's will, the nature of the illness and proposed treatment. Several interviews may be necessary with the family who may be ambivalent about admission and treatment which in turn can influence the patient's attitude.

4. With Guardianship the parent may elect to act as the patient's guardian but, if this is felt imprudent, particularly when the patient is highly manipulative of parents, a Public Guardian can be appointed. Not only is the patient provided with an advocate acting in his or her best interest but the guardian is available to discuss treatment options and make representations to the treatment team.

5. A good rapport between the treatment team, the guardian and the immediate family is essential for effective implementation of compulsory treatment. The lengthy discussion as to the need for restrictive treatment measures and the lack of feasable alternatives goes a long way towards dispelling ambivalence for all parties.

6. Fears, anxieties and guilt must be addressed prior to hospital admission and throughout the treatment process recognising that cooperation is of utmost importance. In this way, the therapeutic alliance may be maintained, and for some patients, enhanced. Dresser (1984a) stated: 'A legal approach permitting most anorectic patients to participate in treatment decision making may further their interest in self-determination without damaging their chances for long-term recovery, and (might) perhaps even increase those chances' (p. 45).

The following case illustrates the implementation and outcome of compulsory treatment under Guardianship.

KT was first admitted to an eating disorders unit at the age of 15 after numerous episodes of self-starvation and dehydration necessitating intensive care admission at the local rural hospital. There was a history of sexual assault followed by drug and alcohol abuse, oppositional behaviour at home and violent clashes with her father who himself had come from a severely emotionally deprived background. KT's weight was 40 kg (BMI = 14.5) and she was dehydrated and hypothermic on admission. She was depressed, hostile, noncompliant in treatment, and after many threats to abscond, did so on a number of occasions (although she always returned). She often expressed suicidal ideation to which her father's response was to state that 'it would be kinder to let her die'. At this stage a decision was made by the treatment team and the family to invoke Guardianship legislation. Her father did not attend the hearing, despite invitation to do so but her mother and sisters were present and they were highly supportive. KT was required to remain in hospital and be treated under a Guardianship Order for 16 months. A Public Guardian was appointed. KT's compliance improved temporarily, she gained weight. She also responded to antidepressants and commenced correspondence schooling. She was able to express anger at her father for deserting her. However, oppositional defiance again supervened and after months of bed rest and pitched battles, a bargain was made with her. She was allowed to return home at New Year although 4 kg below her minimum weight of 56 kg. Dehydration and self-starvation rapidly ensued but after some resistance and delay, readmission was effected when her weight was 41 kg. KT's course was again difficult and she absconded from hospital but was retrieved by her Guardian and returned to treatment. She regained some weight to 50 kg and engaged in psychotherapy but was again discharged prematurely allegedly because she had found accommodation and a part-time job. Rapid weight loss to 41 kg recurred and the Guardian once more threatened retrieval but KT agreed to be admitted to another program run by her original psychiatrist. She made good progress and started to regain weight. She was no longer depressed, had discontinued antidepressants and reported that there had been a rapprochement with her father. She was allowed to work part-time and to continue seeing her psychotherapist from hospital after being discharged at 54 kg. After this she managed Christmas and New Year at home successfully and gained weight to her minimum of 56 kg. Three months later she has been doing well, studying and working part-time whilst living independently. Weight has been maintained and menses have returned. Under the terms of her Guardianship contract, KT is continuing with weekly psychotherapy and is seeing her original psychiatrist and nutritionist monthly. There will be a review of her Guardianship Order shortly. She plans to study Law at University and her success with her correspondence schooling thus far suggests that this ambition is not unrealistic.

IMPLEMENTING SPECIFIC TREATMENT STRATEGIES

Implementation of short-term compulsory medical treatment for anorectic patients in an acute life-threatening state can be relatively easy compared to proceeding with long-term treatment goals (Yager, 1995). In the short term the patient is hospitalised and nutritional rehabilitation is commenced. However, for many patients the course of treatment is complicated further by persistent physiological, psychological, behavioural and social impediments (Yager, 1995). The patient's or her family's goals may be very different from therapist's and for this reason goals need to be assessed, evaluated, monitored and revised throughout treatment (Russell, 1995). The clinician must take into account all these factors when considering different treatment strategies.

For the chronic treatment-resistant anorectic patient it may be necessary to apply more intrusive strategies such as *parenteral and enteral nutrition*. These strategies tend to be confined to intensive care settings and it is the former, which, because of its very accessibility provokes emotional reactions from patients, their relatives, nursing staff and general public by bringing into question the ethical implications of its implementation. The implicit loss of agency, particularly where the procedure is legally enforced, may be deleterious to the treatment goal of taking responsibility and to an already poor therapeutic relationship (Lanceley and Travers, 1993). An innovative use of this technique, whereby patients insert their own nasogastric tubes for overnight supplemental feeding, obviates these objections and may forestall the necessity for more restrictive treatment options such as strict bed rest (Theodoros, Powell and Shepherd, 1995). There are, however, potential medical risks which need careful consideration.

Planning a programme for the treatment resistant anorectic requires time and effort and must include regular consultations and, if necessary, peer supervision. Flexibility is important if treatment strategies need to be changed or if they are not working. As mentioned earlier, therapists must be careful not to give up on a therapeutic relationship because of the patient's resistance. Strict individualised behavioural programmes can be effective for patients who are very resistant to weight gain (Touyz and Beumont, 1996; see also Chapter by Touyz in this volume). These short-term programmes are devised in consultation with the patient. The patient earns a hierarchy of privileges which are linked to incremental weight increases until 4–5 kg is gained. After this the patient continues to gain weight without the individualised programme. Other behavioural strategies for resistant patients, such as room rest and individualised meal supervision, also raise ethical issues for the clinician. Useful strategies for resistant patients have been outlined by Goldner (1989) and Yager (1995).

INTERNATIONAL LEGAL PROVISIONS AND LEGISLATION

We found a limited amount of information on mental health legislation and what was available was difficult to acquire. We noted, however, a considerable lack of consistency in the mental health legislation across countries and even within each country. For example, in the United States each state has different criteria for compulsory commitment to mental health facilities. The states also differ as to whether compulsory commitment can be followed by compulsory treatment. Even after compulsory commitment is followed by compulsory treatment, within each state certain procedures, such as electroconvulsive therapy (ECT), often require a separate court order. Many states have statutory provisions to permit less restrictive outpatient commitment, however, these are not often used (Appelbaum, 1986). Because of lack of uniformity and changes to the many American state mental health laws in the 1970s, the American Psychiatric Association developed its own proposal called: 'APA Model Law' (1983). However, this has not been totally adopted by any state in the USA, although it has influenced public debate and helped shape law reform (Craze, Rees and Ross, 1994).

US Legislation enables doctors and, in some states, clinical psychologists, to detain a mentally disordered person for psychiatric care if one of the following circumstances can be documented: (1) the individual in a danger to self because of suicide risk; (2) the person is a danger to others because of homicide risk; or (3) the person is unable to provide food or shelter because of grave disability. It is the latter circumstance which is used to detain adults with anorexia nervosa. However, whether nutritional neglect qualifies in terms of mental disorder varies within each state and between judges. The time allowed by the courts for such treatment is 17 days, at which time the treatment team must go to court to obtain a conservator, who then has the right to enforce further compulsory treatment for one year. This is granted only if the court holds that there is sufficient evidence for additional treatment against the patient's wishes. In the case of minors this is not needed as parents hold legal authority to undertake treatment for children up to age 18.

The use of the legislation for the admission and treatment of anorexia nervosa depends on the philosophy or policy of the treatment centre in the USA. For example, in the States of Iowa and Maryland, the legislation has been used selectively for compulsory admission and treatment of low weight anorectic patients who refuse treatment and whose lives are threatened. Such treatment centres report that many patients say they would not have given permission, but are clearly grateful after they progress, are thinking clearly, have a greater understanding of their disorder, and have a greater sense of freedom. However, in some treatment centres in the State of California, the legislation is not used for anorexia nervosa. The argument being that it is very difficult or impossible to establish an effective treatment alliance and motivation for change when treatment is initiated in this way.

In Canada, for many years much concern was directed to legal and ethical issues concerning patient rights and compulsory treatment that little emphasis was given to the patient's entitlement to and need for adequate treatment (Roberts, 1989). Each province has its own Mental Health legislation regarding compulsory treatment and there is no reciprocity between provinces. As in the USA the decision to admit and treat have been separated. The clinician makes the decision to admit but the court or tribunal makes the decision to treat. There is provision in some Canadian legislation for the concept of an 'enduring guardian' to be appointed for a person who is mentally ill (Craze, Rees, and Ross, 1994). This was seen to promote the mentally ill person's rights to self-determination. In 1984, the Canadians also embarked on a uniform mental health legislation called 'The Uniform Mental Health Act' which, as in the USA, has not been adopted in any Canadian province although it has significantly influenced debate.

In the United Kingdom, laws for compulsory commitment and treatment are provided under the Mental Health Act (1983). Clinicians control the admission and discharge process rather than the courts but Mental Health Tribunals review admissions and hospitalisation at regular intervals. A report of the Royal College of Psychiatrists (1992) stated that approximately 10 per cent of anorexia patients admitted in England were admitted under this Act. Recently in the UK compulsory treatment for anorexia nervosa was debated extensively in the public domain. It was regarded by the media as coercive and by doctors as compassionate (Tiller et al., 1993; see also Chapter by Dolan in this volume).

There has been a trend for new legislation enacted in some countries to pay more attention to both the rights of patients and their treatment. For example, in the Federal Republic of Germany (FRG), new legislation was introduced in 1992, although we have not been able to ascertain information about its implementation or how it has been applied to anorexia nervosa. Previously the situation in Germany was similar to the current situation in the USA, that is, compulsory commitment and treatment varied from state to state and within a single state. Historically, there were three legal instruments used, custody, guardianship and state commitment law (Nedopil, 1992). Custody was considered too rigid and guardianship was applied instead but frequently abused in its implementation. Sufficient professional guardians could not be recruited so that patients had little contact with their guardian because they had to care for too many patients. Recent amendments to the German laws aimed to safeguard the patient's rights and to stress 'help', 'care', and personal wishes of the patient, while separating the need for support from the question of incompetence (Nedopil, 1992). The person must be over age 18, mentally ill or physically disabled; incapable of taking care of herself; and needing care because of insufficient support. 'Care' cannot be imposed on the person against her will unless mental incapacity is proved. The duties and rights of the 'care person' (or guardian) and limitations to the patient's rights are also decided by the court (Nedopil, 1992).

In Denmark, compulsory procedures were reformed in the Danish Mental Health Act 1989 with the provision for compulsory treatment of life-threatening somatic disease in psychotic patients (Jacobson, Madson and Schultz, 1995). In New Zealand, a new improved Mental Health Bill became law in 1992 which emhasized quality of treatment rather than detention. Patients rights, cultural concerns, Review Tribunals and better assessment procedures were highlighted (Bell, 1992). The Israeli Law of Treatment of Mental Patients, 1955, deals with the question of compulsory admission not compulsory treatment. Becker, Gonen, and Floru (1990) suggest that 'permission to commit should include permission to effect at least the routine methods of treatment' (p. 909).

In Australia, there are different Mental Health Acts operating in each state. In the state of NSW, there are three legal provisions which may be applied in cases of anorexia nervosa requiring compulsory treatment:

(1) Involuntary commitment: the patient is judged to be mentally disordered and in need of treatment because of danger to self;
(2) Legal incompetence: the patient is judged to be legally incompetent to make decisions regarding medical treatment;
(3) Below age of majority: minors can be treated involuntarily when

the parent or guardian consents to treatment. (Newman, Russell, and
Beumont, 1995, p. 54)

The laws governing compulsory treatment of patients suffering
from anorexia nervosa in NSW have undergone major changes in
recent years. Under the Mental Health Act of 1958, these patients
were considered as mentally ill and could be detained involuntarily
in a psychiatric hospital. In a number of instances, these laws were
enforced. During the 1970s, various committees (Edwards Committee, Devison Committee) examined the implications of the
1958 Act to patient's rights, and concluded that reasons for
treatment in a psychiatric hospital were inappropriate and
unnecessary. These developments led to the formulation of the
Mental Health Act 1990, in which mental illness was defined by
the presence of specific psychotic symptoms. Patients with anorexia nervosa were not considered to fulfill these criteria, as ruled
in the case 'JAH vs the Medical Superintendent of Rozelle
Hospital' (1986). Under the Mental Health Act 1990 anorexia
nervosa patients could only be constrained to accept emergency
treatment as 'mentally disordered persons', but these provisions
of the Act allow detention for only three days, which is of little
value in the long-term management of these patients. The history
of JAH is a cautionary tale illustrating the flaws in the current
legislation.

JAH developed anorexia nervosa at the age of 12. She had numerous
admissions to eating disorders units for refeeding and in the early years
of her illness returned to normal weights. Over the years she became
more defiant and when brought before the Supreme Court at 16 was
attempting to leave hospital at a weight of 35 kg. Having been
permitted to do this because a ruling had been made that she was not
mentally ill, she returned home to her parents where she preceded to
become a major management problem. She took regular overdoses of
paracetamol, exercised excessively, was verbally abusive to her parents
and continued to starve herself. A year later her parents charged her
with being uncontrollable and again brought her before the Supreme
Court seeking an injunction to have her treated involuntarily. On this
occasion, she was found by the psychiatrist who assessed her to be
delusional on the grounds that she believed herself to be fat when she
weighed 29 kg. Compulsory treatment under the Mental Health Act
was recommended and JAH was admitted to a public psychiatric

hospital where she was physically restrained and fed nasogastrically when she refused to voluntarily submit to this procedure. When her weight had reached 35 kg she was discharged as a continued treatment patient to a specialised unit but management proved impossible due to rage attacks and noncompliance along with a sense of threat to other patients.

JAH took a number of paracetamol overdoses always out of the hospital, preceded by bingeing and always followed by calling an ambulance. Weight was maintained during this time and a full thickness rectal prolapse was diagnosed. However, surgery was felt to be inadvisable in view of her low weight and she was discharged home. Months later she was readmitted having lost more weight and having developed a severe urinary tract infection. Treatment again proved impossible after an incident when in response to a request that she complete her meal, she threw the plate at another patient and said that she wished to kill herself. JAH was again transferred to the public psychiatric hospital under the Mental Health Act. Months later she was readmitted to another eating disorders unit where she stated that she was grateful to the director as he had never given up on her. One morning in the middle of winter she absconded from the hospital while still severely emaciated and was seen scantily clad and jogging along the road some 5 km away. Three months following her discharge after little progress had been made, JAH was admitted to a rural hospital near her parent's home where she died at the age of 21 of terminal liver and renal failure.

The need for more flexible laws, less coercive than those contained in the Mental Health Act, was recognised in NSW in the late 1980s. A working party was set up to establish a Guardianship Board in NSW under existing legislation, the Disability Services and Guardianship Act 1987. The Board was proclaimed in August 1989 with the powers to appoint guardians and financial managers for people 16 years and over who are unable to make decisions for themselves because of various forms of disability. For anorectic patients, the Board is also able to give consent to certain medical procedures if the person is not capable of giving consent for themselves. Several amendments to the legislation have been made, for example, to allow family members and significant others to be substitute decision makers in the area of medical treatment without having to apply to the Board. Recent debates in Australia have questioned the use of Mental Health Act and suggest it be replaced by modern guardianship legislation (e.g. Campbell, 1994; Rosenman, 1994). For anorectic children under the age of 16 years, the Children's Care and Protection Act of 1978 may be used in NSW. It is a legal requirement that the Department of Community Services be notified in cases where there has been abuse, neglect or collusion, and this directive is clearly relevant to young anorexia patients whose parents do not bring them to treatment.

As in US and Canada, Australia has recently embarked on a project in 1994 to unify and reform mental health laws across Australia and to incorporate United Nations' 'Principles for Protection of Persons with Mental Illness and Improvement of Mental Health Care' and the 'National Mental Health Statement of Rights and Responsibilities'. 'A Model Mental Health Legislation' has been proposed and the project is continuing with the development of a 'Mental Health Rights' framework and 'Rights Analysis' of existing mental health legislation (Craze, Rees and Ross, 1994). Whether anything will ever result from this, remains unclear.

STUDIES OF OUTCOME OF COMPULSORY TREATMENT

There have been few studies on the value of compulsory treatment in terms of patient outcome for any diagnostic category. Szmukler, Bird and Button (1981) compared 150 compulsory admissions under the English Mental Health Act (1959) with 100 voluntary patients at a hospital in a London borough. Not only were there significant sociodemographic and clinical differences between the two groups, there were also differences in outcome at follow-up. Most prominent was a long-term unwillingness to engage in follow-up services on the part of the compulsory patients. The differences persisted when the compulsory patients were compared with a group of voluntary patients matched according to age, sex and diagnosis. A confounding variable, however, was that patients admitted under the Mental Health Act tended, in general, to be those whose illnesses were most severe.

Sensky, Hughes, and Hirsch (1991a) conducted an investigation of general psychiatric patients who, following inpatient treatment under the 1983 English Mental Health Act, were discharged 'on leave' while remaining under the direction of the Act. A group of these 'extended leave' patients was compared with control treatment patients, matched for age sex, and diagnosis and selected because they had not required this form of compulsory community leave. Sensky et al. found that extended leave patients more commonly had a history of recent dangerousness and non-compliance with psychiatric treatment. Positive benefits of extended leave were that compliance to treatment was improved, and the time in hospital and levels of dangerousness were reduced. In an extension of this study, Sensky, Hughes, and Hirsch (1991b) investigated what criteria psychiatrists used when asked to indicate those patients whom they would recommend for treatment with compulsory or extended leave. The findings indicated that their decision depended on criteria from the patient's past, particularly their previous noncompliance with follow-up.

Lindstrom et al. (1994) compared 95 Swedish patients admitted to compulsory treatment to 94 Swedish voluntarily admitted patients to determine which symptoms lead to compulsory intervention. They found schizophrenia and schizophrenia-like psychoses were significantly more common in the compulsory treated patients. The main reasons for compulsory treatment were the presence of pre- and post-admission violent acts and preadmission suicidal behaviour. Unemployment was most common among voluntary admitted patients.

For certain disorders compulsory treatment has enjoyed some endorsement. For instance, there is evidence from the USA that compulsory treatment has been effective in reducing substance abuse (e.g., Gostin, 1991; Maddux, 1988). It has been suggested that compulsory treatment programmes, particularly those used for narcotic addicts in South East Asia, can work if they are extremely authoritarian, receive public support, and are enforced vigorously (Webster, 1978) and that they may reduce the spread of AIDS (Leukefield and Tims, 1990). On the other hand, the effectiveness of compulsory treatment for drug and alcohol dependency has been seriously questioned (Platt et al., 1988).

Our research team conducted a study of 15 anorexia nervosa patients who had been compulsorily admitted and treated under Guardianship Order at four eating disorders centres in Sydney between January 1990 and December 1994 (for details, see Griffiths et al., 1997). To our knowledge, this is the first attempt to look specifically at anorexia nervosa patients who have received compulsory treatment. Retrospective clinical data was collated from the medical files and standardised using a checklist of information on sociodemographic details, family characteristics, clinical background, weight and eating history, health, use of previous services and Guardianship information for the time of admission for compulsory treatment. The sample was compared to a sample of anorexia nervosa patients from a previous study (Beumont, Kopec-Schroeder and Lennerts, 1995). In addition, each patient was contacted and asked to participate in a prospective study of outcome at least one year after the implementation of compulsory treatment. They were asked to provide informed consent to participate in a standardised assessment interview, the Morgan-Russell Assessment Schedule (Morgan and Russell, 1975; Morgan and Haywood, 1988) which has been widely used in treatment outcome and follow-up studies of anorexia nervosa (e.g., Touyz and Beumont, 1984; Gillberg, Rastam and Gillberg, 1994).

A number of similarities and differences between the two samples were found. Some of the differences emerging were that those treated involuntarily were older at the time of admission, their rate of unemployment was higher, admission body mass index was lower, a larger number required specialist medical consultations, and their duration of stay in hospital was longer. The sources of referral, marital status and spread across socioeconomic classes were consistent between the samples. A large number of patients refused prospective follow-up reflecting the general noncompliance in the group.

CONCLUSIONS

In this chapter, a number of issues relating to treatment refusal and the necessity of compulsory treatment in anorexia nervosa were raised. The authors' views from clinical experience and those of others were presented regarding the ethical, medico-legal and psychological aspects of compulsory treatment. Mental health legislation in various countries and studies examining outcome of compulsory treatment were reviewed. To summarise, the views and issues put forward:

1. Treatment refusal is symptomatic of anorexia nervosa.
2. The dichotomy between libertarian and paternalistic ethical views of compulsory treatment may now be outdated.
3. The evidence suggests that anorexia nervosa is a chronic illness with high rates of morbidity and mortality necessitating refeeding in hospital to reverse biological consequences of starvation. The clinician has a duty of care to save the patient's life and, to this end, autonomy may be sacrificed.
4. The increase in the number of anorectic patients seeking palliative care may reflect a general tendency by the clinician or funding authority to give up on treatment-resistant patients.
5. Compulsory treatment can be implemented effectively with careful regard to the patient and her family whereby the therapeutic alliance is strengthened rather than weakened.
6. Various innovative treatment alternatives can be introduced for chronically resistant anorectic patients.
7. Uniformity and reform to international mental health legislation is needed to improve quality of care.
8. The use of Guardianship legislation instead of Mental Health Laws may be a more suitable and less coercive alternative.
9. Studies determining outcome of compulsory treatment for anorexia nervosa are urgently needed.

Underlying compulsory treatment for anorexia nervosa is the clinician's expectation that if weight restoration is reached the patient is more likely to enjoy a full and lasting recovery.

REFERENCES

Appelbaum, P.S. (1986) 'Outpatient commitment: the problems and the promise'. *American Journal of Psychiatry*, 143: 1270–2.

Becker, D., Gonen, H. and Floru, S. (1990) 'Are confinement and treatment synonymous?' *Medical Law* 9: 904–9.

Bell, S. (1992) 'The Mental Health (Compulsory Treatment and Assessment) Act'. *Community Mental Health in New Zealand*, 7: 16–22.

Bergh, C. and Södersten, P. (1996) 'Anorexia nervosa, self-starvation and the reward of stress'. *Nature and Medicine*, 2: 21–2.

Beumont, P.J.V., Russell, J.D. and Touyz, S.W. (1993) 'The treatment of anorexia nervosa'. *Lancet*, 341: 1635–40,

Beumont, P.J.V., Kopec-Schroeder, E. and Lennerts, W. (1995) 'The treatment of eating disorders patients at a NSW teaching hospital: A comparison of State-wide area'. *Australian and New Zealand Journal of Psychiatry*, 29: 96–103.

Birley, J.L. (1991) 'Psychiatrists as citizens'. *British Journal of Psychiatry*, 159: 1–6.

Bruch, H. (1973) *Eating disorders: Obesity, anorexia nervosa, and the person within*, New York: Basic Books.

Campbell, T.D. (1994) 'Mental Health Law: Institutionalised discrimination'. *Australian and New Zealand Journal of Psychiatry*, 28: 554–9.

Craze, L., Rees, N. and Ross, K. (1994). *Model Mental Health Legislation. Volume 1* (Report to the Australian Health Ministers' Advisory Council Working Group On Mental Health Policy). Newcastle: University of Newcastle, Centre for Health Law, Ethics and Policy.

Dresser, R. (1984a) 'Legal and policy considerations in treatment of anorexia nervosa patients'. *International Journal of Eating Disorders*, 3: 43–51.

—— (1984b). 'Feeding the hunger artists: Legal issues in treating anorexia nervosa'. *Wisconsin Law Review*, 2: 297–374.

Fichter, M. (1995) 'Inpatient treatment of anorexia nervosa'. In Brownell, K.D. and Fairburn, C.G. (eds) *Eating disorders and obesity: A comprehensive handbook* (pp. 336–43), New York: Guilford Press.

Gillberg, C., Rastam, M. and Gillberg, C. (1994) 'Anorexia nervosa outcome: Six year controlled longitudinal study of 51 cases including a population cohort'. *Journal of the Academy of Child Adolescent Psychiatry*, 5: 729–39.

Goldner, E. (1989) 'Treatment refusal in anorexia nervosa'. *International Journal of Eating Disorders*, 8: 297–306.

Gostin, L.O. (1991) 'Compulsory treatment for drug-dependent persons: Justifications for a public health approach to drug dependency'. *Milbank Quarterly*, 69: 561–93.

Griffiths, R.A., Beumont, P.J.V., Touyz, S., Russell, J. and Moore, G. (1997) 'The use of guardianship legislation for anorexia nervosa: A report of 15 cases'. *Australian and New Zealand Journal of Psychiatry*, 31: 525–31.

Gull, W.W. (1874) 'Anorexia nervosa (apepsia hysterica, anorexia hysterica)'. *Transactions of the Clinical Society of London*, 7: 22–8.

Jacobson, L.A., Madson, A.L. and Schultz, V. (1995) 'Compulsory procedures in the treatment of somatic diseases in mentally ill patients'. *Ugeskrift for Laeger*, 157: 3319–22.

Lanceley, C. and Travers, R. (1993) 'Anorexia nervosa: Forced feeding and the law'. *British Journal of Psychiatry*, 163: 835.

Leukefield, C.G. and Tims, F.M. (1990) 'Compulsory treatment for drug abuse'. *International Journal of Addictions*, 25: 621–40.

Lindstrom, E., Palmstierna, T., Wallsten, T., Lindstrom, L. et al. (1994) 'Key symptoms in patients with a psychotic syndrome in need for compulsory care'. *European Journal of Psychiatry*, 8: 5–14.

Lucas, A.R., Beard, C.M., O'Fallon, W.M. and Kurlan, L.T. (1991) '50-year trends in the incidence of anorexia nervosa in Rochester, Minn.: A population-based study'. *American Journal of Psychiatry*, 148: 917–22.

Maddux, J.F. (1988) 'Clinical experience with civil commitment'. *Journal of Drug Issues*, 18: 575–94.

Miller, R. (1991) 'The ethics of involuntary commitment to mental health treatment'. In Bloch, S. and Chodoff, P. (eds) *Psychiatric ethics* (2nd ed.), New York: Oxford University Press.

Mitchell, P.B., Parker, G.B. and Dwyer, J.M. (1988) 'The law and the physically ill patient with anorexia nervosa: Liberty versus paternalism'. *Medical Journal of Australia*, 48: 41–4.

Morgan, H.G. and Haywood, A.E. (1988) 'Clinical assessment of anorexia nervosa. The Morgan-Russell Outcome Assessment Schedule'. *British Journal of Psychiatry*, 152: 367–71.

Morgan, H.G. and Russell, G.F.M. (1975) 'Value of family background and clinical features as predictors of long term outcome in anorexia nervosa: Four year follow-up study of 41 patients'. *Psychological Medicine*, 5: 355–71.

Nedopil, N. (1992) 'New laws regulating custody and civil commitment in Germany'. *International Bulletin of Law and Mental Health*, 4: 42.

Newman, L., Russell, J. and Beumont, P.J.V. (1995) 'Issues in the treatment of very low weight anorexics'. In Kenny, D.T. and Soames Job, R.F. (eds) *Australia's Adolescents* (pp. 53–8), Armidale: University of New England Press.

Orbach, S. (1976) *Hunger strike: The anorectic's struggle as a metaphor for our age*, New York: W.W. Norton.

O'Neill, J., Crowther, J. and Sampson, G. (1994) 'Anorexia nervosa: Palliative care of terminal psychiatric disease'. *American Journal of Hospice and Palliative Care*, Nov/Dec, 36–8.

Palazzoli, M.S. (1978) Self-starvation: From individual to family therapy in the treatment of anorexia nervosa, New York: Jason Aronson.

Palmer, R.L. (1980) *Anorexia nervosa,* London: Penguin.

Platt, J.J., Buhringer, G., Kaplan, C.D., Brown, B.S., et al. (1988) 'Prospects and limitations of compulsory treatment for drug addiction'. *Journal of Drug Issues*, 18: 505–25.

Roberts, C.A. (1989) 'Development of mental health services and psychiatry in Canada: Lessons from the past, problems of the present and the future'. *Canadian Journal of Psychiatry*, 34: 291–8.

Royal College of Psychiatrists(1992) *Report to the College Section of General Psychiatry by the Eating Disorders Working Group,* London: Royal College of Psychiatrists.

Rosenman, S. (1994) 'Mental health law: An idea whose time has passed'. *Australian and New Zealand Journal of Psychiatry,* 28: 560–5.

Russell, J. (1995) 'Treating anorexia nervosa: Humbling for doctors'. *British Medical Journal,* 311: 584.

Sensky, T., Hughes and Hirsch, S. (1991a) 'Compulsory psychiatric treatment in the community. I. A controlled study of compulsory community treatment with extended leave under the Mental Health Act: Special characteristics of patients treated and impact of treatment'. *British Journal of Psychiatry,* 158: 792–9.

——(1991b) 'Compulsory psychiatric treatment in the community: II. A controlled study of patients whom psychiatrists would recommend for compulsory treatment in the community'. *British Journal of Psychiatry,* 158: 799–804.

Solomon, A.P. and Morrison, D.A.R. (1972) 'Anorexia nervosa: Dual transference therapy'. *American Journal of Psychotherapy,* 26: 480–9.

Szmukler, G.I., Bird, A.S. and Button, E.J. (1981) 'Compulsory admissions in a London borough: 1. Social and clinical features and a follow-up'. *Psychological Medicine,* 11: 617–36.

Strasser, M. and Giles, G. (1988) 'Ethical considerations'. In Scott, D. (ed.) *Anorexia and bulimia nervosa: Practical approaches* (pp. 204–12), New York: New York University Press.

Theander, S. (1985) 'Outcome and prognosis in anorexia nervosa and bulimia: Some results of previous investigations, compared with those of a Swedish long-term study'. *Journal of Psychiatric Research,* 19: 493–508.

Theodorous, M., Powell, J. and Shepherd, R. (1995) *Self-administered nocturnal enteral supplementation in treatment of anorexia nervosa.* Paper presented at the Second London International Conference on Eating Disorders.

Tiller, J., Schmidt, U. and Treasure, J. (1993) 'Compulsory treatment for anorexia nervosa: Compassion or coercion'. *British Journal of Psychiatry,* 162: 679–80.

Touyz, S.W. and Beumont, P.J.V. (1984) 'Anorexia nervosa treatment: A follow-up investigation'. *Medical Journal of Australia,* 141: 219–22.

——(1997) 'Behavioral treatment to promote weight gain in anorexia nervosa'. In Garner, D.M. and Garfinkel, P.E. (eds) *Handbook of treatment for eating disorders.* New York: Guilford Press.

Treasure, J., Todd, G. and Szmukler, G. (1995) 'The inpatient treatment of anorexia nervosa'. In Szmukler, G., Dare, C. and Treasure, J. (eds) *Handbook of eating disorders* (pp. 275–92), New York: John Wiley.

Vandereycken, W. and Meermann, R. (1984) *Anorexia nervosa: A clinician's guide to treatment*, Berlin-New York: Walter de Gruyter.

Webster, C.D. (1978) 'Compulsory treatment of narcotic addiction'. *International Journal of Law and Psychiatry*, 8: 133–59.

Yager, J. (1995) 'The management of patients with intractable eating disorders'. In Brownell, K.D. and Fairburn, C.G. (eds) *Eating disorders and obesity: A comprehensive handbook* (pp. 374–8), New York: Guilford Press.

CHAPTER SEVEN

Food refusal, forced feeding and the law of England and Wales

Bridget Dolan

I INTRODUCTION

Renowned eating disorders experts have declared that 'it is hard to understand why the compulsory treatment of anorexia nervosa is a contentious issue' (Tiller, Schmidt and Treasure, 1993). This view seems to stem from a purely clinical perspective where the life threatening nature of the disorder with a 20 per cent mortality rate is seen as the ultimate justification for any medical intervention. However, the implementation of any legislation which allows treatment against a person's wishes represents a serious infringement of civil liberties and, as such, should rightly remain an issue of continued debate. Regardless of one's stance on the issues, this debate should not only be from a clinical/medical standpoint but must be informed by an understanding of the legal issues involved.

Public concerns about the legality of treating even detained patients without their consent were raised worldwide in the late 1960s and early 1970s with the rise of the bio-ethics movements (Fennel, 1995). Previously there had been little recognition that a psychiatric disorder and /or compulsory admission did not automatically render a person incapable of making decisions about matters affecting them. However, under the influence of the jurisprudence of the European Court of Human Rights in Strasbourg, many European countries revised their mental health legislation between 1978–1992. The criteria for involuntary admission were reviewed and the image of the patient as a 'citizen with rights' emerged with an increased recognition that compulsorily admitted patients retained their legal rights during their stay in hospital (Legemaate, 1995). Despite this, contemporary comparative analysis of the internal legal position of patients throughout Europe shows a diverse approach. In some countries (e.g. Denmark, England and Wales) there remain extensive powers to treat patients without consent (Vestergaard, 1994), whilst in others (e.g. The Netherlands and Austria) the law limits the powers of the doctors considerably (Legemaate, 1995).

Food refusal is not unique to sufferers of anorexia nervosa, self-starvation is also displayed by those with personality disorder or psychotic disorders in the absence of an eating disorder, and a hunger strike is frequently used as a form of protest by prisoners and detainees. Although many countries now take similar jurisprudential approaches to these issues (Winick, 1994), the actual operation and imposition of the law still varies widely. In an attempt to place the compulsory treatment of anorexia nervosa in its legal context this chapter will address the particular issues related to force feeding within the Law of England and Wales.

To understand the complexities of how the English and Welsh legislation and common law relate to feeding a person against their will, it is necessary to consider not only legal decisions relating to treatment of patients with eating disorders, but also the legality of force feeding detained patients who are refusing food but who do not suffer with an eating disorder. In both these situations it now seems that the courts of England and Wales will endorse force feeding within the 1983 Mental Health Act. However, the common law now takes a rather different view with respect to force feeding those prisoners and detainees who refuse food in the context of politically motivated hunger striking, where the right to self-determination prevails. It also seems unlikely that the courts will intervene to prevent voluntary starvation (even when motivated by a wish not to live) in someone with full capacity and no mental illness. In this paper, each of these issues will be considered in turn and the development of the current legal position will be examined

Under common law a doctor may only administer treatment when a patient gives consent, otherwise they may commit trespass, assault or battery. The patient's reasons for withholding consent may be totally rational, irrational, unknown or even non-existent (Re T [1992]). Thus the ethical principle of self-determination will prevail above medical advice and will protect the right of the patient to decide what is to happen to her. A competent adult is entitled to reject a specific medical or surgical treatment or select an alternative treatment, even if the decision entails serious risk of death. The House of Lords has endorsed the view that a doctor who proceeds to act in the absence of consent will be civilly liable regardless of any justifiable belief that what was done would preserve life or health and in the absence of any hostility (Re F [1990]). Indeed in the tort of battery it is unnecessary for the plaintiff to have suffered any harm from the actions of the doctor to recover damages. However, force feeding without consent has not always been held to be an assault as can be seen in earlier decisions regarding the force feeding of hunger striking prisoners.

2 STARVING PRISONERS

Hunger striking – the refusal of food as a form of protest – is not infrequently used as a political weapon by prisoners, the most infamous recent cases being the fatal hunger strikes of IRA prisoners and the mass hunger strikes by 'emergency detainees' in South Africa in 1989 (Kalk and Veriava, 1991) and by GRAPO members imprisoned in Spain in 1989 (British Medical Association, 1992). However, one of the earliest and perhaps the most effective demonstrations of the use of hunger striking as a prisoner's weapon was that by the British Women's Suffrage movement from 1909–1914.

2.1 THE SUFFRAGETTES

Hunger striking was first used by as a suffragette protest by Mrs Wallace Dunlop who was imprisoned in July 1909 for criminal damage, after daubing extracts from the Bill of Rights on the walls of the House of Commons. She fasted for only 91 hours before the prison authorities, rather than accede to her request to be treated as a political prisoner, released her. Over the next ten weeks 37 suffragettes terminated their imprisonment by hunger striking such that in August 1909 King Edward VII wrote to Herbert Gladstone (then the Home Secretary) and asked whether he had 'seriously considered the advisability of letting these women out of prison' and why 'existing methods, which must obviously exist for dealing with prisoners who refuse nourishment, should not be adopted'(Rosen, 1974). Six weeks later Gladstone ordered prison medical officers to use force to feed all women who refused to eat, and the public and legal controversies over force feeding began.

Mrs Mary Leigh, who had been sentenced to four months hard labour for resisting the police and public order offences was force fed up to three times daily. She described her ordeal to her solicitor: 'I was surrounded and forced back on a chair which was tilted backwards with about ten persons around me. The doctor forced my mouth to form a pouch and held me while the wardress poured liquid from a spoon. . . . On Saturday [I was] forced onto the bed and . . . while I was held down a nasal tube was inserted. It is two yards long with a funnel at the end. The end is put up the right and left nostril on alternate days. Great pain is experienced during the process, both mental and physical. I have been fed through the nostril twice a day. The sensation is most painful – the drums of the ears seem to be bursting and there is horrible pain in the throat and the breast. The tube is pushed down twenty inches. I have to lie on the bed pinned down by wardresses, one doctor stands on a chair holding the funnel . . . and the other who is behind, forces the other end up the nostrils. If the doctor does not think the fluid is going down sufficiently swiftly he pinches my nose with the tube in it and my throat, causing great pain. The after effects are a feeling of faintness, a great sense of pain in the diaphragm below the breast bone, in the nose and the ears.' (McKenzie, 1988).

Mrs Leigh brought an action claiming damages for assault and seeking an injunction to restrain a repetition of the acts against the Home Secretary, Governor and Medical Officer of the Prison. In the court case (*Leigh v Gladstone* [1909]) her counsel submitted that the rules of prisons did not authorise force feeding and that resorting to it so soon after food refusal was a punitive measure used as a means of maintaining prison discipline – this was particularly emphasised as her force feeding had begun after only three days of food refusal.

The submissions did not directly address the legality of force feeding *per se* to save life, but whether its premature use was motivated by malice and therefore an assault. The Lord Chief Justice ruled that as a matter of law it was the duty of the prison officials to preserve the health of prisoners and *a fortiori* to preserve their lives. The only question put to the jury was whether the methods used were proper. After two minutes deliberation the all male jury returned a verdict for the defendants.

Although 116 doctors signed a memorandum against force feeding of the Suffragettes it was clear from evidence at the trial that force feeding was common medical practice. The senior physician at the Bethlem Hospital described how he had administered force feeding thousands of times as often as nine times a day for up to two and a half years. He claimed it took no great medical skill and he had never known it cause detriment pain or injury. Although in a letter to the 'Daily News' in September 1909 J.Kier Hardie M.P. records how force feeding had led to the death of a male prisoner some years earlier (McKenzie, 1988) and in 1917 another prisoner, Thomas Ash, died whilst being forcibly fed (Zellnick, 1976).

2.2 THE CAT AND MOUSE ACT (1913)

Despite Gladstone's victory in court both the hunger striking and force feeding continued unabated. By Summer 1912 there were 102 Suffragettes in prison of whom 90 were being force fed. Reports condemning the practice were published (Savill, Moulin and Horsely, 1912) and some equated the force feeding to the torture currently meted out to political prisoners in Russian Jails (Brailsford and Nevinson, 1909). Gladstone by now had dropped his earlier claim that force feeding was "medical treatment" and acknowledged it to be "an objectionable practice". As public outrage at the treatment increased a new response had to be found. The government responded with legislation and enacted the 'Prisoners (Temporary Discharge for Ill-health) Act' (1913) to allow temporary release of those whose health made detention undesirable. Where the condition was due to their own conduct this release was to be without remission of sentence. The legislation became known as the 'Cat and Mouse Act' as women dodged in and out of prison under its powers. Indeed Mrs Pankhurst was released under the Act at least ten times serving only 30 days of her three year sentence. Force feeding was suspended after the ratification of the Act, however as many of the women avoided re-arrest or continued illegal activities whilst on temporary release making a mockery of the Act force feeding was re-introduced.

Although the case of *Leigh v Gladstone* has been criticised as a 'first instance unreasoned direction to a jury without legal argument on the fundamental point', the position left was that force feeding of hunger strikers was not only legal, but required. If *Leigh v Gladstone* was correctly decided 'then doctors have no discretion in the matter of force feeding: they merely have their ordinary clinical judgement to evaluate the advantages and disadvantages in each case and must resort to force feeding if the former outweighs the latter' (Zellnick, 1976).

2.3 THE IRA HUNGER STRIKERS (1973–1981)

The cases of Suffragettes are of historical interest in terms of the lengths to which the government of the day, as prompted by the King, would go to prevent the women's successful hunger striking. For many years force feeding of prisoners continued without comment until the public debate reopened during the period 1973–1981 when hunger striking by IRA ('Irish Republican Army') prisoners was at its height. Between 1973–74 three IRA prisoners began hunger strike to support their demands for transfer to prisons in Northern Ireland. All were force fed and one died (Miller, 1987). In a statement in the commons on January 30,1974 the Home Secretary, Mr Carr, justified the policy of force feeding saying that: 'Artificial feeding, particularly when accompanied by force against the wishes of the prisoner is horrible and terrible. It is *resorted to only as a last resort and as an alternative to endangering the life* of a prisoner – *an alternative we have never regarded as acceptable in this country*' (Hansard, 1974a).

However, within six months the new Home Secretary (Mr Jenkins) affirmed his disapproval of force feeding and said it should be abandoned unless the prisoner's judgement was impaired by illness (Hansard, 1974b). He stressed that a doctor would be neglecting the duty laid upon him by Parliament if he allowed the health of a prisoner in his charge on hunger strike to be endangered without attempting help (British Medical Journal, 1974). He stated that the daily force feeding of the Price sisters for over five months in prison was not a requirement of law but a medical matter turning solely on the judgement of the responsible medical officer. Yet he also emphasised that no rule of prison practice would *require* artificial feeding. 'The doctor's obligation is to the ethics of his profession and to his duty at common law, he is not required as a matter of prison practice to feed a prisoner against his will ... (He) must have regard not merely to the dangers likely to flow from the prisoner's refusal of food, but also those likely to flow from the process of force feeding'. This statement did nothing to forbid force feeding, it simply left the question to clinical judgement and said that individual medical officers could force feed if they found it right to preserve life in this way. Thus despite some Members of Parliament expressing 'delight that this barbaric practice is now to disappear from our prison system' (Hansard 1974c), the Home Secretary's statement did not actually herald the end of the practice.

That year, Michael Gaughan, an IRA member, had died from pneumonia caused by malnutrition after a 66 day hunger strike at Parkhurst. He had been force fed for 17 days but had put up such resistance that it had been discontinued as the danger of feeding a resisting patient was considered too great. The medical staff were exonerated despite some evidence that the force feeding could have been a factor in causing the pneumonia. Doctors writing to the British Medical Association (BMA) described how the methods used in 1974 had not changed much since the times of the Suffragettes. 'Between the teeth a wooden block is placed, containing a hole through which a greased stomach tube is passed. This process is performed once or twice a day and may be repeated if vomiting occurs. Where resistance is encountered a steel clamp is used to prise open the mouth, and several people may be required to hold the subject still' (British Medical Association, 1992). Although the 1913 'Cat and Mouse Act' was re-enacted within the Prison Act (1952) it was understandably not used for IRA prisoners. It may be relevant that public opinion was sufficiently hostile to IRA prisoners that neither their deaths through hunger strike nor their forcible feeding by the authorities were unlikely to cause too much political discomfort.

A statement issued by the BMA Central Ethical Committee in 1974 did little to clarify the position in saying: 'the doctor must always bear the obligation to preserve human life, but the final decision is for him to make, and it is not for some outside person to seek to override the clinical judgement of the doctor' (British Medical Journal, 1974). The statement made it clear that neither refusal to take part in artificial feeding nor administering the procedures would be seen as professional misconduct 'provided that such procedures were lawful and designed to preserve a prisoner's health' Thus until recently the position seemed to be that whether a prisoner was force fed would depend only on the opinion and stance of a particular prison's medical officer.

The "ethical statement" identified the 'crucial question for decision is whether a doctor ought to stand by and do nothing in a case of what could be tantamount to attempted suicide, even though the consent of the patient has not been given to the intended treatment'. Although this question is never explicitly answered it seems that, in part, the BMA's support of force feeding arose from their construction of food refusal as attempted suicide. An opinion which also seemed to have influenced the decision in *Leigh v Gladstone* where the Lord Chief Justice had declared it 'wicked folly to attempt to starve oneself to death'. Although at the inquest into the death of one prisoner who died after hunger strike, the jury did return a verdict of suicide (The Times, 1976) it is important to recognise that despite the clinical construction of self-starvation as a form of suicide, in legal terms the equation of self-starvation with suicide now seems erroneous (see the cases of *Home Secretary v Robb* and *Airedale NHS Trust v Bland* discussed below).

However, whilst debates about IRA hunger-strikers continued in the UK, worldwide the forcible feeding of political prisoners was a greater cause for concern, particularly the force feeding of political detainees which was occurring under the South African regime gave rise to outcry. In those countries where avenues for legitimate political protest are unavailable the hunger strike remains one of the more important weapons for the prisoner. However it is also in such political regimes that the rights of the prisoner are most likely to be disregarded and force feeding will be administered as retaliative punishment. With this in mind, in 1975 the World Medical Assembly issued the 'Declaration of Tokyo' – a set of guidelines for doctors 'concerning torture and other cruel, inhuman or degrading treatment or punishment in relation to detention or imprisonment' which declared that: 'Where a prisoner refuses nourishment and is considered by the doctor as capable of forming an unimpaired and rational judgement concerning the consequences of such a voluntary refusal of nourishment, he shall not be fed artificially. The decision as to capacity of the prisoner to form such a judgement should be confirmed by at least one independent doctor. The consequences of the refusal of nourishment shall be explained by the doctor to the prisoner' (World Medical Journal, 1976).

However it is noticeable that the declaration remained silent on whether treatment can be provided once a patient is beyond rational thought and as recently as 1991 the World Medcial Association itself suggested that doctors could feed hunger-strikers in the absence of consent in certain circumstances (World Medical Association, 1991). It seemed that despite the declaration of Tokyo the intermittent force feeding of prisoners England continued and the government ignored the call from doctors for legislation to clarify the issue as 'the common law provided so few guidelines only legislation could outlaw the practice altogether.'(British Medical Journal, 1976).

In Britain the lack of a consistent approach was again exposed in 1980–1981 with the hunger strikes of IRA prisoners in the Maze prison. Four prisoners went into comas and their relatives requested medical intervention. The government acquiesced to the relatives' requests and artificially fed the prisoner once they became unconscious or mentally incompetent. Indeed, this seemed to be a common approach internationally. A 1987 review of the practice within the USA, England, Canada and France found that, although countries differed in approach to the initial stages of the hunger strike, there was a uniformity of action once the inmate manifested the effects of starvation – the authorities would intervene to prevent death (Miller, 1987); although in Canada an application for an order requiring provincial authorities to force feed a hunger striker has been refused.

Despite interventions it did seem that Britain was more prepared than the rest of Europe to allow hunger strikers to starve to death. In 1981 there were eleven fatalities as a result of hunger strikes reported in Europe and ten of these were in Belfast (Beresford, 1987). By contrast in the same year in France there were at least 56 episodes of hunger strikes involving hundreds of prisoners with no fatalities (Duhamel, 1984). Of course it is difficult to establish whether the low fatality rate of France is a result of medical intervention or the limited commitment of the hunger striker.

Hunger strikes may not only be fatal for the prisoner concerned but in extreme cases force feeding has also led to the death of the doctor involved. In Spain sixty members of GRAPO (Grupos de Resistenscia Antifascista Primero de Octubre) undertook hunger strikes in protest at their location in separate prisons. Much public debate about the legal and ethical implications of force feeding ensued with judges claiming that force feeding a conscious individual was contrary to Article 5 of the Spanish Constitution which prohibits inhuman or degrading treatments. However the view of the government, that there was an overriding obligation to preserve the health and life of prisoners, prevailed and in 1990 the authorities in Zaragoza and Madrid ordered force feeding despite judicial opposition (British Medical Association, 1992). The Consejo General de Médcicos (Spanish Medical Council) issued an ambiguous circular stating that 'the doctor is obliged to obey the order of the competent authority, whether judicial or administrative' which justified medical intervention where life was at risk or when the patient lost consciousness. When three prisoners in Zaragoza were taken to hospital the head of the nutrition unit, Dr José Ramon Muñoz commenced involuntary feeding. One month later he was shot dead by two members of GRAPO (Le Monde, 1990).

Despite the existence of the Tokyo Declaration hunger strikes and force feeding continue throughout the World. In 1995 and 1996 mass hunger strikes have been reported in countries as politically and geographically diverse as Spain, Azebaijan and Turkey (Amnesty International, 1996a). It is thus surprising that Amnesty International, an organisation which is dedicated to upholding the basic human rights of prisoners and detainees 'takes no position on forcible feeding of prisoners unless it is done in such a way to deliberately cause suffering' (Amnesty International, 1996b).

2.4 A DUTY TO TREAT?

The issue of a doctor's legal duty to preserve life raised in *Leigh v Gladstone* has led some to suggest that it may be a crime not to force feed (Lanham, 1974). Although English and Welsh law does not generally impose liability for omissions, it is clear that when an individual has assumed responsibility for the care of another who can not look after themselves they can not lawfully shed that responsibility without making adequate provisions. Thus a person who fails to feed a baby in their care, or the railwayman who forgets to shut the level crossing gate can be guilty of manslaughter if death ensues. The question has been raised as to whether a common law duty to treat arises with respect to starving prisoners on the point of death. The possible existence of a duty to treat starving prisoners was raised again in 1977 in the criminal case of *R v Stone*.

Mr Stone was a partially deaf, almost blind retired man of low average intelligence. He was charged with unlawfully killing his 61 year old sister, who had moved into his house. She suffered with anorexia nervosa and denied herself meals spending days at a time in her room. She became helpless and ill but did not complain and the Mr Stone did not summon any help. She died from toxaemia from infected bed sores, immobilisation and lack of food. Mr Stone was found guilty of manslaughter. He had assumed a duty to care for the sister and despite the victim refusing nourishment and having made it clear she did not want medical help, he was obliged to summon help or care for her himself.

It seems that in *R v Stone* the victim's inability to care for herself was essential to liability. However, where an alternative is available to the victim who refuses to avail himself of it then the status of dependant is destroyed. Thus failing to force feed a hunger striker would not be subsumed under the existing head of omissions if food water and medical care were provided but refused. Indeed such a liability for omissions was recently considered in *Airedale NHS Trust v Bland*. Lord Keith of Kinkel dismissed the analogy as, having equated feeding with medical treatment, he found no duty on the doctor to continue to treat against the patient's best interests.

2.5 THE CURRENT POSITION

Perhaps the most surprising feature is the remarkable dearth of English case law on the issue despite the frequent occurrence of hunger striking by asylum seeking detainees and convicted prisoners in British gaols over the past decade. There had been no case law since 1909 until the position on force feeding prisoners was clarified in 1995 in the case of *Secretary of State for Home Office v Robb*.

Mr Robb was a 27 year old convicted prisoner who was diagnosed as suffering with a personality disorder. He also had a history of drug addiction and self-harm . He was of sound mind with capacity to make decisions when he began hunger strike and it was noted that he had commenced a hunger strike in custody twice before. A declaration was sought as to whether the Home Office (and prison staff responsible) might lawfully: (1) observe and abide by his refusal of nutrition; (2) abstain from providing hydration or nutrition, by artificial means or otherwise, as long as he retained capacity to refuse the same; (3) in the event of deterioration in his condition, refrain from treatment to prolong his life until he consented to receive the same.

H.H.J. Thorpe in the Family Division of the High Court overruled *Leigh v Gladstone* noting that when that case was decided 'suicide was a criminal act . . . and it was a decision taken in the climate of dramatic conflict between the suffragette movement and the government of the day . . . of little weight or relevance to modern times'. He drew on the authority in *Airedale NHS Trust v Bland* in stating that 'a patient who is entitled to consent to treatment which might or would have the effect of prolonging his life and refuses to consent, and by reason of that refusal subsequently dies, does not commit suicide.' In *Airedale NHS Trust v Bland* Lord Keith of Kinkel had stated the 'principle of sanctity of life is not absolute . . . it does not compel a medical practitioner on pain of criminal sanctions to treat a patient, who will die if he does not, contrary to the wishes of the patient. It does not authorise the force feeding of prisoners on hunger strike'.

H.H.J. Thorpe also considered whether any of the State's interests in preserving life, preventing suicide, protecting innocent third parties and maintaining the integrity of the medical profession countervailed against the individual's right to self determination (such State interests may be taken into account in the United States). He found that 'the principle of sanctity of human life in this jurisdiction is seen to yield to the principle of self determination. . . . Preventing suicide has no application in cases where the refusal of medical treatment and nutrition in the exercise of the right of self-determination does not constitute an act of suicide'. Thus State interests could not outweigh the decision making of a competent adult regardless of the individual's status; the fact of Mr Robb being a prisoner was of no consequence.

It was found that the prison authorities could lawfully abide by Mr Robb's wishes and the declarations sought in (1) and (2) were made. Before the court case Mr Robb had begun eating again thus the more difficult scenario, where the effects of starvation allowed his capacity to make decisions to be called into question, did not arise to be decided upon. Although it seems from the authority in *Bland* (above) that even should a prisoner lose consciousness or capacity it would still not be lawful to treat him under the common law according to clinical judgement of his best interests. His prior refusal of medical treatment would have to be respected and thus it seems likely that the original third point in *Robb* would also be agreed if such a declaration were now sought.

The decision in *Robb* has thus clarified some important issues for doctors faced with a starving prisoner. Firstly it affirms the right to self determination and for the first time states that this is not diminished by a person's status as a prisoner. Secondly it firmly enshrines the right of an autonomous person to make decisions contrary to the doctor's perception of their best interests even if death will result. Finally it suggests that the exercise of self-determination in refusing food is not to be regarded as committing suicide, nor does a compliant doctor aid and abet suicide. Confusion over whether food refusal is to be equated with suicide still remains as despite Thorpe's statement in *Robb* that it was not to be regarded as such, in *B v Croydon H.A.* Hoffman, L.J. (in the Court of Appeal) stated that 'the general law is a person of full mental capacity has the right to choose whether to eat or not. Even if the refusal of food is tantamount to suicide, as in the case of a hunger striker, he can not be compelled to eat or forcibly fed'.

2.6 IMPACT OF "ROBB" AND ADVANCED DIRECTIVES

Advanced directives allow a person, in advance of becoming incompetent, to give instructions about the type of treatment s/he wishes or does not wish to receive in the future should s/he become incompetent. Although such 'living wills' have been legally recognised in the USA since 1976, they have only recently been established as valid in English Law (Robertson, 1995).

Mr Robb had not issued any advanced directive refusing treatment (whilst he retained capacity he did not need one) however if he had it seems that this would have put the position beyond doubt. Indeed the scenario did arise last Summer where a life sentenced prisoner, expressing a wish to die began refusing all food and drink. The man suffered with a personality disorder with a history of substance abuse. Throughout his nine years in prison he had been deemed a chronic suicide risk and had made numerous suicide attempts. He was not mentally ill. After a few days he executed an advanced directive refusing nutrition and treatment should he subsequently lose capacity, although agreeing to treatment with analgesia should it become necessary. The prison were advised by their lawyers that it would be lawful to accede to his wishes, and that any court declaration would be unnecessary, as following the cases of both *Robb* and *Bland* the lawyers considered that if a prisoner with capacity refuses treatment, nothing can be done. Thus no declaration was sought on the advanced directive. After 14 weeks the man died from broncho-pneumonia and cachexia due to starvation.

The Prison Service Health Directorate's current policy is not to force feed any prisoner where an advanced directive is issued. Where a prisoner is of 'sound mind', prison doctors are advised that they need not seek a court declaration unless there are 'exceptional circumstances' (an example of which is given as pregnancy) (Home Office, 1996). In late 1995 a second man died following hunger strike in a British prison, again without any court declaration being sought. The Law Commission paper published in 1995 does however make several recommendations in relation to advanced directives, one of which is that advanced refusal should not preclude taking action necessary to prevent death of the maker *pending a decision of the court* on the validity or applicability of an advanced refusal or on the question of whether it had been withdrawn or altered. Thus they advocate that, where there is any uncertainty over whether an advanced directive is binding, a doctor should be allowed to provide treatment in the interim whilst waiting for a court declaration on the issue (Law Commission, 1995).

3. MENTAL CAPACITY AND CONSENT TO TREATMENT

In the decision in *Robb* a central requirement was the man's capacity to refuse or consent to treatment. All adults are assumed to have legal capacity unless there is evidence to the contrary, and *Robb* clarifies that the status of being a sentenced prisoner is irrelevant in with respect to capacity. However, capacity to form consent becomes of issue when the patient is unconscious, a child or (as in the case of anorexia nervosa sufferers) has a mental illness.

3.1 UNCONSCIOUS OR INCOMPETENT ADULTS

With adult patients who need emergency treatment but who can not consent because they are unconscious, the doctor can, proceed with essential treatment in the best interests of the patient. If a person is found to be incompetent the courts have no jurisdiction to give or withhold consent on their behalf. However the courts can make a declaration as to whether a proposed treatment would be lawful taking into account whether it is (a) for the patient's life, health or well being and (b) in his/her best interests (*Re F (a mental patient: sterilisation) [1989]*).

3.2 MINORS

The Family Law Reform Act (1969) section 8(1) establishes that a child of 16 to 18 has the same capacity as an adult to consent to medical, surgical or dental treatment (*Re W [1993]*). For children under 16 the case of *Gillick v West Norfolk and Wisbech AHA* [1986] establishes that the child's understanding and intelligence will determine whether they can give consent to medical treatment. Thus in the Gillick case a 15 year old could be given contraceptive treatment by a doctor against parental wishes. However *Re W (a minor: consent to medical treatment)* [1993] has clarified that, although when a minor is 'Gillick competent' to *give* consent to treatment this can not be overridden by parents refusal, the reverse will not apply. That is, a minors *refusal* of consent to treatment will not be binding where the parent(s) give valid consent. Indeed, *Re W*, established that a child under 18 years could never have complete autonomy in decisions about their medical treatment as the court retained the power to override consent or refusal even where parents could not.

The case of *Re W* concerned a 16 year old with anorexia nervosa who also displayed self harm and violence to staff. The local adolescent unit wished to transfer her to a specialist unit in London for treatment but she refused to go. The court were asked to decided whether (1) she could be moved to a new treatment unit without her consent and (2) she could be given medical treatment without her consent (this referred not specifically to force feeding but any medical treatment such as administration of drugs etc.).

Despite one doctor's opinion that she had sufficient understanding to make an informed decision, it was agreed that a feature of anorexia nervosa was its capability to destroy an informed choice. However it was unnecessary to decide upon W's capacity to consent, as the court in acknowledging that her views should be taken into account, stated that, since the 1989 Children Act, the child's welfare was of paramount consideration. The court found that under the principles of the Family Law reform Act (1969) no minor of whatever age has the power, by refusing consent, to override consent by someone who has parental responsibility for them. Thus the declarations requested were made.

The final position we are left with after *Gillick* and *Re W* is that in some circumstances a child may be able to give consent to treatment, but not to refuse treatment. The position may seem initially illogical, as others have argued that the right to consent is worthless if not accompanied by the right to refuse (Devreux, Jones and Dickinson, 1993). However, as the consequences of withholding consent are often more dangerous and damaging than the consequences of accepting treatment, refusal can be seen as a higher order decision making, thus justifying a more stringent test of capacity and the greater degree of protection of life (rather than self-determination) offered by the law in such cases (Pearce, 1994).

3.3 MENTALLY DISORDERED ADULTS

It could be assumed that a person with a mental disorder who is detained in hospital is *ispso facto* incompetent. Indeed this was the position taken in the USA by the Michigan circuit court in

Kaimowitz v Michigan Dept. Mental Health (1973). However in England this approach is not followed, instead there is a rebuttable presumption that every adult has the capacity to decide his or her own fate and mentally disordered adults are the same as none disordered adults in this respect (*R v Hallstrom ex parte W* [1986]). Indeed, Part IV of the Mental Health Act explicitly recognises that the 'status' of being a detained mental patient does not destroy capacity to consent in that section 57(2) specifies some treatments (including electroconvulsive therapy and psychosurgery) which may only be given with the patient's consent. However given the importance of the assessment of capacity in medical decisions it is surprising that a legal test of capacity to consent (or to refuse consent) has only recently been scrutinised and clarified in English law in *Re C (an adult: refusal of treatment) [1994]*.

3.4 THE LEGAL TEST OF CAPACITY

Mr C was a 68 year old man with chronic paranoid schizophrenia who was detained in a maximum security psychiatric hospital having being transferred from prison. He was found to have a gangrenous foot and was transferred to a general hospital where the surgeon advised amputation of his leg below the knee to avoid imminent death. Mr C refused consent to amputation, although he did agree to more conservative surgery which removed immediate danger to his life. The doctors believed an 85 per cent chance of death remained and refused to agree not to amputate the leg in the future. Mr C applied to the courts for an injunction to stop the hospital from amputating his leg without his express written consent. The judge found that Mr C was competent to refuse consent for amputation and granted the injunction requested. The decision was somewhat unusual as, despite a recognition of the patient's legal right to refuse treatment, previously the courts have been reluctant to uphold this when such refusal might lead to death (*Re T (an adult: consent to medical treatment)*[1993] and *Re S (adult refusal of treatment)* [1993]). Indeed, *Re C* was the first reported case where the English courts had granted an injunction requiring a doctor not to treat a patient (Stern, 1994).

In *Re C* the process of determining competence was clarified by relating it to three specific stages. The adult patient must be able to : (1) comprehend and retain the information (2) believe it, and

(3) weigh it in the balance and arrive at a choice. If so his/her consent or refusal is valid, regardless of status. The mere fact that a patient's value system is unusual, will not make consent or refusal invalid. However, if the patient's mental illness impairs his or her ability to assess risks then they may fail on the third limb of the test. In *Re C* there was particular examination of the link between the *specific* decision to be made (i.e. amputation of a foot) and the patient's mental condition. Despite Mr C's schizophrenia and delusions he was competent to make decisions about surgery. (It is noteworthy that in the final analysis Mr C's decision seems to have been more 'competent' than the surgeon's as three years later he is still alive with both feet!)

4. COMPULSORY TREATMENT UNDER THE MENTAL HEALTH ACT

In England and Wales the compulsory detention and treatment of mentally ill people can only be conducted under the statutory provisions of the 1983 Mental Health Act (MHA). Scotland also has similar but not identical provisions within the Mental Health (Scotland) Act of 1984. The MHA section of most relevance to anorexia nervosa is Part II, section 3. This section allows a patient to be admitted for treatment providing that:

(a) He is suffering from mental illness, severe mental impairment, psychopathic disorder or mental impairment and his mental disorder is of a nature or degree which makes it appropriate for him to receive medical treatment in hospital.

(b) In the case of psychopathic disorder such treatment is likely to alleviate or prevent deterioration of his condition.

(c) It is necessary for the health and safety of the patient or for the protection of others that he should receive such treatment and it can not be provided unless he is detained under this section.

Two medical practitioners must provide written recommendations stating that these grounds are complied with, and in the case of (c) whether other methods of dealing with the patient are available and, if so, why they are not appropriate.

The objective of the MHA is to allow for treatment of a persons mental disorder, even where the patient is unwilling or unable to recognise the existence of that disorder and their need for treatment. When parliament first introduced these compulsory treatment provisions, Mr Norman Fowler, then Secretary of State for Social Services, stated that the government sought to balance the interests of the patient and the wish to ensure that treatments could be imposed where necessary. Mr Fowler explained that the measures were intended to override the wishes of the patient only in 'strictly defined circumstances'. He added: 'The Bill therefore provides a carefully thought out scheme in which the safeguards are graduated according to the particular category of treatment.' Thus the more invasive the treatment, the more stringent the safeguards in Part IV of the MHA. Section 57 thus requires that controversial treatments such as psychosurgery or surgical implantation of hormones to reduce male sex drive are only undertaken with the patient's consent *and* the authorisation of an independent doctor. Section 58 requires the patient's consent *or* the authorisation of a second doctor for interventions such as electroconvulsive therapy or medication beyond the initial three months.

Treatments specified under section 63 have no such safeguards and neither consent nor a second opinion is required. This is because, during parliamentary debate, it was envisaged that the medical treatment under section 63 would be 'perfectly routine, sensible treatment ... and general nursing and other care'. No special safeguards were introduced because the treatments within section 63 were not considered serious enough to need any safeguards for the patient. Thus, irrespective of a patient's capacity, section 63 of the MHA states that: 'The consent of a patient *shall not be required* for any medical treatment given to him for a mental disorder from which he is suffering if the treatment is given by or under the direction of a responsible medical officer'. These medical treatments which can be given without consent are never specifically defined within the MHA although section 145 partially describes medical treatment as 'including nursing care. Habilitation and rehabilitation under medical supervision'. This description in section 145 is not exhaustive and therefore what may be included is left to the discretion of the responsible medical officer in charge of the patient's care. It is this aspect which has led to cases requiring clarification by the courts. Particularly with respect to whether procedures are specific 'treatments for mental disorder' or alternatively 'part of the treatment of a person who is diagnosed as having mental disorder'.

The objective was never to allow for physical treatment to be carried out under this legislation. Indeed the code of practice states: 'Treatments for physical disorder therefore cannot be given under this part of the Act unless it is a physical disorder that gives rise to a mental disorder and it is necessary to treat the physical disorder in order to treat the mental disorder.' However, as the cases below illustrate, the scope of treatments which have been authorised under section 63 now goes far beyond the 'perfectly routine' treatment initially envisaged by parliament and includes treatment for physical disorders (Dolan and Parker, 1996).

4.1 COMPULSORY TREATMENT AND FORCE FEEDING IN ANOREXIA NERVOSA

The compulsory treatment of anorexia nervosa should not, of course, be equated with forced feeding, many interventions (including psychotherapeutic treatments) are subsumed under the umbrella of compulsory treatment, as often following the compulsory admission to hospital the patient will comply with treatment and re-nourishment packages offered (see other chapters in this book). However, there are cases where food refusal does continue after compulsory admission and then artificial feeding usually by nasogastric tube may be deemed necessary as a last resort.

The position of the courts has always been to uphold force feeding under section 63 in cases of detained anorexia nervosa patients as is illustrated in the recent case of *S.W.Hertfordshire Health Authority v K.B* (1994). KB was an 18 year old woman who in September 1993 was detained under section 3 MHA having suffered anorexia nervosa for $4\frac{1}{8}$ years. She had been fed with a nasogastric tube and in January 1994 (when the court case was heard) she weighed 38kg. The force feeding had been authorised by doctors under sections 58 and 63 MHA.The Mental Health Act Commission had declared that naso-gastric feeding was the administration of food, not medicine and told the doctors to desist. It was estimated that KB would only live for another 14–21 days without food and thus the health authority asked the courts for a declaration on the lawfulness of continued feeding of KB without her consent.

KB argued that feeding by tube was not treatment for her mental illness but was for physical symptoms. The feeding was to increase her weight and thus not for mental disorder as required under section 63 of the Act. The judge however agreed with the Health Authority that as KB suffered with anorexia nervosa relieving symptoms was just as much part of the treatment as relieving the underlying cause. If symptoms are exacerbated by refusal to eat then the mental disorder becomes more difficult to treat and thus naso-gastric feeding was an integral part of treatment, indeed it was necessary to make psychiatric treatment of the disorder possible at all. Thus the judge declared that the detention of KB under section 3 permitted the administration of food or fluids against her will under the provisions of section 63 so long as she remains a detained patient under section 3. As a secondary point the Health Authority had also said that KB did not have the capacity to consent or refuse consent to treatment. The judge agreed although he noted that consent was not required for treatment under section 63 (and thus the issue was irrelevant to his decision). Importantly the effect of this finding was that KB was not being treated *without* her consent as she was deemed not to have the capacity to give or to withhold her consent in the first place.

4.2 FORCE FEEDING A DETAINED PATIENT IN THE ABSENCE OF AN EATING DISORDER

In the subsequent case of *B v Croydon Health Authority* [1995] the Court of Appeal established that when a patient is detained under the MHA and refuses food, they can still retain the capacity to withhold consent to force feeding. However the issue of capacity remains irrelevant as the statute not only permits force feeding but overrides a competent patient's refusal. Ms B was a detained patient suffering with borderline personality disorder coupled with post-traumatic stress disorder in the context of severe childhood sexual abuse. She was detained under section 3 MHA as having 'psychopathic disorder'. She displayed a compulsion to self harm and whilst in hospital, deprived of the means to cut and burn herself, she refused to eat as an alternative means of inflicting harm. At a weight of 32kg she was threatened with tube feeding and applied to the court for an injunction to prevent the hospital taking this action without her consent. It was argued by Ms B's lawyers that food was 'medicine' within the terms of section 58 and thus either the patient's consent or certification by a second opinion by a doctor was required. However the court found that ordinary food was *not* medicine within the meaning of section 58 but was 'treatment' within the broad definition of section 145 (above) and thus tube feeding fell within the scope of section 63 and could be administered without the patient's consent.

The question remaining was whether tube feeding was treatment for Ms B's 'mental disorder', as required within section 63. It was established in *re KB* (see 4.1. above) that tube feeding is treatment for the mental disorder in anorexia nervosa, but Ms B's 'mental disorder' was borderline personality disorder not an eating disorder. The court said it was too 'atomistic' to attempt to discriminate between treatment for a mental disorder (as in anorexia nervosa) and treatment for the consequences of a mental disorder (as with Ms B's personality disorder) and agreed with the judgement in *re KB* that 'relieving symptoms was just as much treatment as relieving the underlying cause'. Forced feeding came within section 145 of the Act and it was *for* the mental disorder even if it was ancillary to the core treatment (of psychotherapy) if it was 'nursing and care concurrent with the core treatment or as a necessary pre-requisite to such treatment'. Thus it was held that force feeding would have been lawful and her appeal was dismissed. The lower court had found that Ms B did have capacity to refuse consent, although two of the judges in the Court of Appeal expressed doubts about this, they found it unnecessary to re-open the issue as they had already decided that capacity was irrelevant to treatment under the Statute. Interestingly Mr Justice Thorpe, in the court below, had also concluded that force feeding was contrary to Ms B's best interests, although this issue was (surprisingly) not addressed in the Court of Appeal.

Although the decision in *B v Croydon H.A.* may be welcomed by doctors, it can also be seen as a severe infringement of civil liberties. Gunn (1995) has argued that the object of the MHA was not to enable physical treatment to be carried out under statute and that legislation permitting such infringements of personal liberty should be strictly interpreted. Although the distinction between treatment for mental and physical disorder is difficult to draw, he submits that the fact a treatment is necessary for the treatment of a mental disorder to take place does not make it treatment for the disorder itself. Indeed it seems from *Re C* (see

3.4 above) that the fact that treatment keeps someone alive (and thus makes other treatment possible) does not make it treatment for the mental disorder itself. Although there is admittedly a closer association between Ms B's food refusal and her borderline personality disorder than between Mr C's gangrenous foot and his schizophrenia, it could be argued that if society wishes to authorise such treatment this should be explicitly stated in legislation rather than requiring judges to stretch the Mental Health Act to permit it.

Fennel (1995) has also noted that the decisions in *Re KB* and *B v Croydon HA* means that detained patients who are force fed now have no safeguards beyond the clinical judgement of the doctor to ensure that treatment is in their best interests. Since force feeding is not deemed to fall within the special category of treatments in section 57 (requiring consent) or even section 58 (requiring second opinions if consent is not obtained) there can be no scrutiny of a single doctors decision to administer treatment. The dangers of patients' rights being disregarded in such circumstances are not merely hypothetical, but are demonstrated in a recent case which has extended the powers under the MHA even beyond the bounds of *B v Croydon HA* and has authorised a Caesarean section to be conducted against a woman's express wishes and without seeking a second opinion under section 63 as 'treatment for her mental disorder' (Dolan and Parker, 1996).

In each of these cases the integrity of the doctors and the clinical team caring for the patient is unquestionable. The reluctance of the courts to allow a patient to starve to death is also understandable. However, it seems that MHA which was originally enacted to protect the rights of patients, now affords far greater protection to their doctors when administering treatment without consent. This does not necessarily mean that the treatments applied are of themselves inappropriate or improper. But achieving a balance between the patients right to self determination and their right to treatment when mentally ill is a complex task. However, if society wishes to authorise such physical treatments this should be explicitly stated within the legislation and introduced only after an opportunity for public scrutiny of the issues concerned, rather than requiring judges to stretch the boundaries of the MHA beyond its initial remit. As Gunn (1995) stated, if the MHA creates a lacuna 'it should be filled not by judicial creativism but by Parliament after careful public debate of the issues involved.'

5. ADVANCED DIRECTIVES AND THE MENTAL HEALTH ACT

A final issue to consider is the effect of advance directives on the provisions of the Mental Health Act. As has been described above, advanced directives issued by a competent patient will be legally binding. However, given that consent is irrelevant under MHA, it seems likely that advanced directives would be equally ineffective. The author is unaware of any cases which have specifically tested this issue although it was raised in 1993 in *Broadgreen NHS Trust v DW*.

Miss DW was a single thirty year old woman with a five year history of anorexia nervosa detained under section 3 MHA (1983). At a weight of 29.5 kg she refused food and the hospital applied to the courts for a declaration that artificial feeding was lawful. The view was that she did not have capacity to make decisions, however her lawyers argued that when her attitudes were last known she did have capacity. The doctor agreed that earlier in her illness he speculated that she would also have refused the artificial feeding. However, despite some evidence to support this in the patient's writings, the situation was hypothetical as it had never been specifically put to her in order for her to express a firm view in the event of a life threatening situation. The judge contrasted this situation from that of a Jehovah's witness who has consistently expressed a belief that a blood transfusion should not be given whatever the circumstances. Feeding was then authorised under section 63 of the Act as treatment for her anorexia nervosa. One report of the case states that the judge 'remarked, however, that had the patient made an advanced directive about force feeding the outcome might have been different'. However, this comment does not appear in the transcript of the judgement and it is submitted that it would not accurately reflect the current legal position (Lancely and Travers 1993).

Advanced directives are instructions about the kind of treatment a person wishes to have should they lose capacity, they are in effect simply prospective declarations of consent to/refusal of future treatment. Should the anticipated event later arise an advanced directive will then have the same force as a *current* capable consent or refusal and will override common law duty of a doctor to treat an incapable or unconscious patient. Yet as current consent is irrelevant to treatment under section 63 it would follow that consent framed within an advanced directive would also be irrelevant. Indeed Gordon (1996) has noted that if advanced directives could survive the MHA then the implementation of the statute and liability to be detained would be dependant upon a prior contingency rather than a patient's clinical condition. This would undermine the entire legal basis for treatment under the MHA.

6. CONCLUSIONS

It seems to be legally settled that in England and Wales patients with anorexia nervosa can be compulsorily admitted and artificially fed regardless of absence of consent under the provisions of section 63 of the MHA. Regarding the other scenarios discussed above the present situation seems to be that:

(1) If a person is competent to refuse treatment/feeding then it would be a breach of common law to override their refusal (*Home Secretary v Robb*; *Re C*). It is immaterial if they are a sentenced prisoner.

(2) An advanced directive forbidding artificial feeding/treatment will be binding should a competent person subsequently lose capacity (*Re C*); subject to (6) and (7) below.

(3) If a person is not competent, treatment can be declared lawful by the courts following a best interests approach ('*Bolam*' test) (*Re F*).

(4) Even if a minor is competent to refuse treatment this can be overridden following a best interests approach (*Re W*).

(5) If a person is detained under MHA and has capacity, a treatment *not connected* with the mental disorder can only be given with their consent. Any advanced directive will also be binding in this respect (*Re C*).

(6) If a person is detained under MHA any treatment *connected* with the mental disorder can be given under section 63 and the possession of capacity or consent is irrelevant (*B v Croydon H.A.*).

(7) As possession of capacity or consent is irrelevant to treatment for mental disorder it is submitted that an advanced directive

(which embraces provisions for future lack of capacity) will also be irrelevant and thus an advanced directive will be ineffectual in preventing treatment *connected* with the mental disorder in a detained patient under section 63 MHA.

Finally, it should be remembered that most of these cases are declarations of the courts which merely declare the rights and duties of parties and do not alter the legal position. It is debatable whether the cases have general interpretation or whether a doctor should still seek a declaration on every case (or at least if unusual circumstances arise). On balance it is suggested that as long as doctors follow principles of the existing declarations and act with good faith and reasonable care (within the '*Bolam*' test), they will be protected from civil proceedings and indeed section 139 MHA explicitly affords protection from civil and criminal proceedings in the case of detained patients.

REFERENCES

Amnesty International (1996a) *Amnesty International Index*, EUR 55/01/96.

——(1996b) Personal communication.

Beresford, D. (1987) *Ten Men Dead*, London: Grafton.

Brailsford, H. and Nevinson, H. (1909) Correspondence. *The Times*, October 5.

British Medical Association (1992) *Medicine betrayed*, London: Zed Books.

British Medical Journal (1974a) 'Medicolegal: Inquest on hunger-striker'. *British Medical Journal*, 52–3.

——(1974b) 'Ethical statement: Artificial feeding of prisoners'. *British Medical Journal*, 2: 52.

——(1976) 'Medicolegal: Force-feeding in prison'. *British Medical Journal*, 2: 823–4.

Devreux, J., Jones, D. and Dickinson, D. (1993) 'Can children withold consent to treatment?' *British Medical Journal*, 306: 1459–61.

Dolan, B. and Parker, C. (1996) 'Caesarean section: A treatment for mental disorder'. *British Medical Journal*, in press.

Duhamel, O. (1984) 'Esquisse d'une typologie des grèves de la faim'. Chapter in *La grève de la faim*, Paris: Economica.

Fennel, P. (1995) 'Force feeding and the Mental Health Act (1983)'. *New Law Journal*, 145: 319–20.

Gordon, R. (1996) 'Advanced directives and users of treatment'. *Mental Health Law and Consent to Treatment,* London: IBC.

Gunn, M. (1995) 'Treatment without consent'. *Journal of Forensic Psychiatry,* 6: 411–15.

Hansard (1974a) *868 H.C.* Debs., col. 442 (January 30).

—— (1974b) *877 H.C.* Debs., col. 451 (July 17).

Home Office (1996) *DDL (96)* (January 1).

Kalk, W.J. and Veriava,Y. (1991) 'Hospital management of voluntary total fasting amongst political prisoners'. *Lancet,* 337: 660–2.

Lanceley, C. and Travers, R. (1993) 'Anorexia nervosa: Forced feeding and the law' (letter). *British Journal of Psychiatry,* 162: 835.

Lanham, P. (1974) *Criminal Law Review* , 206.

Law Commission (1995) *Law Commission Consultation Paper: Mental Incapacity,* No. 231.

Le Monde (1990) March 29.

Legemaate, J. (1995) 'Involuntary admission to psychiatric hospital: Recent European developments'. *European Journal of Health Law,,* 2: 15–32.

McKenzie, M. (1988) *Shoulder to shoulder,* New York: Vintage Books

Miller, W.P. (1987) 'The hunger striking prisoner'. *Journal of Prison and Jail Health,* 6:(1), 40–61.

Pearce, J. (1994) 'Consent to treatment during childhood: The assessment of competence and the avoidance of conflict'. *British Journal of Psychiatry,* 165: 713–16.

Robertson, G.S. (1995) 'Making an advanced directive'. *British Medical Journal,* 310: 236–8.

Rosen A. (1974) *Rise up women!* London: Routledge and Kegan Paul.

Savill, A.F., Moullin, C. and Horsely, V. (1912) 'Preliminary report on the forcible feeding of suffrage prisoners'. *Lancet,* ii: 549–51.

Stern, K. (1994) 'Competence to refuse life sustaining treatment'. *Law Quarterly Review,* 119: 541–5.

The Times (1976) February 17.

Tiller, J., Schmidt, U.,and Treasure, J. (1993) 'Compulsory treatment for anorexia nervosa: Compassion or coercion?' *British Journal of Psychiatry,* 162: 679–80.

Vestergaard, J. (1994) 'The Danish Mental Health Act of 1989: Psychiatric discretion and the new legislation'. *International Journal of Law and Psychiatry, 17: 191–210.*

Winick, B.J. (1994) 'The right to refuse mental health treatment: A therapeutic jurisprudential analysis'. *International Journal of Law and Psychiatry,* 17: 99–117.

World Medical Association (1991) *News Release*, June 3.
World Medical Journal (1976) pp. 87–8.
Zellnick, G. (1976) 'The forcible feeding of prisoners: An examination of the legality of forced therapy'. *Public Law*, 2: 153–87.

LAW REPORTS

A. G British Columbia v Astaforoff (1984) 4. W.W.R. 385.
Airedale NHS Trust v Bland (1993) 1 All ER 821.
B v Croydon H.A (1995) 1 All ER 683.
Bolam v Friern Barnet Management Committee (1957) 2 All ER 118.
Broadgreen NHS Trust v DW (1993) 6th May, 93/WG/1025 QBD Liverpool (unreported).
Gillick v West Norfolk and Wisbech AHA (1986) 1 FLR 224.
Leigh v Gladstone (1909) 26 TLR 139–142.
Prisoners (Temporary Discharge for Ill-health) Act (1913) 3 Geo. 5 Ch. 4.
R v Hallstrom ex parte W (1986) 1 QB 1090.
R v Stone (1977) 2 W.L.R. 169.
Re C (an adult: refusal of treatment) (1994) 1 FLR 31.
Re F (a mental patient: sterilisation) (1990) 2 AC 1.
Re S (adult: refusal of treatment) (1993) Fam, 123.
Re T (adult: refusal of treatment) (1992) 4 All ER 649
Re T (an adult: consent to medical treatment) (1993) Fam 95, CA.
Re W (a minor: medical treatment) (1993) 1 FLR 1.
S.W.Hertfordshire Health Authority v K.B (1994) 2 FCR 1051.
Secretary of State for the Home Office v Robb (1995) 1 All ER 677.

CHAPTER EIGHT

A plea against compulsory treatment of anorexia nervosa patients

Günther Rathner

INTRODUCTION

Every treatment will be confronted with the dilemma of enhancing personal well-being and respecting the person as self-determining individual. Treatment of anorexia nervosa has to face an additional therapeutic dilemma: encouraging greater autonomy and freedom in the patient, while at the same time taking control over the patient's food intake and body weight (Bruch, 1986). But it is time to rethink the ethical foundation of our treatment approaches. The age of 'doctors know best' is gone. A Medline search, for example, showed a more than tenfold increase of scientific papers on treatment refusal in medical journals from 1984 to 1996. However, only a handful of these papers concerned eating disorders, thus it looks like we are still in a quite 'safe' position compared to other areas of medicine.

This chapter is devoted only to anorexia nervosa, as I could not find a single reference to compulsory treatment of normal-weight bulimia nervosa patients. This is surprising, as the defendants of the compulsory treatment position could also use the self-harm argument to justify compulsory treatment for many bulimic patients. This may be because bulimia nervosa has a lower mortality than anorexia nervosa as far as we know (Patton, 1988; Sullivan, 1995) and thus represents less danger to the patient and a less thrilling therapeutic enterprise for the clinician. Another factor is the form of the disorder: the self-starvation of the anorectic patient is an outward sign with all the possibilities for countertransference, while bulimic behaviors are usually performed in secret. The experience of a 'strong will' and utmost self-control shown in starving oneself may elicit stronger counter-transference feelings of breaking this will (see Chapter by Dolan in this volume) than the failing self-control in bulimia nervosa; the latter may stimulate guidance, help, and paternalistic behaviors. In essence, 'control' (in anorexia nervosa) may favour a symmetric escalation of imposing even more control by the clinician, whereas 'no control' (in bulimia nervosa) may elicit a more lenient approach from the therapists.

Both the limited research record on compulsory treatment in anorexia nervosa and a scarce body of case reports call for a critical evaluation of compulsory treatment and for a tentative summary of alternatives to compulsory treatment. This chapter puts the issue of compulsory treatment in the broader context of law and ethics, the patient-doctor relationship, and the research on involuntary admission and compulsory treatment both in general medicine and psychiatry, in order to set the scene for alternatives to compulsory treatment. Much of each section focuses on gaps in our empirical knowledge and on recourse to opinions, values, and prejudices rather than facts. Specifically, by disguising different masks of paternalism in psychiatric and psychological treatments, we will argue for *service* as the best conceptualisation and basis for the therapeutic relationship.

Before commenting upon the position of others, it is perhaps appropriate to explicitly state my own position and actual practice in treatment. I would argue against the use of involuntary admission and compulsory treatment in cases of anorexia nervosa. I have never used it, although with one of my patients I have used the threat of involving the court when her mother attempted to discharge her.

MEDICAL PATERNALISM AND NONCOMPLIANCE

The encounter between patient and health care providers is characterized as the focus of the entire health care enterprise. The basic issue that underlies this relationship is the relative knowledge and power on part of the doctor, and the suffering, pain, fear of the future, and eventually life-threat on part of the patient. Both patients and doctors share the burden of clinical decision with ethical implications, but mainly patients have to tolerate the consequences. According to Max Weber's classical definition, power is the chance to carry through his/her will, irrespective of the grounds of this chance. A contract is called a voluntary agreement, but the *relative power of involved parties is unbalanced*; this is usually the case in treatment. As known, the word 'patient' stems from the Latin '*pati*' (to suffer).

The core of traditional medicine has been paternalism (Thomasma, 1983). Thus, the clash between paternalism and autonomy lies at the heart of many ethical problems in medicine. Paternalism is the interference with a person's liberty of action justified by reasons referring exclusively to the welfare, good, happiness, needs, interests or values of the person being coerced (Hermann, 1990). This would imply that the best interests are defined by the doctor. One of the temptations of the paternalistic model derives from the relative ease of decision making for the doctor. Obedience is then euphemistically termed 'compliance'. In the paternalistic model inevitably noncompliance enters the stage: between one third and one half of patients fail to comply with medical advice and prescriptions (Donovan, 1995; Bebbington, 1995). Refusal of treatment can be re-labelled as *open noncompliance*, whereas drop-out, not following the prescribed treatment, not taking certain drugs etc. would be *covert or silent noncompliance*. It has been argued that compliance is a false goal and that the traditional concept of compliance, which ignores the patient's role in medical decision making, is outmoded in modern health care systems, where chronic illnesses and questioning patients predominate (Donovan, 1995).

Social changes have brought forward new concepts of the therapeutic relationship, i.e. *participatory shared decision making* (doctor and patient are mutual contributive partners in the pursuit of the shared value and goal of good health) and *advocacy*, the patient being the decisional authority (Grundstein-Amado, 1991). Both these models have many aspects in common and seem to fit better to the reality of illness and treatment, as in most cases (except for unconscious patients) the patients decide what will be done or not, meeting their own beliefs and personal circumstances. For example, patients may experiment with prescribed drugs to find a lower but still active dose with fewer side effects. Nowadays, however, there are growing economic barriers to the exercise of patients' rights such as the increasing proportion of people without any health insurance and the growing influence from managed-care organizations to reduce costs (Levinsky, 1996; see also chapter by Andersen in this volume). This might have the impact of re-establishing the old medical power hierarchy.

Some still justify paternalism against the 'antipaternalistic' rights position of the 1970s (Silber, 1989). The more modern version, the differentiation of *weak versus strong paternalism* (Thomasma, 1983) or *reasonable versus hardline paternalism* – the latter permits overriding a competent person's wishes or choices – (Hermann, 1990; Kopelman, 1990) seems to introduce the old-fashioned concept in 'new clothes'; sometimes reasonable paternalism is favoured in minors, aged or incompetent subjects. The principle of beneficence should not be used to back paternalism of each provenance. Beneficence, acting for the good of others, is an inherently ethical principle of medicine.[1] Most often it is expressed by the axiom of non-harm. Autonomy stems from the Greek for 'self-law or rule'. It has been argued that beneficence is primary to autonomy (Thomasma, 1983). However, as the word tells us, beneficence has to be based on the needs of the patients. Very likely there will be a lack of congruence of values between any particular patient and any one physician in a pluralistic society. Interventions that would be entirely justified on objective medical grounds, but which are contrary to and undermine the beliefs and values of the patient, may not satisfy the principle of beneficence, because the 'good' valued by the doctor could undermine the 'good' valued by the patient. Accordingly, *without respect for autonomy, the wishes of the patient will not be known.*

The matter is not to defend a reasonable against a hardline paternalism. In essence, paternalism is the unjustifiable overturning of self-rule by ignoring a patient's wishes; it leads away from treating a person to curing a disease. Therefore, I am arguing that we need to change completely our point of view: we have to *serve* our clients, be they minors or adults, to *our* best knowledge and to *their* needs. This would imply to *place the decisional authority in the patient*, 'which permits medical information to be acted upon by the patient in conformity with his or her own values and beliefs in such a way that the ultimate treatment decision will be consistent with the patient's character and give further expression to his or her personhood' (Hermann, 1990). This position has the advantage of reflecting the realities of health care and avoiding the noncompliance path.

WHAT IS COMPULSORY TREATMENT?

INFORMED CONSENT

Autonomous decision making in matters affecting the body and mind is one of the most valued liberties in a civilized society. The values of bodily integrity and self-determination are deeply embedded in the philosophy of Western civilization; rights of liberty and self-autonomy are secured by constitutions. Liberty rights are applicable also to children, as it is not disputed that a child, in common with adults, has a substantial liberty interest in not being confined unnecessarily for medical treatment (Cichon, 1992). The right of *self-autonomy* protects the right to make fundamental decisions in matters concerning one's person. This right exists in the legal doctrine of informed consent, which is considered a basic principle of ethical behavior in psychiatry since the 1950s.

Compulsory treatment can be defined as *any treatment against the informed consent of the patient*. The latter refers to the consent which is obtained after the patient has been adequately instructed about the ratio of risk and benefit involved in the procedure as compared to alternative procedures or no treatment at all (Kirby, 1983). A valid consent must be voluntary and uncoerced, the patient must be capable of understanding the nature of the procedure (i.e. specific competence), and the patient must have an adequate level of information concerning the procedure (Roth, Meisel and Lidz, 1977; Appelbaum and Roth, 1982; Kutner, Ruark and Raffin, 1991; Jones, 1995). Implementation of informed consent is not a singular event, but implies the integration of informing the patient into the continuing dialogue between physician and patient that routinely should be part of diagnosis and treatment (Lidz, Appelbaum and Meisel, 1988). This process model of consent implies more talk and less paper.

REFUSAL AND COMPETENCE

Informed consent necessarily implies *informed refusal*, otherwise the right to consent would seem to be no more than the right to agree with the doctor. Treatment contrary to the patient's wishes is almost always unethical, because it has the effect of offending against the principle of respect for autonomy. Even if the patient's decision appears unwise, foolish, or life-threatening, the law requires that it be respected if competently made (Cichon, 1992). Thus, a competent adult is entitled to refuse medical treatment even in circumstances where the likely consequence is serious harm or even death (Jones, 1995). But every rule has its exceptions.

The two main reasons for overriding the right to consent or refusal by law are *incompetence in adults* and the *age of minority*. Perhaps the most dramatic area of the recognition of patient's rights to refuse is that involving life-sustaining medical treatment.[2] The three most frequent types of non-psychiatric patients referred for competency evaluation are the following: those who have inflicted harm on themselves, the elderly with cognitive deficits, and those who present management problems (Myers and Barrett, 1986). Thus, competence issues arise also in physical illness (Wear and Brahams, 1991). But there is no single simple test for competency, as *the concept of competence is social and legal, and not merely psychiatric or medical* (Roth et al., 1977). Mental illness is not equivalent to incompetence, as mental illness is selective and competence has to be related to the decision making task at hand (specific competence; Kopelman, 1990). Some kind of involuntary admission and compulsory treatment in mental disorders is legal in most countries.[3] The relative easiness of compulsory treatment in mental illness and the almost complete lack of compulsory treatment in physical illness such as cancer should make us suspicious about the underlying values of the medical system.

If a patient has been evaluated as incompetent, there are three guidance principles to proceed: the *best interests standard* (acting so as to promote maximally the good, i.e. well-being, of the incompetent individual), *substitute judgement* (surrogate decision making by family, court, physician, or institutional ethics committee), or *advance directives* (implementing a living will or durable power of attorney, that the individual executes while being competent). Both the best interests and the substitute judgement standard are problematic (Gunn, 1991). The substituted judgement standard was developed in an attempt to afford respect to the personal values of the incompetent patient. However, substituted judgement (e.g. by a proxy) may be an unacceptable legal fiction: 'What the incompetent would do if he or she could make a choice is simply a matter of speculation' (Kluge, 1989). This standard often camouflages the fact that in reality the proxy is making an independent decision for the incompetent individual (Cichon, 1992). The patient's best interests are defined as 'objective, societally shared criteria' (Greco et al., 1991). The operative guideline is what a 'reasonable person' would do if competent. This reference to ordinary people or the allegedly ordinary common sense has been criticized as sanism (prejudice against mentally disabled) and pretextual thinking in law (Perlin, 1993, 1994); it ignores the unique individuality of human beings, as the choice to undergo treatment is not a common but an individualized one (Hermann, 1990; Gigliotti and Rubin, 1991). Despite these problems, the best interests standard might still be the least problematic legal guideline if needed in this vexed area.

THE CONTINUUM OF COERCION AND COMPULSION

Unfortunately, in the field of eating disorders compulsory treatment is sometimes wrongly equated to other terms such as imposed, forced or coercive treatment. However, these do not mean the same thing. Likewise, compulsory treatment should not be muddled up with forced feeding or tube feeding. Obviously, *each* treatment includes some (or more) coercive, but necessary elements, e.g. insulin injections or dietary restrictions for diabetes. This is also the case in anorexia nervosa. It is *necessary to disentangle coercion and compulsion*, the coercive elements of treatment in anorexia nervosa usually are to secure the necessary weight gain.

In contrast to compulsory treatment *voluntary treatment* seems not so well defined; for example, there are many informal pressures on psychiatric patients by family, police, and hospital staff to accept voluntary admission. In science the continuum approach has many advantages over the categorial approach; the same is true for compulsion and coercion. There are various social pressures that family, friends, relatives, schools, and (mental) health care personnel use in an attempt to get the sufferer to accept the idea of seeking help: request, reasoning, persuasion, barter, bargaining, begging, gentle prodding, enticement, selective information, manipulation, deceiving, blackmail, threat, even various forms of physical force. These informal coercive actions form a continuum with the formal coercion of compulsory treatment at the other end. Although it is difficult to draw the line, it is important to be aware of the difference between acceptable coercion and unacceptable compulsion.

The crucial difference to compulsory treatment is the *patient's consent to the coercive elements of treatment*. With regard to forced feeding, in a literal sense 'forced' is not even possible in babies, as every mother knows, as they spit, turn their head, close their mouth and so on. Why then should it be possible in adolescent or adult anorexia nervosa patients? Sometimes they might be fed with a spoon by a nurse in the framework of a nursing regime (Russell, 1977), but this hardly can be labelled forced treatment. The same is true for tube feeding: some inpatient treatment programs include tube feeding as time-limited procedure in case of insufficient weight gain. Again, this is part of the treatment contract and would not mean that the patient is put in bodily restraints. In some countries (e.g. USA) a committed patient could not be forced to undergo an intrusive psychiatric treatment without a hearing; this is also recommended in Europe (Council of Europe, 1994). Electroconvulsive treatment or psychosurgery are usually considered intrusive, but tube feeding is not (Hughes, Eckert and McManus, 1985). See also Slomka (1995) for the physiological meaning of tube feeding in contrast to the social meaning of food and drink.

INDICATIONS FOR COMPULSORY TREATMENT

COMPULSORY TREATMENT IN ANOREXIA NERVOSA

Most descriptions of treatment programs for anorexia nervosa reserve only a few lines – if any – for ethical issues and compulsory treatment. The general statement seems to be that clinical interventions come first and compulsory treatment should be used only as a last resort (e.g. Crisp, 1980; Dresser, 1984; Vandereycken and Meermann, 1984). Compulsory treatment seems to be justified by the immediate danger to the patient (self-harm, ultimately mortal danger) and the beneficence motive of society and the health care system.

In general psychiatry, there is a trend for compulsory treatment to decrease. A vast amount of research has been done on factors influencing civil commitment rates (e.g. Davies et al., 1996; Myers and Barret, 1986; Cournos, McKinnon and Stanley, 1991; Bagby et al., 1991; Sensky, Hughes and Hirsch, 1991a; Perris et al., 1985), outpatient commitment (e.g. Scheid-Cook, 1991; Sensky, Hughes and Hirsch, 1991b), all including follow-up data (Hiday, 1992), on drug treatment refusal and its long-term effects (e.g. Cichon, 1992), and finally on physician's decision making in usually competent patients with mild to moderate psychiatric disorders leading to the acceptance of the 'second best alternative' by the doctor (e.g. Geiselmann, 1994).

In contrast, empirical research in anorexia nervosa is rare. It is a stricking fact that no comparative study of treatment outcome of compulsorily treated anorexia nervosa patients versus matched voluntary patients exists. Nor has any study been published which has followed up anorexia nervosa patients under compulsion at least for one year after termination of compulsory treatment; only anecdotal reports are available so far, which give minimal information making it impossible to evaluate the case. Why such a reluctance to look at the course and outcome of compulsory treatment in a scientific way, when more than 500 papers a year are published on eating disorders?

We briefly mention some of the scattered case reports and comments (see also the Chapter by Dolan in this volume). Hughes et al. (1985) reported the case of a 22-year-old anorectic who was compulsorily tube fed, but the authors did not mention the patient's weight. In contrast, Mitchell, Parker and Dwyer (1988) described the case of a 19-year-old patient who refused to be weighed (said to be 40 kg) and was not committed to inpatient treatment despite the severity of the illness (three years duration of anorexia nervosa, two previous unsuccessful involuntary admissions and two admissions with premature discharge by the patient). Hébert and Weingarten (1991) described a fatal case aged 22 years with almost eight years of hospitalisation, several compulsory treatments including body restraints, where finally the ethics committee, parents, and doctors decided not to start further aggressive treatment. In discussing this case, Goldner, McKenzie and Kline (1991) considered periods of commitment and active, aggressive intervention necessary to prevent death, while Leichner

(1991) argued that the fatal outcome of the Hébert and Weingarten case might be due to the lack of specialized units. O'Neill, Crowther and Sampson (1994) reported the 'successful caring for terminal illness': a 24-year-old anorectic women (7 years of illness, osteoporotic fractures of lumbar spine, weight not reported, obviously severe hospitalism due to years spent in psychiatric units) was given morphine in a hospice and died within eight days. Russell (1989) presented three case vignettes of compulsory admission, including a follow-up of an improved case. Missliwetz, Ellinger, and Risser (1991) reported autopsy of two Austrian cases aged 16 (body mass index or BMI of 9.7) and 26 years (BMI 10.8; previous compulsory treatment) who died at home. A 16-years-old anorectic orphan (BMI 12.2) had been transferred from a local authority care to a special unit elsewhere against her will (Roberts, 1992, Langslow, 1994). Interestingly, the Council of Europe (1983) stated that before transferral the patient's wishes should be taken 'as far as possible ... into account'. In Israel, an involuntary admission of a 20-year-old anorectic (BMI 15.2) by the district psychiatrist was cancelled after her appeal at the district psychiatric commission (Altmark, Sigal and Gelkopf, 1995). Goldner (1989) and Tiller, Schmidt and Treasure (1993) have argued for compulsory treatment in their reviews. Dresser (1984) holds the best interests standard for compulsion applicable if a good program is available and if the anorectic has never before been exposed to skilled treatment. All available case reports speak for the application of the 'best interests' standard, the life-threatening risk of anorexia nervosa usually being the argument. 'Surrogate decision making' mainly by parental consent is the main method in minors. I am not aware of cases in which 'advance directives' have been used in anorexia nervosa.

A war of words is not useful to clarify the extremely complicated matter of compulsory treatment in anorexia nervosa. For example, the empty phrases 'caring versus neglect' (those who treat compulsorily are caring, those who do not, neglect their patients fate) or duty to care versus ommission are in fact a ban to thinking. Similarly, the alternatives compassion (Tiller et al., 1993) or devotion ('Legal interventions demonstrate the clinician's devotion to the patient', Yager, 1995) versus coercion have put forward. However, this disguises the true alternative compulsion versus coercion. In addition, these emotionally loaden statements might be indicative of countertransference feelings such as therapeutic zeal. For example, one of the early arguments against the right to refuse was that it would exert an antitherapeutic effect on the professional's enthusiasm (Kapp, 1994). But the therapist must question his indispensability and omnipotence; rescue fantasies increase the risk of ill-considered therapeutic activism.

At present, we do not know the frequency of involuntary admission and compulsory treatment in eating-disordered patients due to the almost complete lack of data. It is not known whether tertiary referral centres (i.e. specialized units with a 'negative' patient selection) have higher rates of compulsory treatment than other units. Only few figures are available, pointing in the direction of high variation. Russell (1989) has presented some data from the Maudsley Hospital in London: compulsory treatment longer than four weeks up to six months averaged 11.6 per cent of his case load. However, he indicated a slowly rising trend since the 1983 Mental Health Act. Also in London, at St. George's Hospital, Crisp (1980) has reported a roughly 1.5 per cent compulsory treatment rate (6 out of 400 patients). Lehmkuhl and Schmidt (1986) in Germany have found a 5.9 per cent rate for adolescent and young adult patients; their patient's mean BMI at the time of compulsory admission was 13.0 (range 11.4–14.1), the mean age 18.6 years. However, these case vignettes fail to present follow-up data.

The attitudes of medical professions towards compulsory treatment might be influenced by their attitudes towards certain diagnoses. Fleming and Szmukler (1992) have found, although in a general hospital and not a specialized unit, that eating disorder patients were less liked than patients with schizophrenia and were seen as responsible for their illness almost to the same degree as overdose takers. Attitudes to patients with suicidal acts showed the same sympathy-hostility dimension. In addition, the more 'physical' and less 'psychological' the illness, the more sympathetic the attitude. Anxiety in the case of a 'stubbornly' starving patient can suddenly turn into hostility and anger. It is reasonable to suppose that diffences in attitudes of staff will add to inconsistencies in treatment and contribute to unfavorable outcomes. Although the knowledge of eating disorders in lay people is nowadays much better than that of physicians in the 1970s, even attitudes of trained physicians nowadays can be influenced by the sympathy-hostility change (Vandereycken, 1993).

IATROGENESIS AND COMPULSORY TREATMENT

Surprisingly, the issue of *iatrogenesis* has not received much attention in the eating disorder field (Garner, 1985). Iatrogenesis refers to any adverse condition resulting from the application of a treatment as well as the failure to provide adequate care when it is warranted. Obviously, eventual negative or even fatal effects of treatment on the illness and the afflicted subject are a difficult field. Crisp (1980), for example, has cautioned that overambitious or coercive treatment may precipitate depression and suicide in chronic patients.

What are the differences with the usual treatment, when one treats a patient against her/his will? In the best case we assume none except for compulsory treatment itself, and in any other case undue harshness, control etc. One major principle should not be overlooked: there are subjects one can not treat. The myth of omnipotence in medicine conceals the difficulty to admit failures, not being able to help. So why use compulsory treatment, except for the therapist's compassion to treat? If one would analyse thoroughly a compulsory treated patient's history, some interactions might show that the treatment is unduly harsh, thus stimulating or enhancing the patient's resistance or refusal. In addition, in the usual course of treatment there are many steps patients may experience as coercive; in case of admission, the hospital per se is a coercive environment. So why threatening a patient with a possible compulsory treatment? We should only ask for her willingness to *start* therapy. In this respect, we need the patient's verbalised consent. For the further steps in treatment, we sometimes do not require explicit verbalisation, but just signs of cooperation. This reminds us of the legal concept of behavioral oriented standards of consent ('cooperated appropriately'; Appelbaum and Roth, 1982), again including the threshold problem. Finally, the patient's actions count more than words.

UNPROVEN VALUE OF COMPULSORY TREATMENT

As shown above, we have no research-based data to evaluate the efficacy of compulsory treatment in anorexia nervosa. We have to rely on clinical opinions. Crisp (1980), for example, only occasionally had recommended detention and was certain that the patients would otherwise have died; several of such patients fully recovered and were pleased to be alive. In contrast, one of the cases of Lehmkuhl and Schmidt (1986) died three years after compulsory treatment. Lanceley and Travers (1993) reported a successful trial to section a case, which 'eroded further the poor therapeutic relationship'; the patient continued to struggle with anorexia.

Few data exist on the percentage of patients who refuse voluntary treatment (drop-outs) and their eventual outcome. In Crisp's (1980) series, 30 per cent declined the offer of treatment, and their outcome appeared to be poor. It is known that a high proportion of cases (one third up to 50 per cent; a rate matching the noncompliance rate in medicine and psychiatry) drop out prematurely (Vandereycken and Pierloot, 1983; Szmukler, Eisler, Russell and Dare, 1985). Most drop-out studies implicitly hold the assumption that the doctor's proposal to continue treatment is right. This is challenged by the finding that at short-term follow-up drop-outs showed no major differences; except for a smaller weight gain, compared to patients who had completed the proposed treatment (Vandereycken and Pierloot, 1983). Non-acceptance of doctor's advice may not automatically mean bad prognosis. Moreover, dropping out from a treatment with a therapist not experienced in eating disorders might be a wise choice!

COMMON PITFALLS OF COMPULSORY TREATMENT

TREATMENT REFUSAL AND COMPETENCE

Anorexia nervosa has been subsumed into disorders presenting subtle forms of patient incompetence. Gutheil and Bursztajin (1986) argue that this subtlety is mainly due to the denial of illness. These authors provide also guidelines to present incompetence in an effective manner in court; one of them is to return to court when a different judge is sitting! This is one example how psychiatrists try to treat their patients by hook or crook (Conference Report, 1981); as known, the vast majority of treatment refusals is overriden by the courts. However, the denial argument reminds of a 'catch-22' situation in which a patient's denial of the need for treatment is taken as evidence of that very need. Nevertheless, the dilemma of denial in the assessment of competency is not a fiction: those who deny the presence of illness are the most challenging groups in this regard (Roth et al., 1982). Denial, however, is also a major characteristic of alcoholism (Siegal et al., 1995). Despite these distortions in thinking, compulsory treatment is not advocated in this (mainly male!) patient group.

It has been argued that the gratitude afterwards of patient and parents would speak for compulsory treatment. This reminds of methodological flaws of many patient's satisfaction studies with involuntary admission and compulsory treatment, which were conducted while patients were still under commitment (Hiday, 1992). As one cannot overrule a competent patient's decision on the chance that the person might be grateful later, this argument assumes incompetence of the patient (Kleinmann, 1989).

The common medical practice seems to be that competence is mainly questioned if a patient refuses medical advice (Mebane and Rauch, 1990). On the other hand doubful competence in the case of consent is hardly brought to court. Medical ethicists have commented wryly on this situation (Culver and Gert, 1990, 1982). To demand a more stringent standard for competence in the case of refusal, i.e. a higher 'tariff' or penalty (Buchanan and Brock, 1989) seems to be another catch-22 argument, as it contains several debatable points.

First, it assumes that the doctor is right about what is in the patients best interest. Except for some clear-cut cases where refusal would result in immediate danger of death, the patients' best interests are not at all a medical matter, but a matter of values. In addition, in many illnesses the prognostic ability of medicine is severely hampered and this is also the case in anorexia nervosa. Psychiatrists are very often incorrect in predicting dangerousness (Monahan, 1988). Despite this, prognoses are given in exact percentages; this reminds of a mathematician's saying that uncertainty is blurred by increasing precision behind the comma!

Second, this position implies that treating the patient even against her wishes will still help her. However, as Beumont has put forward in a panel on compulsory treatment of an anorexia nervosa women (Mitchell et al., 1988), treatment of anorexia nervosa necessitates the patient's cooperation: 'If one is going to enforce treatment one must be reasonable confident that the treatment is going to bring about some beneficial effect . . . However, if it were only a case of forcing this women to receive treatment for her anorexia nervosa, that is nonsensical. To admit her to hospital, is not to persuade her to undergo treatment: to undergo treatment she has to cooperate. She has been in hospital on several occasions, but never once she really cooperated. I think that we are unable to treat her, so that we cannot make the claim that we are going to force her into treatment. It is not possible unless we obtain her cooperation'. *Basically, cooperation of the patient is always necessary in medicine, except in the case of the unconscious patient.*

Fortunately, there is no single or well-accepted definition of specific incompetence with respect to medical decisions. Competence is typically questioned only when a patient chooses a treatment course other than that advocated by the doctor. It has been argued that anorexia nervosa is no conscious choice (Tiller et al., 1993)[4] and that the effects of starvation seriously distort an anorectic patient's ability to make treatment decisions (Dresser, 1984). But why is this argument only used in case the patient refuses a certain type of treatment? Scrutiny is rare when a patient assents, even if the patient is not fully competent. However, the refusal of treatment does not necessarily indicate incompetence. The psychodynamic basis of a patient's refusal should be explored prior to determination of incompetence, including also an assessment of the patient's need for autonomy. Some treatment refusal may be secondary to a need to exercise control and *control is the essence of the struggle in anorexia nervosa*. In addition, compulsory treatment may cause substantial injury to the already fragile self-esteem of anorexia nervosa patients. Autonomy should be maximized to avoid the situation in which the patient feels that the only way to maintain some control over her life is by refusal of treatment. If this is true for general medicine patients, why not for anorectic patients?

THE RISK OF SYMMETRIC ESCALATION

Discussing about involuntary admission and compulsory treatment it becomes clear that conflicting values and interests are at stake. The main risk of compulsory treatment is symmetric escalation. In anorexia nervosa, the most common argument is that in life-threatening situations compulsory treatment is justified. However, without the patient's cooperation, forced treatment plans like forced feeding, nasogastric tubes or total parenteral nutrition are usually short-lived and likely to fail. Patients, for instance, can pull out tubes placed against their will. Would one then encase their arms in plasters? What if they can free themselves or move too much in case of total parenteral nutrition, which requires patient cooperation to prevent complications and death? Thus, in my view, no doctor or no hospital in the world can keep somebody alive for a longer period of time, if the patient does not want to be kept alive and afterwards seek alternatives to her previous life. This statement ('nobody except herself') should be delivered explicitly to the anorexia nervosa patient, because it points to the core issue, the struggle for control.

Eating disorders should not be muddled up with suicide, although suicide is one of the main causes of death in (chronic) anorexia nervosa. Legally, suicidal patients have to be admitted into hospitals in most countries. However, the day-to-day interactions show the same danger of symmetric escalation: suicidal ideas, attempts, contention, discharge, midnight phone calls, admission and so on. Basically, the most important therapist's message to these patients is: 'It's not me or the ward who will keep you alive, it will be you or nobody. You will give us the opportunity to work with you and to check possible less dangerous alternatives to your current situation. However, this is only possible if you stay alive'. This position reflects the walking on the edge: although there might be no legal right to commit suicide, there is a factual opportunity to do so. The above statement of the therapist tries to overcome this dilemma. In my view, the same is true for eating disorders: besides the denial at the surface, their massive ambivalence towards their illness and their deep fear of change, *it is the patient who decides to give others some opportunity to help her.* One might say, she treats herself partly through another person (the therapist), partly through the so-called healthy parts of her self.

Compulsory treatment can be conceptualized as *a trap laid out by the patient*: somebody else takes the decision and the patient can rebel, or see how it works and rebel later, but does not feel responsible. The problem of who controls whom is a major source of concern. *Anorectics are both terrified and desirous of being controlled.*[5] Being controlled is equated with being cared for, but on an infantile level; in a way their sadistic-masochistic relationship to their body might expand to their social relations. Their *tremendous difficulties in decision making* (Bruch, 1973, 1979) are strongly related to the issue of control. A typical example are their endless ruminations about the decision to eat or not to eat (that bit). At many times, due to feared future consequences, no decision at all is made, which results in the fact that *time or context will decide instead of the subject.*

These difficulties in decision making are *seductive* to parents and doctors. They may feel invited to take the decision for the daughter/patient. The latter may oppose, not verbally but by starving which, in inversing the previous role relationship, results in feelings of helplessness in the carer. Thus, anorexia nervosa subjects often act '*as if*'. This almost permanent struggle about control, specifically concerning her body and life, is a strong invitation to symmetric escalation. However, power struggles around eating and self-control are masking the real tasks, all the issues of adult relationships. Thus, one should resist any trial by the patient to frighten and coerce the clinician with the threat of becoming sicker. There might be two groups of anorexia nervosa patients: some take treatment efforts not too literally and eventually eat their way out of the hospital; others take the struggle too literally and 'enact' confinement. Systemic family therapy has told us to move in the complementary position, i.e. to be weak, in order to avoid the endless symmetric escalation.

ALTERNATIVES TO COMPULSORY TREATMENT

There are few possible alternatives to compulsory treatment left in the 'armamentum' of the therapist. The crucial issue is successful engagement of the patient and the family, gaining co-operation and not forcing treatment.

ENGAGING THE PATIENT AND THE FAMILY

Engagement means that the patient achieves ownership of her recovery program. From the first assessment onward, any treatment should involve the patients and her most important relatives; this is true both for minors and adults (Vanderlinden and Vandereycken, 1989). So one should start with engaging patient and family to prevent further situations which might create the idea of compulsion. Even the compulsory patient should be helped to become a voluntary patient at the very earliest opportunity if some greater impact on the course of events is sought (Crisp, 1980).

Crisp (1980) states that his approach – the 'kindling process' for the anorectic – is rooted in the notion that the anorectic or some part of her must wish for change and escape from the illness for this to be a therapeutic possibility. The therapist needs to be a mentor, a guide who is observant and perceptive, and who helps the patient develop aptitudes to self-initiated behavior so that she can become an active participant in the treatment process (Bruch, 1986). Despite the patient's negative attitude, good therapeutic communication can be established. However, the attitude towards treatment remains tenuous, and the tendency to interrupt exists. The most important preconditions for the therapist are a strong empathic interest for the patient and the family and that she/he knows what she/he does. The therapists needs to be someone who can help without being overindulging, who can be sensitive without being seductive, and be considerate without being fearful. These patients require thoughtfulness with encouragement, responsiveness with realism, and calmness with strength.

To achieve the patient's engagement in treatment is only possible via a positive therapeutic relationship. The assessment plays a crucial role in engaging the patient. For several years we have used a thorough telephone interview and letters of all family members before the first personal contact. The telephone interview has been inspired by the Milan Family Therapy School (DiBlasio, Fischer and Prata, 1986). Usually, the first phone contact is made by a parent. This call with the head of the unit lasts about 30 minutes and includes a short assessment to rate the severity of the case; in addition, the referral context and the expectations of patient and family are clarified to prepare for the first family interview. As inspired by Bruch (1973) we ask each family member to write us a letter explaining one's viewpoint on the current situation. These letters not only reveal worthwhile insights into family dynamics, but are also very useful to engage the whole family in the future steps of treatment.

The aim of anorectics to be in control of their lives and feelings is appropriate, but their means to reach this goal are self-limiting and sometimes dangerous. *Anorexia nervosa subjects try to freeze time and social relationships; in this regard, they must fail as neither of the two are controllable.* The issue of control leads to the *control paradox of anorexia nervosa*: under a certain weight the anorexia gets out of control, which is perhaps the most scaring experience for them. What once began as a solution evolves, over the course of the illness, to a problem in itself. It is absolutely essential to ask them at the assessment whether they still feel in control of their weight; most of the cases in a downward spiral of weight loss will then confess their loss of control. The deep fears associated with it will only be disclosed later on in treatment. Thus, in a strict sense, treatment of anorexia nervosa in the first place is aimed at *reestablishing the anorectic control*, which includes that they increase their weight to a safer 'control' level at first. In chronic cases, this may be the ultimate goal of treatment to avoid (possibly lethal) complications of the disorder.

The core problems of anorexia nervosa, according to Bruch (1973), are their profound sense of ineffectiveness, their lacking self-awareness, and their lack of feeling in control of themselves, not even owning their body and its functions. When the patient feels control over her fate, rather than being at the mercy of physicians, cooperation in treatment will increase. A complete transparency of the treatment program from the very onset increases the patient's sense of control. The element of personal choice is essential to effective treatment as the patients need help with their impaired sense of autonomy. The only non-negotiable element of treatment is the necessary 'healthier weight' (Russell, 1977), its level depending on the *aims set by the patient* (see below). The abnormal nutrition must be improved, but without depriving the patient of her sense of autonomy (Bruch, 1983). Thus, the therapist's conclusion is: we can offer you help, but under certain preconditions. Because of the psychophysiological consequences of starvation, weight gain is the only precondition but the most feared one on the patient's part.

A family-oriented treatment (family therapy or family counselling) has the capacity to engage patient and family. The age of the patient is no barrier to involving parents (Vanderlinden and Vandereycken, 1989; Crisp and McClelland, 1996). Family treatment of eating disorders has moved beyond the old-fashioned concepts of early family therapy, which unfortunately included the assumption of family pathology on the one hand and of implicit scapegoating on the other (Vandereycken, Kog and Vanderlinden, 1989). Research has shown that family therapy is the treatment of choice in adolescent anorectics with a duration of illness of less than three years (Russell, Szmukler, Dare and Eisler, 1987).

Recent research has expanded the application of family therapy to adult anorexia nervosa cases. Crisp et al. (1991) have found no difference in one year follow-up in three different treatment modalities (inpatient, outpatient individual and family therapy, and outpatient group therapy). In conclusion: 'There is evidence that the best method of treatment is to work with the family ... The success of family therapy doesn't mean that the family is pathogenic' (Russell and Treasure, 1989).

As one has to reach the patient where she can be reached, the therapist utilizes some of the many informal (coercive) social pressures in an attempt to persuade the patient to start the treatment, while carefully clarifying and confronting possible pathogenic manoeuvres of the family such as cheating, manipulating etc. An ongoing firm and joint decisional process of parents with respect to treatment options and growing-up might reduce the duration of the illness not only in adolescents, but also in adults.

TAKE YOUR TIME

A failure to obtain consent to treatment does not necessarily mean that treatment has to be compulsory. It is usually better to delay it until attitudes and relationships have changed, which could be just as easily be the professional's attitude as the patient's. If patients and families are not yet prepared to accept the treatment offered, the time for intervention might not be there and the illness may need more time to breed true (Russell, 1977). To postpone the decision means to put the timing in the patient's hands. Resistance to treatment at a given time does not necessarily mean resistance to change; it could be resistance to imposed change (Vandereycken and Meermann, 1984). Kalucy, Crisp, and Harding (1977) noted that the more the patient complains, resists and attempts to renegotiate her position, the better the ultimate progress.

To take *a break in treatment* can be a useful systemic intervention in the course of treatment when an impasse occurs: 'We are unable to treat you (now)'. By this statement the therapist moves in a complementary position, showing her/his weakness. A break necessarily implies that a new appointment will be arranged in some months.

Just like in any other illness there are certain steps before a patient arrives at the doctor's office. The first step is the *self-diagnosis* of a problem. This step is usually delayed in anorexia nervosa as their success in weight loss gives them a personal sense of worth. This leads to denial of illness, which might be overstated as a central characteristic of anorexia nervosa. The denial charac-terizes mainly the first phase of the illness; after several months or one to two years of the illness (maybe accompanied by the development of out-of-control behavior such as bingeing and vomiting) the disadvantages outweigh the benefits and the patients are able to accept their problem and to look for help. Only in a very few cases this denial may last till the very end. The second step is *self-treatment*, usually including all informal help systems (family, friends, relatives, teachers, priests, self-help groups, bib-liotherapy etc.). This might include presenting to a doctor with some symptom and not disclosing the basic problem. If there is a diagnostic delay by the doctor they can treach themselves by having done something (worthless), or they can reassure them-selves that nobody will understand their problem. If this fails (although there is still the possibility of spontaneous remission) help is sought in the health care system.

In addition to patient's characteristics, family factors and infor-mal coercive actions may determine the help-seeking process in anorexia nervosa. Usually there is a wide variation of the interval between onset and first presentation, ranging from about nine months till several years; determinants of the help-seeking process in anorexia nervosa have not been investigated yet. In addition, the proportion of untreated cases in the community is still unknown.

For a specialized unit, weight restoration would not pose major problems as the hospital is a safe and coercive environment per se (for roughly two thirds of patients who are compliers). After discharge, however, the maintenance of status and prevention of relapse pose a major problem. With growing experience the necessity of a first inpatient phase in treatment of anorexia nervosa is put in question, indicating no difference of outpatient to inpatient treatment for anorexia nervosa, at least at one year follow-up (Crisp et al., 1991; Treasure et al., 1995). It is our principle since many years to start with outpatient treatment in almost every case.

TREATMENT OF MINORS

Although minors are legally incompetent, differences in treatment of anorexia nervosa with adult cases may be overrated. It is a myth that a 16-year-old anorectic would be easier to treat than a 23-year-old patient (this is the age range of the case reports on compulsory treatment). The only difference is that involvement of the family is mandatory in each adolescent case, as there remains some real or legal dependence on parents. It may be that adolescents are more inclined to defer to perceived parental wishes. However, individuals differ widely in their conformity to social expectations and requests by authority. In addition, anorexia nervosa lends itself to a preferred reaction to wishes of others in all but one topic, eating. In minor patients, it seems that psychotherapy intuitively uses the existing law that the parents can override a minor's decision. However, the therapist still has to work with the anorectic minor, and without her there will be no treatment result just like in adults. In adolescents, it is as difficult to gain trust as in adults. It seems that in adolescents there is more reluctance to act with compulsory treatment; it might be that in youngsters the therapist does not feel urged to act as a parent, because the real parents are in charge of their care. I am not aware of any published case were a parental refusal of treatment of their anorectic minor (if she refuses, too) was overruled by the court (see also Chapter by Dolan in this volume).

In most countries minors under the age of 18 years have no absolute right to give or refuse consent to treatment. Parental consent is required unless in emergency situations, which force the doctor to act on the principle of necessity. Thus, minor's decisions can be overruled by the parents or the court. However, there is no magic age when children suddenly become competent to give consent. The age of majority moved downwards in many countries to 18 years, underpinned by societal influences and changes. There are some legal exemptions where minors are considered with equal rights as adults (e.g., military service, parenthood, living alone, or self employment) and the '*mature minor rule*' has been applied in the USA to minors above 15 years of age (consent to medical treatment without parental permission; Leikin, 1983; Wertz, Fanos and Reilly, 1994). Many countries have divorce laws indicating that children up from age 10 have to be asked about their placement and children aged 14 years can decide about their placement.

A review of the limited empirical data suggests that adolescents, especially those aged 14 and above with some individual variability, may have as well developed decisional skills as adults for making informed health care decision: the capacity to think abstractly, to consider multiple factors, to hypothesize, and to predict future consequences, all necessary ingredients for the consent process (Weithorn and Campbell, 1982). It has been shown that in decision making 14-year-olds scored as high as 18- and 21-year-old on choice of reasonable outcome, sound reasons, and understanding of implications of their decision (Wertz et al., 1994). In a survey (Alderson, 1993), children themselves set the highest threshold age for consent to surgery at 14 years, like parents do on average (13.9 yrs), but in contrast to health care professionals who choose a much lower age (10.3 yrs).

A new term, *assent*, has been introduced to distinguish a minor's agreement to a proposed procedure from the legal concept of binding consent. Assent has been defined as affirmative agreement and not merely as an absence of dissent; it has been recommended from the age of seven years on (Wertz et al., 1994; Abramovitch et al., 1991). In expanding the statement of the Committee of Bioethics (1995) in pediatrics, many pediatricians propose that 'children and adolescents should *always* be included in health care decisions to the extent of their capacity and willingness to do so, i.e. they should *never* be excluded' (Bartholome, 1995). Even in the most extreme cases (the rare life-or-death decisions) it has been argued for greater involvement of children in decision making related to the extremely difficult matter of the use of life-sustaining treatment (Evans, 1995). Obviously, also children and adolescents have the need to be in control of what happens to them. Clearly, a delicate balance has to be struck between that need of control and the need to do what is deemed to be in their best interest; in children and adolescents there might be even *a greater risk to exploit the 'best interests' argument to overrule the patient's wishes* than in adults. If assent is to be honored, then dissent should be binding. If not, a promise has been broken, showing disrespect for the minor, which leads to mistrust of the physician or parents or both. The binding nature of dissent avoids many situations, in which the only way a child can get the attention of grown-ups is to, at least temporarily, say 'NO'.

Similarly to adults, in minors too the position of refusal is challenging. Two different notions have been proposed: Devereux, Jones and Dickenson (1993) would see no difference between giving and withholding consent, because the right to consent is worthless if it is not accompanied by the right to refuse consent; McCall-Smith (1992) argued that refusal to give consent is a higher-order of decision making than merely giving consent; this would be justified by the potentially dangerous and highly responsible decision to withhold consent and would necessitate a more stringent test of competence than in assessment of consent competence.

AIMS OF TREATMENT

The aims of treatment have a major impact on the treatment itself. Several tricky questions have to be answered such as who decides on treatment goals and when? The process of reviewing and eventually changing goals is a mutual process between caregiver, patient, and family. This would mean to re-evaluate a therapist's concepts of cure. Supposedly there are different aims for a 17-year-old anorectic with 4 years duration of illness, for a 30-year-old women with a history of 13 years of anorexia, and for a 42-year-old women with 20 years of anorexia nervosa. In every case the anorectic has also *the right to be helped to survive with her illness* (Crisp, 1980). Chronic cases may confront therapists with their unrealistic concepts of 'cure'; they force us to look toward supporting these individuals in their decision to remain anorectic, helping them to stabilize their anorexia nervosa and lead the fullest possible life with it (Vandereycken and Meermann, 1984). However, hesitation to prematurely accept the limited goal of becoming a 'controlled anorectic' in cases with less than ten years duration of illness is warranted. Chronic cases limp along in an anguished state of chronic ill health with a narrow social life, pushing themselves to top performance in their professional or vocational lives, or alternatively failing in their professional expectations, without ever having the satisfaction of true fulfillment.

It is not appropriate for all cases to aim for a full recovery. A better approach may be to treat the patient on an outpatient basis whenever her weight becomes dangerously low and allow her to gain some weight but not to achieve full recovery; if out-patient treatment fails, admission should be proposed. The task is to set realistic aims for chronic cases; about 45 kg could be a stable anorectic weight for an average-sized women (165 cm). However, maintenance in a chronic sufferer still is treatment. Even in chronic cases the *creation of hope* is indispensable and might be favorable compared to the idea of 'terminal care' for anorexia nervosa (Ramsay and Treasure, 1996). One must always offer the patient a chance to change. A positive self-fulfilling prophecy of the therapist and the treatment team is useful: things can change (at least one or more issues, hardly ever all or everything) irrespective of what has happened before. To consider the past, the present, and then 'feed-forward' to the future (a useful technique in family therapy) might be adopted.

TERMINATION OF THE TREATMENT BY THE THERAPIST

The ultimate possibility (but only after years of treatment) may be the refusal, on the part of the therapist, to provide further treatment (Bruch, 1983). This is no simple 'take it or leave it' choice. The therapeutic ultimatum should only happen in a situation which Story (1983) has called the 'malignant autonomy of symptoms'. It is especially critical not to pretend that such a decision is other than an ultimatum. 'If the therapist can safely trust his or her countertransference feelings about a patient and pay special vigilance to unconscious issues of rescuing, wishes to intimidate and bully, or to shame the patient and extricate himself from a treatment impasse by abondoning the patient, thus freeing himself of feelings of guilt and failure, there is then time to say, "It's me or starving yourself" or "It's me or vomiting" or whatever. Such an ultimatum is a strenuous but at times unavoidable effort to get behind the smoke screen of the stereotyped anorexic symptoms and to thereby get chance to explore with the patient the latent and excluded material that has been outside of aware- ness and never before faced' (Bruch, 1983, pp. 309–10). Such a statement must derive from the therapist in her/his containing, holding, and securing function for the patient (Story, 1983). It is not a cure, but a means to restore basic interactional conditions between patient and therapist. *The message is that both the patient and the therapist have the free decision to say yes or no; the patient has even the right to just say no.* Basis of this ultimate ressort is the therapeutic relationship. I myself have refused treatment only in two exceptional cases, after prolonged course of treatment (3–4 years) and multiple unsuccessful admissions: one of them is now a student with an amazingly stable 'ideal' anorectic weight; the other patient, once again in downward spiral of weight loss, has decided half a year after termination to go to another specialized inpatient unit. The therapist has to tolerate discontinuing the work with the patient, although she/he would also regret it. Therapist's reflections include: it is not me who must cure this patient; if I have failed after prolonged and considerable efforts, another treatment or no treatment at all might be a better alternative.

To take a break in treatment or to terminate treatment has also been suggested by Crisp and McClelland (1996) in their minimum treatment package for primary and secondary care (general practitioners or non-specialized units): the failure to achieve a steady weight gain leads to discharge from the treatment. Behind this option for non-specialized therapists probably lies the hope that somebody else in health care might provide a 'net' for that patient.

FURTHER RECOMMENDATIONS

Finally, I want to give some recommendations which may help clinicians to avoid treatment traps or impasses.

Do not predict fatal consequences at a certain weight. Some of my patients confessed proudly that they are now five kilograms below the weight predicted earlier as the fatal point of no return. It is not clear whether anorectics do not really believe that they may die from the condition or its complications. They might 'delusionally' believe that they can starve their body to death and yet have the mind or spirit survive (Zerbe, 1993). This might be an example of the 'anorectic game' of reality testing and therapist's testing. The latter would coincide with some adolescent's cognitive 'flirt with death'.

Request a second opinion from a senior and experienced therapist when an impasse occurs.

The *stepped-care approach* to treatment of eating disorders seems to be in line with the legally least restrictive alternative doctrine.[6] Obviously outpatient treatment would be a less restrictive setting than inpatient treatment. This would call for the development of appropriate outpatient facilities and more specialized eating disorders units, even in a time of budgetary restrictions of health care.

A last requirement should be the *transferral to a specialized eating disorders unit before any action towards compulsory treatment is started.* The European Convention of Human Rights in its section on psychiatric patients states that the decision to commit a patient should be taken by a 'competent national authority' (Council of Europe, 1994).

CONCLUSIONS

The issue of compulsory treatment in eating disorders has been the topic of a public debate at the Inaugural Meeting of the European Council on Eating Disorder (ECED) in 1989 in London with Gerald Russell and Bob Palmer as speakers, and again at the Fourth General Meeting of the ECED in Dublin in 1995 with Sarah McCluskey and myself as debaters. At the end of these debates, the audience was asked to make a 'vote'; each time the majority of experts (roughly two thirds) voted in favor of compulsory treatment. Although most experts seem to have no doubts, this chapter has shown that the current body of research on compulsory treatment in anorexia nervosa is very much in a state of conjectures and refutations. Much empirical research remains to be done in evaluating the impact of involuntary admission and compulsory treatment on anorectic patients.

To develop my argumentation that compulsory treatment is unnecessary in anorexia nervosa, and to provide a basis for alternatives to compulsory treatment, I have discussed the legal and ethical domain and the changing practice of medical and psychological help provided for sufferers. Specifically, the dynamics of the patient-doctor relationship, the heritage of the paternalistic medical model creating the problem of noncompliance, and the current status of research into treatment consent and refusal had to be tackled to disentangle compulsion from coercion (and its many modes, ranging from persuasion, protection, instilling hope to confrontation). Saving life is one issue, ignoring patient's wishes and decision making is another one; the latter approach would not obtain the cooperation of patients necessary for treatment in anorexia nervosa. Derived from Weber's definition of power, the differences between compulsion and coercion have to be refined as only gradual ones. As the usual treatment in anorexia nervosa involves many coercive elements, in my view this is enough: *compulsory treatment in anorexia nervosa would be one coercion too much.* To conclude, the judicial system does not provide the ideal forum to make medical decisions. An US Supreme Court judgement stated: 'Our legal system cannot replace the more intimate struggle that must be borne by the patient, those caring for the patient, and those who care about the patient' (Kutner et al., 1991).

When finishing this paper, a tentative 'one sentence answer' came into my mind: *the only alternative to compulsory treatment is treatment, nothing else*; treatment according to the wishes of patients and relatives and to the present state-of-the-art, to our best knowledge and intentions. This is hard enough, when confronted with a stunningly starving patient and her family. However, it is the only way not to get stuck in a symmetric escalation of control, to achieve the cooperation of the sufferer and her loved ones, and to help them to wake up their sleeping sense of self and their uniqueness.

ACKNOWLEDGEMENTS

I would like to thank Dr Chris Evans (St George's Hospital, London) for helpful criticism on earlier drafts of this chapter.

FOOTNOTES

1. The principles of ethical analysis form a triangle: *patient autonomy* (following a competent patient's wishes), medical *beneficence* (helping the patient) and *justice*; within this context justice means fairness to the individual and protection of the rights of others, globally the society (Grundstein-Amado, 1991; Culver and Gert, 1982; Buchanan and Brock, 1989). Beneficence lies at the heart of the best interests standard: restoring the patient's health to the greatest possible standard. The best interests standard is an almost universal argument, as beneficence is often used to override a patient's refusal. 'Experience should teach us to be most on guard to protect liberty when ... purposes are beneficent ... The greatest dangers to liberty lurk in insiduous encroachment by men of zeal,

well-meaning but without understanding' (Justice Brandeis, quoted in Cichon, 1992, p. 344).

2. In general medicine, following the development of intensive care and its limitations, there seems to exist a slight trend to counteract the medicalization and denial of death in Western societies (e.g. McCue, 1995) by putting forward that not all what is possible should be done and that dying should be as humane as possible (e.g. Pijnenborg et al., 1995; Quill and Brody, 1995; Jecker and Schneiderman, 1995). However, I would strongly oppose drawing a line from futility to triage based on limited resources and competing health care demands (Gatter and Moscop, 1995). Although ethical discussions in medicine are rather new and date back to the Nuremberg trial, one should remind that corrosion begins in microscopic proportions and no society is immune against inhumanism (Alexander, 1949).

3. Legemaate (1995) excellently reviewed the diversity of the European national regulations with respect to the scope of legal regulation, the general approach (medical or legal), the criterion (serious danger to oneself or others versus patient's health interests, the latter in the UK, Denmark, France), the emergency and the ordinary procedure (decision-making procedure, who certificates, duration, regular review process, conditional discharge/probationary release, lodge an appeal), and the patient's internal legal postition ('patient's rights'). It is important to differentiate between legislation for involuntary admission to psychiatric hospitals and patient's rights. As for Austria, patient's rights are dispersed in several peripheral legislative acts and form a sketchy patchwork at best (Pichler, 1995); the future direction might be procedural safeguards rather than substantive rights.

4. In contrast, Bruch (1979) has emphasized that the anorectic is not a passive victim in the whole development, in particularily the development of the illness. This active participation and perpetuation of the illness seems to me at least one element in the process of anorexia nervosa, except in the out-of-control stage of the illness (see below). In addition, the needs of an anorectic should be viewed too from *her* point of view: she wants to stay thin but would not like to stand the trade offs of that position. Thereby she tries to create a *'quadratic circle'*, but in vain. Immanently her position would not look so strange because it is logic. Underneath her pursuit of thinness she would like to get something else which is not so different from other human beings, love; but she fears she might not get it.

5. Recently we had to decide about the date for discharge of a patient

after her second admission. We asked her to make a proposal, implying that we would follow her proposal. It took her much time to decide, but finally she managed to do so, and was sure that we would override her proposal. As we said, 'Okay, that's the date of discharge', she shouted immediately: 'That's unfair; I'm a minor!'

6. The essence of this doctrine is that the government may not pursue its ends, however compelling, by means which unnecessarily encroach upon fundamental rights (Cichon, 1992). Thus, it has to be shown that no less restrictive (or drastic) means such as involuntary admission or compulsory treatment are available to achieve the same purpose; this would mean that *less severe measures have been tried and found unworkable*. The principle of the least restrictive alternative is equally applicable to alternate treatment dispositions *within* the hospital. This doctrine has been supported by the United Nations General Assembly which has adopted principles for policy in mental health: 'Every patient shall have the right to be treated in the least restrictive environment and with the least restrictive or intrusive treatment appropriate to the patient's health needs and the need to protect the safety of others' (United Nations, 1992). I do not agree with the interpretation by Buchanan and Brock (1989, p. 350), that the least restrictive alternative doctrine is superfluous and that its only useful role seems to be a reminder that the mere convenience of others, such as family or treatment staff, does not justify employing restrive or intrusive treatment alternatives. The latter is unethical (without the least restrictive alternative doctrine), as therein a treatment device is used as punishment.

REFERENCES

Abramovitch, R., Freedmann, J.L., Thoden, K. and Nikolich, C. (1991) 'Children's capacity to consent to participation in psychological research: Empirical findings.' *Child Development*, 62: 1100–9.

Alderson, P. (1993) *Children's consent to surgery*. Buckingham: Open University Press.

Alexander, L. (1949) 'Medical science under dictatorship.' *New England Journal of Medicine*, 241: 39–47.

Altmark, D., Sigal, M. and Gelkopf, M. (1995) 'Partial insanity: when the judiciary and the psychiatric world collide.' *Israel Journal of Psychiatry and Related Sciences*, 32: 109–13.

Appelbaum, P.S. and Roth, L.H. (1982) 'Competency to consent to research: A psychiatric overview.' *Archives of General Psychiatry*, 39: 951–8.

Bagby, R.M., Thompson, J.S., Dickens, S.E. and Nohara, M. (1991) 'Decision making in psychiatric civil commitment: An experimental analysis.' *American Journal of Psychiatry*, 148: 28–33.

Bartholome, W.G. (1995) 'Informed consent, parental permission, and assent in pediatric practice' (letter). *Pediatrics*, 96: 981–2.

Bebbington, P.E. (1995) 'The content and context of compliance.' *International Clinical Psychopharmacology*, 9, Suppl 5: 41–50.

Bruch, H. (1973) *Eating disorders. Obesity, anorexia nervosa, and the person within*, New York: Basic Books.

——(1979) 'Island on the river: The anorexic adolescent in treatment.' *Adolescent Psychiatry, 7: 26–40.*

——*(1983) 'Treatment in anorexia nervosa.'* International Journal of Psychoanalytic Psychotherapy, 9: 303–12.

——(1986) 'Anorexia nervosa: The therapeutic task.' In Brownell, K.D. and Foreyt, J.P. (eds) *Handbook of eating disorders* (pp. 328–32), New York: Basic Books.

Buchanan, A.E. and Brock, D.W. (1989) *Deciding for others: The ethics of surrogate decision making*, Cambridge: Cambridge University Press.

Cichon, D.E. (1992) 'The right to "just say no": A history and analysis of the right to refuse antipsychotic drugs.' *Luisiana Law Review*, 53: 283–426.

Committee on Bioethics (1995) 'Informed consent, parental permission, and assent in pediatric practice.' *Pediatrics*, 95: 314–17.

Conference Report (1981) 'Refusing treatment in mental health institutions: values in conflict.' *Hospital and Community Psychiatry*, 32: 255–8.

Council of Europe, Committee of Ministers (1983) *Recommendation R (83) 2, 'concerning the legal protection of persons suffering from mental disorder placed as involuntary patients'.*

Council of Europe, Parliamentary Assembly (1994) *Recommendation 1235 'on psychiatry and human rights'.*

Cournos, F., McKinnon, K. and Stanley, B. (1991) 'Outcome of involuntary medication in a state hospital system.' *American Journal of Psychiatry*, 148: 489–94.

Crisp, A.H. (1980) *Anorexia nervosa: Let me be*, New York-London: Academic Press.

Crisp, A.H., Norton, K., Gowers, S., Halek, C., Bowyer, C., Yeldham, D., Levett, G. and Bhat, A. (1991) 'A controlled study of the effect of therapies aimed at adolescent and family psychopathology in anorexia nervosa.' *British Journal of Psychiatry*, 159: 325–33.

Crisp, A.H. and McClelland, L. (1996) *Anorexia nervosa. Guidelines for assessment and treatment in primary and secondary care*, East Sussex: Psychology Press.

Culver, C.M. and Gert, B. (1982) *Philosophy in medicine.* New York: Oxford University Press.

——(1990) 'The inadequacy of incompetence.' *Milbank Quarterly*, 68: 619–43.

Davies, S., Thornicroft, G., Leese, M., Higgingbothan, A. and Phelan, M. (1996) 'Ethnic differences in risk of compulsory psychiatric admission among representative cases of psychosis in London.' *British Medical Journal*, 312: 533–7.

Devereux, J.A., Jones, D.P.H. and Dickenson, D.L. (1993) 'Can children withhold consent to treatment.' *British Medical Journal*, 306: 1459–61.

DiBlasio, P., Fischer, J.M. and Prata, G. (1986) 'The telephone chart: A cornerstone of the first interview with the family.' *Journal of Strategic and Systemic Therapy*, 5: 31–44.

Donovan, J.L. (1995) 'Patient decision making: The missing ingredient in compliance research.' *International Journal of Technology Assessment and Health Care*, 11: 443–55.

Dresser, R.J.D. (1984) 'Legal and policy considerations in treatment of anorexia nervosa patients.' *International Journal of Eating Disorder*, 3: 43–51.

Evans, J.L. (1995) Are children competent to make decisions about their own deaths? *Behavioral Science and Law*, 13: 27–41.

Fleming, J. and Szmukler, G.I. (1992) 'Attitudes of medical professionals towards patients with eating disorders.' *Australian and New Zealand Journal of Psychiatry*, 26: 436–43.

Garner, D.M. (1985) 'Iatrogenesis in anorexia nervosa and bulimia nervosa.' *International Journal of Eating Disorder*, 4: 701–26.

Gatter, R.A. and Moskop, J.C. (1995) 'From futility to triage.' *Journal of Medicine and Philosophy*, 20: 191–205.

Geiselmann, B. (1994) 'Informed refusal: The patient's influence on long-term treatment.' *Pharmacopsychiatry*, 27: Suppl: 58–62.

Gigliotti, G.A. and Rubin, J. (1991) 'The right to refuse treatment: An application of the economic principles of decision-making under uncertainty.' *International Journal of Law and Psychiatry*, 14: 405–16.

Goldner, E. (1989) 'Treatment refusal in anorexia nervosa.' *International Journal of Eating Disorder*, 8: 297–306.

Goldner, E., McKenzie, J.M. and Kline, S.A. (1991) 'The ethics of forced feeding in anorexia nervosa' (letter). *Canadian Medical Association Journal*, 144: 1205–6.

Greco, P.J., Schulmann, K.A., Lavizzo-Mourey, R. and Hansen-Flaschen,

J. (1991) 'The patient self-determination act and the future of advance directives.' *Annals of Internal Medicine*, 115: 639–43.

Grundstein-Amado, R. (1991) 'An integrative model of clinical-ethical decision making.' *Theoretical Medicine*, 12: 157–70.

Gunn, A.E. (1991) 'Risk-benefit ratio: The soft underbelly of patient autonomy.' *Issues in Law and Medicine*, 7: 139–53.

Gutheil, T.G. and Bursztajn, H. (1986) 'Clinician's guidelines for assessing and presenting subtle forms of patient incompetence in legal settings.' *American Journal of Psychiatry*, 143: 1020–3.

Hébert, P.C. and Weingarten, M.A. (1991) 'The ethics of forced feeding in anorexia nervosa.' *Canadian Medical Association Journal*, 144: 141–4.

Hermann, D.H.J. (1990) 'Autonomy, self determination, the right of involuntarily committed persons to refuse treatment, and the use of substituted judgement in medication decisions involving incompetent persons.' *International Journal of Law and Psychiatry*, 13: 361–85.

Hiday, V.A. (1992) 'Coercion in civil committment: Process, preferences and outcome.' *International Journal of Law and Psychiatry*, 15: 359–377.

Hughes, J.R., Eckert, E.D. and McManus, K.M. (1985) 'Tube feeding as a psychiatric procedure.' *American Journal of Psychiatry*, 142: 1127–8.

Jecker, N.S. and Schneiderman, L.J. (1995) 'When families request that "everything possible" be done.' *Journal of Medicine and Philosophy*, 20: 145–63.

Jones, M.A. (1995) 'Ethical and legal responses to patients who refuse consent to treatment.' *British Journal of Urology*, 76, Suppl. 2: 9–14.

Kalucy, R.S., Crisp, A.H. and Harding, B. (1977) 'Prevalence and prognosis in anorexia nervosa.' *Australian and New Zealand Journal of Psychiatry*, 11: 251–7.

Kapp, M.B. (1994) 'Treatment and refusal rights in mental health: Therapeutic justice and clinical accomodation.' *American Journal of Orthopsychiatry*, 64: 223–34.

Kirby, M.D. (1983) 'Informed consent: What does it mean?' *Journal of Medical Ethics*, 9: 69–75.

Kleinman, I. (1989) 'The right to refuse treatment: Ethical considerations for the competent patient.' *Canadian Medical Association Journal*, 144: 1219–22.

Kluge, E.H. (1989) 'The ethics of forced feeding in anorexia nervosa: A response to Hébert and Weingarten. *Canadian Medical Association Journal*, 144: 1121–4.

Kopelman, L.M. (1990) 'On the evaluative nature of competency and capacity judgements.' *International Journal of Law and Psychiatry*, 13: 308–29.

Kutner, J.S., Ruark, J.E. and Raffin, T.A. (1991) 'Defining patient competence for medical decision.' *Chest*, 100: 1404–9.

Lanceley, C. and Travers, R. (1993) 'Anorexia nervosa: Forced feeding and the law' (letter). *British Journal of Psychiatry*, 163: 835.

Langslow, A. (1994) 'Who controls the fate of a teenager with anorexia nervosa?' *Australian Nursing Journal*, 8: 36–8.

Legemaate, J. (1995) 'Involuntary admission to a psychiatric hospital: Recent European developments.' *European Journal of Health Law*, 2: 15–32.

Lehmkuhl, G. and Schmidt, M.H. (1986) 'Wie freiwillig kann die Behandlung von jugendlichen Patienten mit Anorexia nervosa sein?' (How voluntary can the treatment of young anorexia nervosa patients be?) *Psychiatrische Praxis*, 13: 236–41.

Leichner, P. (1991) 'The ethics of forced feeding in anorexia nervosa' (letter). *Canadian Medical Association Journal*, 144: 1206.

Leikin, S.L. (1983) 'Minor's assent or dissent to medical treatment.' *Journal of Pediatrics*, 102: 169–76.

Levinsky, N.G. (1996) 'Social, institutional, and economic barriers to the exercise of patient's rights.' *New England Journal of Medicine*, 334: 532–4.

Lidz, C.W., Appelbaum, P.S. and Meisel, A. (1988) 'Two models of implementing informed consent.' *Archives of Internal Medicine*, 148: 85–1389.

McCall-Smith, A. (1992) 'Consent to treatment in childhood.' *Archives of Disease in Childhood*, 67: 1247–8.

McCue, J.D. (1995) 'The naturalness of dying.' *Journal of the American Medical Association*, 273: 1039–43.

Mebane, H.M. and Rauch, H.B. (1990) 'When do physicians request competency evaluations?' *Psychomatics*, 31: 40–6.

Missliwetz, J., Ellinger, A. and Risser, D. (1991) 'Plötzlicher Tod infolge Anorexia nervosa' (Sudden death due to anorexia nervosa). *Beiträge zur Gerichtlichen Medizin*, 49: 343–52.

Mitchell, P.B., Parker, G.B. and Dwyer, J.M. (1988) 'The law and a physically-ill patient with anorexia nervosa.' *Medical Journal of Australia*, 148: 41–4.

Monahan, J. (1988) 'Risk assessment of violence among the mentally disordered: Generating useful knowledge.' *International Journal of Law and Psychiatry*, 11: 249–57.

Myers, B. and Barrett, C.L. (1986) 'Competency issues in referrals to a consultation-liaison service.' *Psychosomatics*, 11: 782–9.

O'Neill, J., Crowther, T. and Sampson, G. (1994) 'Anorexia nervosa: Palliative care of terminal psychiatric disease.' *American Journal of Hospice and Palliative Care*, 11, (6): 36–8.

Patton, G.C. (1988) 'Mortality in eating disorders. *Psychological Medicine*, 18: 947–51.

Perlin, M.L. (1993) 'Decoding right to refuse treatment law.' *International Journal of Law and Psychiatry*, 16: 151–77.

——(1994) 'Law and the delivery of mental health services in the community.' *American Journal of Orthopsychiatry*, 64: 194–208.

Perris, C., Malm, U., Stancati, G. and Minnai, G. (1985) 'Patients admitted for compulsory treatment to selected psychiatric units in Italy and in Sweden.' *Acta Psychiatrica Scandinavica*, Suppl 316: 135–49.

Pichler, J.W. (1995) 'Patients rights in Austria: Still under construction.' *European Journal of Health Law*, 2: 77–83.

Pijnenborg, L., van der Maas, P.J., Kardaun, J.W.P.F, Glerum, J.J., van Delden, J.M. and Looman, C.W.N. (1995) 'Withdrawal or withholding of treatment at the end of life.' *Archives of Internal Medicine*, 155: 286–92.

Quill, T.E. and Brody, R.V. (1995) '"You promised me I wouldn't die like this!" A bad death as a medical emergency.' *Archives of Internal Medicine*, 155: 1250–4.

Ramsay, R. and Treasure, J. (1996) 'Treating anorexia nervosa: Psychiatrists have mixed views on use of terminal care for anorexia nervosa' (letter). *British Medical Journal*, 312: 182.

Roberts, E. (1992) 'Refusal of treatment by 16-year-old.' *Lancet*, 340: 108–9.

Roth, L.H., Meisel, A. and Lidz, C.W. (1977) 'Tests of competency to consent to treatment.' *American Journal of Psychiatry*, 134: 279–84.

Roth, L.H., Appelbaum, P.S., Sallee, R., Reynolds, C.F. and Huber, G. (1982) 'The dilemma of denial in the assessment of competency to refuse treatment.' *American Journal of Psychiatry*, 139: 910–13.

Russell, G.F.M. (1977) 'General management of anorexia nervosa and difficulties in assessing the efficacy of treatment.' In Vigersky, R.A., (ed.) *Anorexia nervosa* (pp. 277–90), 'New York: Raven Press.

——(1989) *Opposing the motion: Compulsory treatment of anorexia nervosa is more beneficial for the therapist than the patient.* Paper read at the Inaugural meeting of the European Council on Eating Disorders, London.

Russell, G.F.M, Szmukler, G.I., Dare, C. and Eisler, I. (1987) 'An evaluation of family therapy in anorexia nervosa and bulimia nervosa.' *Archives of General Psychiatry*, 44: 1047–56.

Russell, G.F.M. and Treasure, J. (1989) 'The modern history of anorexia nervosa: An interpretation of why the illness has changed.' *Annals of the New York Academy of Science*, 575: 13–30.

Scheid-Cook, T.L. (1991) 'The validity of social control critiques: Psychiatric medication, side effects and outpatient commitment.' *Sociological Focus*, 24: 59–77.

Sensky, T., Hughes, T. and Hirsch, S. (1991a) 'Compulsory psychiatric treatment in the community I. A controlled study of compulsory community treatment with extended leave under the Mental Health Act: Special characteristics of patients treated and impact of treatment.' *British Journal of Psychiatry*, 158: 792–9.

——(1991b) 'Compulsory psychiatric treatment in the community II. A controlled study whom psychiatrist would recommend for compulsory treatment in the community.' *British Journal of Psychiatry*, 158: 799–804.

Siegal, H.A., Rapp, R.C., Kelliher, C.W., Fisher, J.H., Wagner, J.H. and Cole, P.A. (1995) 'The strengths perspective of case management: A promising inpatient substance abuse treatment enhancement.' *Journal of Psychoactive Drugs*, 27: 67–72.

Silber, J.S. (1989) 'Justified paternalism in adolescent health care.' *Journal of Adolescent Health Care*, 10: 449–53.

Slomka, J. (1995) 'What do apple pie and motherhood have to do with feeding tubes and caring for the patient?' *Archives of Internal Medicine*, 155: 1258–63.

Story, I. (1983) 'Anorexia nervosa and the psychotherapeutic hospital.' *International Journal of Psychoanalytic Psychotherapy*, 9: 267–302.

Sullivan, P.F. (1995) 'Mortality in anorexia nervosa.' *American Journal of Psychiatry*, 152: 1073–4.

Szmukler, G.I., Eisler, I., Russell, G.F.M. and Dare, C. (1985) 'Anorexia nervosa, parental "expressed emotion" and dropping out of treatment.' *British Journal of Psychiatry*, 147: 265–71.

Thomasma, D.C. (1983) 'Beyond medical paternalism and patient autonomy: A model of physician conscience for the physician-patient relationship.' *Annals of Internal Medicine*, 98: 243–8.

Tiller, J., Schmidt, U. and Treasure, J. (1993) 'Compulsory treatment for anorexia nervosa: Compassion or Coercion?' *British Journal of Psychiatry*, 162: 679–80.

Treasure, J., Todd, G., Brolly, M., Tiller, J., Nehmed, A. and Denman, F. (1995) 'A pilot study of a randomised trial of cognitive analytical therapy vs educational behavioral therapy for adult anorexia nervosa.' *Behaviour Research and Therapy*, 33: 363–7.

United Nations (1992) 'Resolution 46/119 concerning "Principles for the protection of persons with mental illness."' *International Digest of Health Legislation*, 43: 413–23.

Vandereycken, W. (1993) 'Naughty girls and angry doctors: Eating disorder patients and their therapists.' *International Review of Psychiatry*, 5: 13–18.

Vandereycken, W. and Meermann, R. (1984) *Anorexia nervosa: A clinician's guide to treatment*, Berlin-New York: Walter de Gruyter.

Vandereycken, W. and Pierloot, R. (1983) 'Drop-out during in-patient treatment of anorexia nervosa: A clinical study of 133 patients.' *British Journal of Medical Psychology*, 56: 145–56.

Vandereycken, W., Kog, E. and Vanderlinden, J. (1989) *The family approach to eating disorders*. London: PMA Publications.

Vanderlinden, J., Norré, J. and Vandereycken, W. (1992) *A practical guide to the treatment of bulimia nervosa*. New York: Brunner/Mazel.

Vanderlinden, J. and Vandereycken, W. (1989) 'The place of family therapy in the treatment of chronic eating disorders.' *Journal of Strategic and Systemic Therapy*, 8: 1, 18–23.

Wear, A.N. and Brahams, D. (1991) 'At the coalface: To treat or not to treat. The legal, ethical and therapeutic implications of treatment refusal.' *Journal of Medical Ethics*, 17: 131–5.

Weithorn, L.A. and Campbell, S.B. (1982) 'The competency of children and adolescents to make informed treatment decisions.' *Child Development*, 53: 1589–98.

Wertz, D.C., Fanos, J.H. and Reilly, P.R. (1994) 'Genetic testing for children and adolescents. Who decides?' *Journal of the American Medical Association*, 272: 875–81.

Yager, Y. (1995) 'The management of patients with intractable eating disorders.' In Brownell, K.D. and Fairburn, C.G. (eds),*Eating disorders and obesity: A comprehensive handbook* (pp. 374–8), 'New York-London: Guilford Press.

Zerbe, K.J. (1993) 'Whose body is it anyway? Understanding and treating psychosomatic aspects of eating disorders.' *Bulletin of the Menninger Clinic*, 57: 161–77.

CHAPTER NINE

Ethical considerations in the implementation of behaviour modification programmes in patients with anorexia nervosa: A historical perspective

Stephen W. Touyz

INTRODUCTION

Despite all the advances in our understanding of anorexia nervosa, the treatment of this condition remains difficult and controversial (Touyz and Beumont, 1987). Many forms of treatment have been advocated over the years but few have stood the test of time. Venables, in the early 1930s, suggested practical guidelines for the management of patients with anorexia nervosa which makes very interesting reading even today. He suggested that (1) every patient could be persuaded to eat normally (2) the condition to be hysterical and that no patient should remain uncured (3) the doctor should sit down with the patient and fight for every mouthful of food which could take an hour or two per meal (4) the doctor should never lose his temper and (5) one must cure the anorexia before one starts on the psychology of symptoms. He was also most enthusiastic about the outcome in anorexia nervosa and believed that all patients would eventually eat normally and everyone with the condition would be cured (Venables, 1930). We now know that this is not the case (Touyz and Beumont, 1984; Herzog et al., 1992). He also alluded to the difficulties inherent in treating patients with anorexia nervosa by referring to the frustration that doctors endure and warns, despite this, tempers should never be lost!

Garner (1985) has echoed similar sentiments warning of the iatrogenic dangers in treating patients with anorexia nervosa and he quotes from Morgan's (1977) paper to illustrate his concern. Morgan examined the attitudes towards 'fasting girls' and concluded that clinicians 'have great difficulty ... in disengaging ... from an attitude which implies that resistance to eating could be controlled with adequate exercise of will on her part. We are of course anxious to feed those who take insufficient food, but if frustrated, our anxiety quickly turns to hostility at what seems to be unnecessary self-imposed disease' (p. 1655).

Venables went on to assert that meaningful psychotherapy could only be achieved once the patient had commenced regaining weight. Further, support for this contention has come from the work of Keys and colleagues (1950) who found that many of the symptoms reported by patients with anorexia nervosa arose when volunteers were starved to about 75 per cent of their original body weight. Most clinicians treating patients with anorexia nervosa would now agree that certain aspects of the psychopathology of anorexia nervosa are likely to be directly related to the effects of starvation per se (Fairburn and Cooper, 1987) and that meaningful psychotherapy is best achieved once refeeding has commenced (Danziger et al., 1989).

So how does the clinician overcome the difficulty of getting patients with anorexia nervosa to reverse their weight losing behaviours and to eat in a more appropriate manner? Many patients hospitalised with anorexia nervosa refuse to cooperate with the management plan and may even continue to lose weight whilst in hospital despite encouragement to the contrary. A dedicated nurse may spend an hour or more with an angry, hostile patient whilst she slowly and painstakingly eats her meal, endeavouring to allay the patient's fears of losing control over her eating and becoming fat. It is not too difficult to understand the nurse's frustration and feelings of impotence when she finds that the patient has induced vomiting five minutes after completing her meal! Unfortunately, consultant clinicians are not immune from developing feelings of counter-transference either, especially when confronted by a rude and angry patient who steadfastly continues to lose weight despite the treating team's best efforts. It is therefore not surprising that Brotman et al. (1984) found that patients with anorexia nervosa tended to generate more anger, stress and helplessness in medical residents than did diabetic or obese patients. Furthermore, psychiatric and paediatric residents reported significantly more negative affect than those in medicine. However, what is probably of more concern, is the fact that the psychiatry residents were of the opinion that their own dysphoric mood state influenced the quality of care delivered to their anorexia nervosa patients.

It is therefore not too difficult to understand as to why a single case study published just over thirty years ago describing the successful treatment of an anorexia nervosa patient, using a new therapeutic technology, had such an immediate and profound impact on the field of anorexia nervosa (Bachrach et al., 1965). In fact by 1983, most North American psychiatrists and clinical psychologists (Whyte and Kaczkowski, 1983) had been seduced by the optimistic reports regarding the effectiveness of such behavioural programmes in promoting rapid weight gain even in the most recalcitrant patient. There was also the considerable appeal in the relative ease of implementation of such programmes especially by inpatient staff. This led to their immediate incorporation into the prevailing therapeutic armamentarium, without regard to the important fact that such programmes could eventuate in them being applied in a rigid somewhat mechanical manner without regard for the therapeutic relationship and important individual differences amongst patients (Garner, 1985).

The aim of this chapter is to critically examine the evaluation of behavioural strategies promoting weight gain in anorexia nervosa with specific attention being directed at those ethical and moral issues which necessarily pertain to such interventions. We should remain painstakingly aware of the first rule of medicine, *primum non nocere*, whilst being cognisant of the fact that 'voluntary treatment remains the formidable, elusive, yet mandatory goal in the treatment of anorexia nervosa' (Dresser, 1984, p. 50).

Historically, the basic operant paradigm for refeeding patients with anorexia nervosa, comprised the isolation of patients from material and social reinforcers and their return made contingent upon specified amounts of weight gain or caloric intake. In most cases, the decision to implement such programmes has been pragmatic and atheoretical (Bemis, 1987). Now to the history of the development of such programmes.

Bachrach and colleagues (1965) were the first to introduce the concept of operant techniques in the management of anorexia nervosa. The patient, a 37-year-old woman with severe weight loss, was isolated in her hospital room without amenities and was not permitted to engage in any recreational activities. At the outset, all meals were served with one of the therapists present and verbal reinforcement in the form of conversation was provided only when she ate. Later, additional rewards such as going for walks and having visits from relatives were made contingent on satisfactory eating behaviour. After initially gaining weight, her weight stabilised at 27 kg and it was then discovered that she had in fact been secretly vomiting. At this stage, it was decided that reinforcement was best made contingent on weight gain rather than eating behaviour per se. She was subsequently discharged from hospital after gaining 14 lbs (6.4 kg) and at one year follow-up she weighed approximately 30 lbs (13.6 kg) more than she had done at admission. She was reported to have been maintaining her weight well. Furthermore, improvements in both her social adjustment and physical health were documented.

The successful utilisation of this new behavioural technology in treating patients with anorexia nervosa spawned a plethora of reports in the published literature, but unfortunately few included experimental control procedures (Halmi, 1985). An exception to this was a study by Leitenberg and colleagues (1968) who elegantly described two experimental case studies in which they investigated the effects of selective positive reinforcement in achieving weight gain. Each patient was subjected to a non-reinforcement phase during which physical complaints and comments about eating were ignored. This was followed by selective positive reinforcement for both the amount of food eaten and weight gained. The introduction of selective positive reinforcement led in both cases to the restoration of a normal body weight which the patient was able to maintain in the short-term. Perhaps the most interesting finding to emerge from this study was that the removal of reinforcement did not result in the expected decrease in caloric intake. The authors pondered as to whether eating behaviour had unwittingly been reinforced, as the reward for leaving hospital after successful weight gain, had not been rescinded. Furthermore, the patient was in fact receiving regular feedback from her own observations that she was successfully gaining weight and external praise at this stage may have been redundant. Halmi (1985) has cautioned against underestimating the contribution that self-observed signs of progressive improvement may play in the maintenance of behavioural change especially with regard to cross-over studies.

These two studies laid the foundation for the subsequent popularity of operant techniques in the treatment of patients with anorexia nervosa. The popularity was based on the rapid weight gain achieved during refeeding and the relative lack of perceived side-effects when compared to medication and nasogastric tube feeding. Garfinkel and Garner (1982) in fact point out that prior to 1970, only five investigators reported utilising an operant paradigm in refeeding patients with anorexia nervosa (Azerrad and Stafford, 1969; Bachrach, Erwin and Mohr, 1965; Blinder and Ringold, 1967; Leitenberg, Agras and Thomson, 1968; Stumphauzer, 1969) but this had increased by at least five fold by the end of the next decade.

The data emanating from the studies tended to confirm that the majority of patients did in fact gain weight without any documented harmful side-effects. But the clouds before the storm were already beginning to gain momentum.

Hilde Bruch (1974, 1978) disagreed with those who insisted that the implementation of rigid behavioural programmes were without dangers contention and has expressed grave concern regarding the use of such interventions in treating patients with anorexia nervosa. In a paper entitled 'Perils of behaviour modification in anorexia nervosa', Bruch (1974) strongly criticised behaviour therapists for their naive assumption that the restoration of a normal body weight (the most prominent symptom) was sufficient treatment for those patients. It was her impression that most behaviourally orientated programmes failed to take into account the major deficits in the personality development of these patients, namely: low self-esteem, self doubt, lack of autonomy and an inability to lead a self-directed life. She also indicated that behavioural programmes had an adverse psychological effect on patients who would gain weight under the 'pressure of persuasion, force or threats' and would literally 'eat their way out of hospital'. Bruch (1974) concluded by saying that 'it is generally known that true benefit is derived from such weight gain only if it is part of an integrated treatment programme with correction of the underlying individual and family problems'.

Stunkard (1972), in a more positive vain, portrayed behaviour modification as a creative approach but emphasised the need to *individually* tailor each patient's programme to the specific variables that maintained the patient's behaviour.

What clinical findings have emerged from this wealth of research on the use of behaviour modification in the treatment of patients with anorexia nervosa and what implications does this have for contemporary clinical practice? After their extensive review of several case reports and uncontrolled studies, Fairburn and Cooper (1987) concluded that the specific value of behavioural techniques in promoting weight gain was still unproven. They were very critical of the scientific correctness of the above studies citing numerous methodological inadequacies including small sample sizes, lack of prospective design, inadequate diagnostic criteria, the concurrent use of medication, psychotherapy and operant conditioning programmes thereby making it virtually impossible to derive at the conclusion that operant conditioning programmes in fact facilitated weight gain. However, they were of the opinion, despite the above shortcomings, that operant paradigms did promote weight gain in the short-term. What was clearly amiss in the published literature were studies comparing the effectiveness of weight gain and its maintenance thereafter in different forms of treatment including operant based ones. What has been investigated, however, is the relative effectiveness of various operant weight restoration programmes.

OPERANT CONDITIONING PROGRAMMES: THE DAWN OF A NEW ERA?

Most of the traditional operant programmes developed for anorexia nervosa patients during refeeding have been unnecessarily harsh. The iatrogenic dangers of facilitating increasingly rapid rates of weight gain have been well documented (Touyz and

Beumont, 1997). Bemis (1987) has challenged the notion that more rapid refeeding is necessarily better and cautioned that common sense must prevail because at 'some point the short-term economic advantage of increasing speed is cancelled out by its clinical disadvantage'. The risk of developing bulimic symptoms under such circumstances should not be underestimated. Bruch (1978) concluded that operant conditioning programmes may well facilitate a more rapid weight gain during refeeding, but strongly cautioned that their effectiveness could be offset by the psychological damage they may cause in some patients: 'Its very efficiency increases the inner turmoil of patients, who feel tricked into relinquishing control over their bodies and their lives' (Bruch, 1978, p. 652).

Garner (1985) has also alluded to reports in the literature 'which capture the extraordinary degree of frustration, anger and maltreatment which have prevailed under the guise of behaviour modification.' There is no justification whatsoever to implement harsh behavioural regimens to punish patients who have not complied with treatment. To this end we compared the effects of 'strict' and 'lenient' operant conditioning programmes in promoting weight gain in 65 anorexia nervosa patients (Touyz et al., 1984). In a consecutive series, 31 patients were treated using a traditional strict bed-rest programme, with an individualised schedule of reinforcers for each 0.5 kg weight gained, whereas the next 34 patients were treated with a lenient and flexible behavioural programme. After an initial week of bed-rest, a contract was made with each patient to gain a minimum of 1.5 kg per week. Provided they complied with this requirement, patients were free to move around the unit. They understood that if they failed to achieve the weekly target of weight gain, they would be required to spend the following week on bed rest. No further restrictions were imposed and patients had unlimited access to their personal possessions. In all other aspects, the treatment regimens for the two groups were similar. All the patients received nutritional counselling, supporting psychotherapy, group therapy and occupational therapy, and the duration of hospital stay was approximately 9 weeks for both treatment groups.

The mean daily weight gain did not differ between the strict and lenient programmes (0.21 kg versus 0.20 kg) and a similar proportion of patients in each group reached their target weight. This weight gain during refeeding on both programmes compared favourably with the best figures reported by other authors using behavioural techniques. Thus Agras and coworkers (1974) cited a rate of 0.20 kg/day using a programme which included large meals, reinforcers for weight gain and feedback. Halmi et al. (1975) reported the same rate after using a programme of strict bed-rest and reinforcers contingent upon weight gain. Bhanji and Thompson (1974) obtained a slightly lower rate (0.16 kg/day) using a similar programme. Agras and Werne (1978) reported much lower rates of weight gain in regimens using psychotherapy or counselling as the principal form of therapy.

There were practical advantages in using the lenient programme compared to the strict one. The lenient programme was seen as more acceptable by most of our patients, and there was a general consensus among staff members that patients on the lenient programme were better motivated towards other aspects of treatment than those on the strict programme. The lenient programme also required less nursing time, and so was more economical, and it provided less opportunity for patients to manipulate individual staff members in connection with their treatment. As a result, the staff were able to use their time more constructively in both group therapy and supportive psychotherapy with patients. This was very much in keeping with our overall aim of providing a comprehensive integrated approach to treatment. As stated previously, Bruch (1974) has stressed the importance of an integrated approach in treating patients with anorexia nervosa. She has suggested that inpatients gain weight under the 'pressure of persuasion, fear or threat' so that there is a high rate of relapse. We believe that our lenient treatment programme, despite its behavioural basis, provides sufficient opportunity for psychotherapeutic contact and for patients to maintain their autonomy during treatment to avoid these criticisms (Touyz et al., 1984; APA Practice Guidelines For Eating Disorders, 1993).

NASOGASTRIC FEEDING: THE ALTERNATIVE APPROACH?

Despite the encouraging results that have emerged from our lenient flexible approach to promote weight gain (Touyz et al., 1984, 1987), not all patients gain weight consistently on this regimen and a minority even lose further weight. In such situations, a clinician may feel tempted or even justified to institute nasogastric tube feeding or parenteral refeeding. However, there is now significant recognition of the danger of rapid refeeding (e.g. severe fluid retention and cardiac failure; Garfinkel and Garner, 1982). In fact, the APA Practice Guidelines for Eating Disorders (1993) specifically state that these interventions should not be used routinely, but rather be considered only for those more severely malnourished anorectic patients.

The psychological distress that can be inflicted on patients who are literally forced to endure nasogastric feeds is best expressed in the following vignette:

> I didn't know what it was going to involve. I hated pain ... I was afraid, so scared. The tube looked so hard and so long, I began to cry ... the hideous piece of plastic tubing was being forced down my left nostril ... I was screaming ... my head thrashed wildly on the bed whilst my body squirmed or moved like a wounded fish out of water.
>
> I cried ... Nothing can or will ever remove the memory of that tube. However, this tube was going to save my life ... But I decided that I didn't want this tube inside of me nor the fluid flowing into me through the tube. The most sensible thing in my eyes to do was to pull it out. But I didn't want any pain.
>
> I gently pulled the tube protruding from my nose and it was sore. I was so afraid and scared of what I could do to myself and also scared of what the staff would do to me ... I lifted my feeble arms and fingers. I placed the tube between my thumb and forefinger and gently yanked it. Something moved inside me. I could now feel the tube inside my stomach. My mind ran amuck. I was so confused. Out came the tube, one hell of a long tube. I hadn't realised how long it actually was. (I later found out that it was 3 feet long). (Touyz and Beumont, 1993, p. 68)

This vignette graphically illustrates why tube feeding should only be considered in rare instances in which the patient is in imminent danger and/or completely unresponsive to more conservative methods.

THE HUMANE APPROACH: BRIEF REWARD PROGRAMMES (BRPS)

Despite our cogent criticisms of the routine implementation of strict operant conditioning programmes for refeeding patients with anorexia nervosa (Touyz et al., 1984, 1987), there is some justification not to abandon this strategy altogether. When confronted by a recalcitrant patient in hospital, who fails to gain weight on a more lenient programme, then we believe it to be both necessary and justifiable to implement a stricter operant conditioning programme but in a modified form. We have recently introduced the concept of 'Brief Reward Programmes' (BRPs) as an adjunct to refeeding those patients who have not responded to our more lenient approach (Touyz and Beumont, 1997).

The major focus of the BRPs is to provide both an incentive and/or face saving mechanism for the non-compliant patient to commence eating and gaining weight. Thus, instead of the traditional operant conditioning programme which necessitated the patient remaining in relative isolation on the ward, often for several months and at times for the entire admission, BRPs are developed to ensure that the patients' confinement to their room is limited to a few weeks at best. The hierarchy of reinforcers should be individualised as with all operant programmes, but the entire hierarchy of reinforcers should be restricted to a 4–5 kg range. Thus should the patient manage to gain 1 kg per week, then the entire duration of such a programme would be approximately five weeks. By this time, the patient is usually complying better with treatment and is able to continue to gain weight without the individualised programme.

When we place patients on a BRP, they are told from the outset that their progress will be reviewed on a regular basis and, if they do well with regard to their weight gain, they may be given an opportunity to come off the programme prior to completing it with the clear understanding that if they fail to continue to gain an agreed weekly weight, they will have to return to the BRP until it is successfully completed.

There are several advantages in using BRPs with patients who fail to respond to more lenient approaches to refeeding:
• Patients can see the light at the end of the tunnel in that such programmes are designed to assist them in commencing the refeeding process and are therefore by nature short lived. Traditional operant conditioning programmes require the patient to reach their goal weight before it is terminated and one usually remains on it no matter how well one is doing.
• Since only a minority of patients will require BRPs, there is the

added incentive of gaining weight so as to resume the normal ward programme and not to be seen to be different to one's peer group.

• There is less danger of patients 'literally eating their way out of hospital' (Bruch, 1974).

• It is seen as less punitive by the majority of our patients.

It is our belief that such programmes warrant further investigation.

CONCLUSIONS

With so much water under the bridge since Bachrach and his colleagues (1965) introduced operant conditioning principles to the treatment of patients with anorexia nervosa, what can one conclude about the ethical and moral justification of implementing such programmes in routine clinical practice?

It is our opinion, after a thorough and careful analysis of the published literature as well as our extensive clinical experience in the treatment of patients with anorexia nervosa spanning a quarter of a century, that behaviour modification techniques do have an important contribution to make, especially during the refeeding phase of treatment, provided they are used in an appropriate manner and as part of an integrated treatment programme comprising individual and group psychotherapy, family therapy, nutritional and exercise counselling. Garner (1985) has stressed the importance of distinguishing between the coercive use of negative reinforcement and properly applied behaviour therapy based upon the systematic contingencies underlying the disorder. It is absolutely imperative that behavioural principles are applied in a manner which focuses on the individual needs and concerns of the patient. It may surprise many that in a recent study by our group (Griffiths et al., 1997) which investigated patients' perceptions of imposed bed rest, anorectic patients reported that such programmes were both necessary and helpful in their treatment but when applied too harshly, created boredom which was unhelpful in the treatment process.

Finally, Agras and Kraemer (1984) have suggested that the Body Mass Indices (BMI) of patients on admission have shown a marked decline over the past 50 years. Since a lower admission rate has been purported to be associated with a poorer outcome, those data suggest that patients with more severe anorexia nervosa are being admitted to hospital today than was the case fifty years ago. If this is indeed the case, then there is an even greater need to develop more humane effective and integrated treatment programmes for patients with anorexia nervosa (Touyz and Beumont, 1997).

However, the proof of the pudding is in the eating and the ultimate test of treatment programmes in patients with anorexia nervosa is to demonstrate improvement at longer-term follow-up. This has sadly not been the case. Herzog (1996) in a plenary address to the 21st European Conference on Psychosomatic Research in Bordeaux, France, bewailed the fact that his extensive review of the published literature revealed that only five well-controlled studies have been published pertaining to the treatment of anorexia nervosa. This area of research endeavour is clearly in need of urgent address especially when one considers that even these better controlled studies lacked adequate follow-up data.

REFERENCES

Agras, W.S. and Kraemer, H.C. (1984) 'The treatment of anorexia nervosa: Do different treatments have different outcomes?' In Stunkard, A.J. and Stellar, E. (eds) *Eating and its Disorders* (pp. 193–207), 'New York: Raven Press.

Agras, W.S. and Werne, J. (1978) 'Behavior therapy in anorexia nervosa: A data-based approach to the question.' In Brady, J.P. and Brodie, H.K.H. (eds) *Controversy in Psychiatry* (pp. 655–75), Philadelphia: Saunders.

American Psychiatric Association (1993) 'Practice Guidelines for Eating Disorders.' *American Journal of Psychiatry*, 150: 207–28.

Azerrad, J. and Stafford, R.L. (1969) 'Restoration of eating behaviour in anorexia nervosa through operant conditioning and environmental manipulations.' *Behaviour Research and Therapy*, 7: 165–71.

Bachrach, A.J., Erwin, W.J., and Mohr, J.P. (1965) 'The control of eating behaviour in an anorexic by operant conditioning techniques.' In Ullman, L.P. and Krasner, I. (eds) *Case Studies in Behavior Modification* (pp. 153–63), 'New York: Holt, Rinehart and Winston.

Bemis, K. (1987) 'The present status of operant conditioning for the treatment of anorexia nervosa. *Behavior Modification*, 11: 432–63.

Bhanji, S., and Thompson, J. (1974) 'Operant conditioning in the treatment of anorexia nervosa: A review and retrospective study of 11 cases.' *British Journal of Psychiatry*, 124: 166–72.

Blinder, B.J. and Ringold, A.L. (1967) 'Rapid weight restoration in anorexia nervosa' (Abstract) *'Clinical Research*, 15: 473.

Brotman, A.W., Stern, T.A. and Herzog, D.B. (1984) 'Emotional reactions of house officers to patients with anorexia nervosa, diabetes and obesity.' *International Journal of Eating Disorders*, 3: 71–7.

Bruch, H. (1974) 'Perils of behaviour modification in treatment of anorexia nervosa.' *Journal of the American Medical Association* 230: 1419–22.

——(1978) 'Dangers of behaviour modification in treatment in anorexia nervosa.' In Brady, J.P. and Brodie, H.K.H. (eds) *Controversy in Psychiatry* (pp. 245–654), 'Philadelphia: Saunders.

Danziger, Y., Carel, C.A., Tyano, S. and Mimounty, M. (1989) 'Is psychotherapy mandatory during the acute refeeding period in the treatment of anorexia nervosa?' *Journal of Adolescent Health Care*, 10: 325–31.

Dresser, J.D. (1984) 'Legal and policy considerations in treatment of anorexia nervosa patients.' *International Journal of Eating Disorders*, 3: 43–51.

Fairburn, C.G. and Cooper, Z. (1987) 'Behavioural and cognitive approaches to the treatment of anorexia nervosa and bulimia nervosa.' In Beumont, P.J.V., Burrows, G.D. and Casper, R.C. (eds) *Handbook of Eating Disorders. Part 1: Anorexia and Bulimia Nervosa* (pp. 271–98), Amsterdam: Elsevier Biomedical Press.

Garfinkel, P.E. and Garner, D.M. (1982) '*Anorexia Nervosa: A Multidimensional Perspective*, New York: Brunner/Mazel.

Garner, D.M. (1985) 'Iatrogenesis in anorexia and bulimia nervosa.' *International Journal of Eating Disorder*, 4: 701–26.

Griffiths, R., Gross, G., Russell, J., Thornton, C., Beumont, P.J.V., Schotte, D. and Touyz, S.W. (1997) 'Perceptions of bedrest by anorexia nervosa patients.' *International Journal of Eating Disorders* (in press).

Halmi, K.A. (1985) 'Behavioral management for anorexia nervosa.' In Garner, D.M. and Garfinkel, P.E. (eds) *Handbook of Psychotherapy for Anorexia Nervosa and Bulimia* (pp. 147–59), New York: Guilford Press.

Halmi, K.A., Powers, P. and Cunningham, S. (1975) 'Treatment of anorexia nervosa with behavior modification.' *Archives of General Psychiatry*, 32: 93–6.

Herzog, T. (1996) 'Toward evidence based psychosomatic medicine: How and what can we learn from intervention studies for eating disorders?' (abstract). *Proceedings of the 21st European Conference on Psychosomatic Research*, Bordeaux, France, p. 18.

Herzog, W., Rathner, G. and Vandereycken, W. (1992) 'Long-term course of anorexia nervosa: A review of the literature.' In Herzog, W., Deter,

H.-C. and Vandereycken, W. (eds), *The Course of Eating Disorders: Long-term follow-up studies of anorexia and bulimia nervosa* (pp. 15–29), Berlin-New York: Springer-Verlag.

Keys, A., Brozek, J., Henschel, A., Mickelsen, O. and Taylor, H.L. (1950) *The Biology of Human Starvation.* Minneapolis: University of Minnesota Press.

Leitenberg, H., Agras, W.S. and Thomson, L.E. (1968) 'A sequential analysis of the effect of selective positive reinforcement in modifying anorexia nervosa.' *Behaviour Research and Therapy*, 6: 211–18.

Morgan, H.G. (1977) 'Fasting girls and our attitudes to them.' *British Medical Journal*, 24: 1652–5.

Stumphauzer, J.S. (1969) 'Application of reinforcement contingencies with a 23-year old anorexia patient.' *Psychological Reports*, 24: 109–10.

Stunkard, A. (1972) 'New therapies for the eating disorders: Behavior modification of obesity and anorexia nervosa.' *Archives of General Psychiatry*, 26: 391–8.

Touyz, S.W. and Beumont, P.J.V. (1984) 'Anorexia nervosa: A follow-up investigation.' *Medical Journal of Australia*, 141: 219–22.

——(1987) 'Anorexia and bulimia nervosa: A personal perspective.' In Beumont, P.J.V., Burrows, G.D. and Casper, R.C. (eds) *Handbook of Eating Disorders, Part 1, Anorexia Nervosa and Bulimia*, (pp. 1–11), Amsterdam: Elsevier Biomedical Press.

——(1993) 'Overcoming anorexia nervosa: The struggle to survive despite innumerable odds.' In Schwartz, S. (ed.) *Australian Cases in Clinical Psychology* (pp. 53–72), Jacaranda (Australia): John Wiley.

——(1997) 'Behavioural treatment principles to promote weight gain.' In Garner, D.M. and Garfinkel, P.E. (eds) *Handbook of Psychotherapy for Eating Disorders* (2nd ed.), New York: Guilford Press.

Touyz, S.W., Beumont, P.J.V. and Dunn, S.M. (1987) 'Behaviour therapy in the management of patients with anorexia nervosa. A lenient, flexible approach.' *Psychotherapy and Psychosomatics*, 48: 151–6.

Touyz, S.W., Beumont, P.J.V., Glaun, D., Phillips, T. and Cowie, I. (1984) 'A comparison of lenient and strict operant conditioning programmes in refeeding patients with anorexia nervosa.' *British Journal of Psychiatry*, 144: 517–20.

Venables, J.F. (1930) 'Anorexia nervosa: A study of the pathogenesis and treatment of nine cases.' *Guy's Hospital Report*, 80: 213–14.

Whyte, B.L. and Kaczkowski, H. (1983) 'Anorexia nervosa: A study of psychiatrists' and psychologists' opinions and practices.' *International Journal of Eating Disorders*, 2: 87–92.

CHAPTER TEN

Counting the cash: Ethics and market forces in relation to the provision of treatment for eating disorders

Sue Robinson, Stuart Lieberman, Chris Dare and Andrew Curry

The burden of the therapist has been altered by changes made in the ways money is resourced, or the cash counted, in health services. Clinicians now must give fundamental consideration to the financial relationships which underpin the relationships between consumers, users, and providers of services. These developments have engendered new conflicts between the clinical judgements of practitioners (or providers) and their financial assessments. In attempting to resolve these there are few ethical guidelines available, either in the public or private sectors. This chapter examines how changes in the political, social, and economic context of health provision, in particular in relationship to money and values, impact upon clinical treatments of patients, specifically for anorexia nervosa. This new environment already affects the everyday duties of the therapist, yet there has been little analysis of the dynamics of these political and economic pressures. Although some of the examples draw on the reforms to the British health service, the issues raised are relevant to all market-based health reforms.

It will be argued that the development of market-based systems, without the corresponding development of appropriate ethical frameworks, leads to a breakdown of trust generally in the provision of health services, and specifically in the therapeutic encounter. In turn this breakdown of trust has significant costs for health services, which are not accounted for in market-oriented

accounting systems. The roots of the dilemmas raised by the new financial relationships between providers, consumers, and users can be summarised thus:
a) the accessibility of information about the available routes to therapy;
b) the expectations users can be permitted about the outcome of treatment;
c) the controversy about long term provision.

Health provision must be funded, and a financial relationship lies at the base of all patient care. The development of market systems has made relationships between user, provider, and consumer visible (an intentional outcome) but has done so in a manner which, perhaps contrary to the intentions of market reformers, is neither transparent, neutral nor predictable. The relationships between need and provision are complicated further by the fact that while the *user* of the service is an individual or a family, the *consumer* will usually be an institution, for example an insurance company (in the private sector) or a health service fundholder (in the British public health sector). When the interests of users and consumers conflict the provider or practitioner can find themselves in the middle. Anorexia nervosa affords illustrations of these obligations in one particular field, but also has relevance for other areas of medicine for the following reasons.

1) The death rate for anorectics is high in comparison both with the population as a whole and with other types of psychiatric disorder. Figures for the UK suggest that the annual suicide rate is 5,000 in a population of 50 million, or 0.01 per cent of the population (Office for National Statistics, 1994). For anorexia nervosa the longer term death rate is estimated in some studies to be as high as 18 per cent (Ratnasuriya, Eisler, Szmukler, and Russell, 1991); and while the statistical comparison is not exact, the contrast between the two figures is stark enough to convince.
2) There is often an initial stage of denial, manifested in a reluctance to accept treatment during the first stages of illness in anorexia (Vandereycken and van Deth, 1995).
3) There are no agreed clinical causes or cures for anorexia, and this contributes to a paucity of preliminary information about the range of available treatments accessible to users. Similarly the

gatekeepers of resources have no direct obligation to users to be explicit about the values which underpin their resource allocation.

The developments characterised above have taken place within a political culture which has sought 'to promote the market as the sole organising principle of economy and society ... Wherever possible – from the National Health Service to the provision of pensions – market forces have been promoted and state intervention rolled back' (Hutton, 1995). If Britain has been in the vanguard of the market experiment, it has hardly been alone. As the authors of a recent review of OECD (Organisation of Economic Co-operation and Development, 1995) health care policy observed: 'All OECD countries have introduced reforms, although some have only done so recently'. While the details vary from country to country, the report identifies common issues:

● At the level of hospitals, clinics, and other health resources, 'The central requirement for improving efficiency is to clarify and strengthen the role of health funders.'
● The funders become agents of cost control on behalf of central government, enforcing budget limits and becoming accountable for contracting arrangements with providers.
● Funders are intended to become more effective purchasing agents for health users, accountable for the quantity and quality of medical services provided.

As the study observes, 'These changes often require increases in the costs of administering the system'.

THE SOURCE OF CONFLICT

The language of the OECD report is typical of much current discussion of health provision, which is not to say that it is improper either to discuss cost in relation to health care, or the relationship between health care and health outcome. The key effect of redesigning health systems to make costs more visible is – at the local or hospital level – to make the role of the purchaser both more influential and more visible. (Historically in state systems, the role of the 'purchaser' was effectively just a mechanism for transferring resources.)

However, in making visible the financial process of health care a conflict of interest has been created within health systems. The new language of public service provision makes much of notions borrowed from market economists such as 'consumer sovereignty' and 'accountability'. Health care reformers, often using market models, look to market mechanisms to deliver accountability (the authors of the OECD report refer to the need for 'competition' and 'monitoring'). However, medical professionals have long had a framework which, they believed, made them accountable to the best interests of the patient; it is a non-financial model which has evolved from the Hippocratic oath.

In Britain, the difference lies in the location of the duty of care. Within the market place, when a customer enters a shop to buy goods, we are enjoined *caveat emptor*: buyer beware. Within health care, a different expectation both exists and is legally enforced. The user (even if they are the direct purchaser of the clinical care) has the legal right to expect that the provider will act in the user's interests, will undertake clinical interventions governed by the requirements of good practice, and has no right to undertake treatment specified purely by the user.

Ruark and Raffin (1988) cite six basic principles of medical ethics: to preserve life; to alleviate suffering; to do no harm (quoted by Hippocrates as *Non nocere*); to tell the truth; to respect the patient's autonomy; and to deal justly with patients. Usually this is summarised by medics into four main principles: autonomy; beneficence; avoid maleficence; and justice (behave fairly). Even within this ethical framework, there is little guidance as to which principle should take precedence if they conflict. The same clinicians, or providers, who consider that they are accountable to their patients for their treatment through an ethical system imbued by training and by professional culture, now find that they are also accountable to purchasers of health services for delivery of care within budgets and according to measurable objectives and service delivery indicators.

In acute and general medicine, the conflict leads to disputes over issues such as 'health rationing'. In the area of therapy, which exists in an associative relationship to general and acute services, the conflict becomes more severe. This is because therapeutic services, more so than core health services, are likely to have a variety of funders (health care purchasers, research grants, other public funders) sometimes concurrently, sometimes at different times. Each of the funders has their own objectives, while the therapeutic service may concurrently treat individuals and families. The clinical assessments of the patient's needs, and the organisation's assessment of the ability to deliver a service to a patient, may also require a careful assessment of the purchaser's (or funder's) objectives.

The assessment of such objectives requires that the welfare of patients is considered alongside possible treatment outcomes and likely costs. All these criteria are influential in the setting of priorities, even though it is evident that conflicts will exist between them. For an anorectic, where the patient's condition can be critical, causation is mostly psychological, but the effects are strongly physiological as well as mental, the potential for conflict between proposed treatment and cost can be significant. This is exacerbated because there is no certain cure and clinicians therefore tend to offer treatments in keeping with their own training, values, and ideology.

Further, the issue of outcomes is also less clear-cut than it appears initially. Findings about the successful outcomes of treatments for anorexia nervosa are largely inconclusive but Russell, Smzukler, Dare and Eisler (1987) suggest that 'family therapy is an effective treatment for those patients whose illness commences at a relatively early age and has not become chronic. A second, more tentative finding is that individual supportive psychotherapy is more effective than family therapy [for those] in whom the illness commences at a somewhat older age.' However, research on outcome does not generally relate the benefits of different treatments to their costs.

Priorities and choices make visible the value systems which underpin selection: the question of how the value of health is measured against financial worth becomes a question of politics. As the OECD (1995) report notes, the driver for health reform has been a desire by governments to cut health expenditure as a proportion of their overall expenditure, driven by a belief that current levels of spending on welfare services are unsustainable (the so-called 'fiscal crisis of the state'). There is not space here to explore this argument, but it should be noted that some commentators (Hutton, 1995) have argued that the notion of the 'fiscal crisis' is itself an ideological construction by those opposed to welfare spending.

The political effect of financial reforms is explored by Shaoul

(1996) in her analysis of UK health reforms. She distinguishes between 'marketisation' (market-mimicking mechanisms such as purchasers' and 'providers') and 'corporatisation' (reconstituting the hospitals as self-funding entities). She argues that the accounting rules imposed on the British health service trusts will reduce the revenue base of the hospitals, and redirect some of that revenue to the government, while affording local management little of the autonomy of action they would need to achieve their targets. Shaoul concludes that this financial regime requires hospital trusts to focus on particular types of health care, in particular those which offer a high throughput of patients and low equipment costs. This requires a new emphasis on maximising utilization of medical equipment and buildings, and promotes medical solutions to health care rather than preventive medicine. (The same conclusion is reached by the OECD report.) All of this drives the public health system towards the financially driven health care model of the private sector.

Writing specifically about eating disorders, Vogler (1993) concluded that in the United States 'medicalisation increases directly with economic profitability'. Vogler's argument, in summary, is that, 'Political and economic influences dealing with the issue of control of women's bodies are compounded by the medical claims that highlight the hazards of eating disorders. Private hospital treatment programs have, therefore, emerged as a solution to the individual's efforts to control their eating behaviour.' The availability of medical insurance to pay for psychiatric treatment in hospital settings is a critical factor, underlining the role of a funder in the clinical decision-making process: 'Because out-patient care for eating disorders ... is minimally reimbursed by current coverage provisions of most insurance companies all patients are given the psychiatric diagnosis ... in order to receive maximum insurance benefits. Second, the profit making incentives of doctors and institutions make it more profitable to provide fully re-imbursed inpatient treatment rather than limited reimbursed out-patient treatment.'

Responses to the market changes by clinicians working with anorexics have included self-help manuals (e.g. Fairbairn, 1995; Schmidt and Treasure 1993) and preventive educational strategies, such as those pioneered in Norway (Gresko and Karlsen, 1994). Financial relationships also inhere in the emergence of self-help manuals; here the market interface between user and provider is constructed by publishers and educational funders. One approach from theorists (Jaggar and Bordo, 1989) and clinicians (Fallon, Katzman and Wooley, 1994) has been to reframe the issues facing anorectics in terms of the social and economic environment in which they find themselves. One can sympathise with their approach, but such analyses will not help direct resources into patient care until they are shared by managers, fundholders, and the boards to whom they are accountable.

RESULTS, OUTCOMES, AND TRUST

To identify more fully the hidden costs of the market reforms, a brief review of current developments in thinking on the market is necessary. Recent writing on the market has identified its limitations. Ormerod (1995) criticises the assumptions which are essential in neo-classical economic theory to ensure that markets 'clear', matching supply and demand. These require that all buyers and all sellers have perfect knowledge about all transactions at all times, past, present, *and* future. Ormerod observes that such perfection applies in scarcely any market. It certainly does not apply in a complex market such as health.

The social shortcomings of the market are identified by the British political philosopher John Gray (1993). 'The market is not free-standing or self-justifying ... [It] lacks ethical and political legitimacy unless it is supplemented or complemented by other institutions that temper its excesses and correct its failures.' Mulgan (1993) notes that 'marketisation' in organizations promotes competition within them, replacing co-operation and collaboration, while Parston (1993) suggests that many recent public sector reforms have ignored fundamental differences in the purpose of management in the public sector as against the private. 'The ends of public sector organisations are social. Their driving force is more social return on investment, better social results: a more widely educated public, in the case of schools, for example; a healthier population, in the case of the health service'. Yet reformers have assumed that implementing private sector processes will of itself result in improved public services.

The history of Britain's market-based reforms is therefore a strange one. Even as health provision was reorganised on market lines, as business leaders were recruited to the managing boards of Britain's newly created hospital trusts, and the British model was represented internationally as a way forward in health care, management theorists were already addressing the limitations of narrowly market-based approaches. This was more than academic fashion. It was a response to the failure of market-oriented methods to deliver long-term value in the private sector; a search for the elements missing from the market model. In his book *Trust*, the influential conservative theorist Francis Fukuyama (1995) argues that this missing element is 'social capital'. In both public and private sectors, such social capital might include, for example, training, shared expertise or resources, and shared support services. It is dissipated in narrowly focussed market reforms. Fukuyama goes further, identifying the importance to business of shared values: 'If people who have to work together in an enterprise trust one another because they are all working to a common set of ethical norms doing business costs less.'

Management writers now identify value in organisations as deriving from the people within them, not from the control model inherent in market mechanisms. They endorse ideas such as 'continuing self-organisation' built on 'shared meanings and understandings' (Morgan, 1993); curiosity and innovation (Peters 1995); learning, empowerment, and dissent (Handy 1989, 1993); and teamwork (Belbin, 1981). All of these values are identifiable as elements of strategies to protect and develop social capital within the firm or organisation. Therapeutic services, with their necessary emphasis on shared understandings, collaborative work, research, and innovation (all elements of social capital), have more in common with current business thinking than previous market models. It is also evident that there are hidden costs to the market system in the health service. If users are to trust a service, they must feel that the service shares their values about the basis of treatment and care. The market reforms have fragmented such assumptions, such that individual users now have to try to establish at the level of individual clinicians or service providers whether they have values in common (given the paucity of available inform-ation this is time-consuming both for potential patient and for the health service unit involved). Because of this decline of trust, patients are more likely to seek redress if necessary through formal procedures such as the UK Patients' Charters, Ombudspeople, or even the law, rather than resolving grievances informally at local level. Other costs are more likely to be incurred, in particular in increased administration. These costs diminish the available health resource but do not appear as costs in the income and expenditure flows of the health purchaser or health provider.

In terms of anorexia nervosa the hidden costs are concealed by the ways patients profit from the treatment. These are not just computed in terms of take-up of treatment but also in the effectiveness of outcomes. An intrinsic element of anorexia nervosa is the subversion of bodily needs to the service of others and the displacement of anger into patterns of starvation. Bruch (1973) showed that anorectics have an illness which has taught them to be compliant. Many conceal their desires by caring for others and are employed in helping and caring professions (Orbach, 1985; Fallon et al., 1994). It is unlikely that this sort of clientèle will risk future treatment relationships by making demands and contravening what appear to be the best medical or therapeutic diagnoses, even though they may smoulder underneath.

In general adult eating disorder patients are viewed with ambivalence by mental health professionals. It is important to recognise that people who both feel undeserving and who arouse complex emotional responses in professionals, require careful support to enable them to benefit from treatment. When the structures of health provision defer to market forces, priorities are determined by the interests of the better off. While anorectic patients tend to come from families who are relatively affluent, with the middle-class advocacy which typically follows, this is not the case for bulimic patients. Nor are social systems structured by market forces designed with the needs of secretive people in mind. Anorexia nervosa is characterised by the patient's terror of taking nourishment, and by a wish (often ill-disguised) to hide the psychological and physical effects of the condition.

In the psychotherapy of the individual, the therapist is confronted with the patient's difficulty in accepting help for themselves from within the treatment. The following transference intervention is pertinent to an anorectic patient: 'You find yourself having to refuse emotional support or nourishment from me in the same way as you refrain from eating. You feel you are no more deserving of possible therapeutic nurture than you are of nutritional nurture.' When a service for eating disorder patients is 'cash starved' there is a painful isomorphism.

ETHICS AND CLINICAL ISSUES

The introduction of any kind of market mechanism, be it a shadow market, an internal market, or a hybrid, has a number of effects on health management processes which raise ethical questions.

1) Decision making authority is placed in the hands of a few. This has advantages and disadvantages. It may mean closer supervision of spending, but in practice this leads to less imagination and creativity, which reduces innovation and, in the long term, increases costs. In the UK, patients have rights to ask to be referred to consultants acceptable to them, but unless their general practitioners are fundholders the health authority has to agree to pay for such a referral.

2) Services become fragmented into competing market areas. Spending on anorexia nervosa, for example, is pitched against other competing claims in psychiatry. While competition for resources is an inevitable feature of health resource allocation, in the market environment fragmentation and competition are augmented, and encourage second guessing. This in turn undermines trust, which is one of the cornerstones of the doctor-patient relationship.

3) Confusion is created in which the wider perspective of the issues relating to a patient's care, and the wider possibilities of their care, are eclipsed. This leaves clinicians uncertain about what treatments make the optimal financial use of resources. Because the tally of accounts can fall between different departments and budgets, patients can feel no one has their overall well being at heart.

4) The concentration of National Health Service (NHS) resources which is an inevitable consequence of the UK reforms means that services are less localised. Patients therefore have less access to specialist resources, which may also be at greater distance, with adverse consequences for equity of care.

This confusion is combined with a lack of moral pointers. In attempting to resolve conflicts, the therapist can become bound up in a tangled and sometimes destructive web. The following clinical examples explore the principal dilemmas identified at the outset:

a) the accessibility of information about the available routes to therapy;

b) the expectations users can be permitted about measurements of treatment outcome;

c) the controversy over long term provision.

THE ACCESSIBILITY OF INFORMATION ABOUT AVAILABLE ROUTES TO THERAPY

There are currently few guiding principles to instruct therapists or users how to resolve possible conflicts arising from financial interests in selecting a cure. At present therapists appear free to inform users, or not, of such issues according to personal preference. The information available to users about treatments appears scarce, haphazard and even contradictory. With the proliferation of different types of therapy and counselling organisations patients can find it hard to know where to seek advice and there are few ways for potential users of services to evaluate resource-based clinical compromises.

The processes which impel a patient in the direction of one therapy or another are difficult to document, but they are not usually accidental. When people instigate the therapy process, a kind of 'tagging' occurs which pushes them in one particular therapeutic direction or another. This happens when the search for therapy begins: with the phone book; the general practitioner; the advice of a friend; or whatever. Already the branches are starting to multiply. The inception of any therapeutic journey combines a filigree of the patient's problems, their chance for information, and the theoretical framework of the referrer, culminating in a visa to the next stage. At different embarkation points patients' therapeutic passports are stamped in ways that direct their journey towards a particular agency or therapist. At some level this mapping is instigated long before the journey's outset, when the problems became troubling enough to require the help of an external agent. It is puzzling that so little has been written about the mechanics of this period, which may be termed 'the acquisition of therapy stage'.

Given the points made earlier (about the life-threatening nature of anorexia nervosa; the stage of denial at onset; the erratic availability of information about possible treatments and their effectiveness; the clinician's interest in ensuring the viability of their service; and the pressures to provide treatment as cheaply as possible) it is not surprising that the diagnostic process is imbued with financial as well as clinical components. Transparent mechanisms regulating the ethical obligations for clinicians and administrators to inform potential users about the limitations and advantages of specific care programmes have not yet evolved. A complete list of available treatments is generally not available or is restricted to those encompassed by the budget of the institution or health authority. Clinicians are no longer encouraged to act as a kind of patient's representative helping the user to gain the best possible treatment (which might be outside the institution or geographical region which serves as the first port of call). Not only is there now no incentive for workers to undertake the advocacy rôle, but prohibitions are sometimes imposed, forbidding referrals to specialist services except by budget controllers. Nor are clinicians furnished with pointers outlining how conflicts should be resolved if there are differences between patients' wishes and/or competing professional views about the cheapest available treatment.

Clinical Example
Jan had had multiple problems for many years and had received many different kinds of short-term support, including family therapy, assertion therapy, cognitive behavioural therapy, and treatments for other symptoms, such as acrophobia in connection with her inability to travel except in certain cars. By the time she was referred to an NHS psychotherapy department the stamp in her passport to therapy seemed to be 'survivor of abuse' because her difficulties appeared to be connected with traumas suffered as a child. Her disassociation about these traumas was so severe it was impossible to know how she found her way into the support services in the initial stages of her various treatments. She herself was reluctant to disclose much about this although she could remember some specific horrifying experiences which she consigned to 'my awful life in Essex'.

In the context of a NHS psychotherapy department her treatment options were limited: individual therapy, group therapy for survivors, or referral for treatment elsewhere. For Jan, the 'survivor' label was relatively new, emerging in the last three years when she remembered instances of abuse. These memories returned only after talking with a counsellor. As for her eating problems, she half admitted using laxatives and feeling fat and overweight, even though she knew she was very thin, walking wherever she could, partly so as not to have to travel in cars and partly to expend calories. She was excessively fastidious about certain foods; for instance, she would not cook in metal pans because particular metals contained poisons. She refused to consume certain food with fibre, such as potatoes and bananas, because she believed they were contaminating. Her eating disorder symptoms had not been addressed in any of her previous treatments and indeed had barely been acknowledged. Her counsellor was determined Jan should be referred to a specialist hospital which treated whole families, while her general practitioner and psychiatrist saw this specialist centre as an expensive option. The counsellor had no access to money for treatment because she worked in a voluntary organisation but remained the clinician in most regular contact with the patient. Jan herself hardly had any contact with those who managed the budgets. The clinicians with direct links to the financial administrators were precisely the ones who required firm indicators justifying treatment at what they regarded as the costly family service.

The dilemmas for the therapist were several-fold: discerning clinically the best course of treatment for Jan; calculating the responses of others about whether and how long it might take to convince those holding the purse strings to fund it; and in persuading Jan to take up whatever option was proposed even if it did not fit with what she wanted. These decisions had to be taken in the knowledge that if one form of treatment did not work, the funders were likely to baulk at further expense. Delays were likely because of the inclusion of these business elements, and political predicaments were inherent in these choices. Just making information available would have repercussions, steering Jan toward one treatment centre or another. Knowledge of different treatments was theoretically available, Jan had only to acquire it. Yet it was not similar to clear transactional information found in the foreign currency markets. There were different ifs, buts and maybes at different stages of intervention. It was more akin to the processes of game theory than the market. Naturally Jan listened most to the clinician, the counsellor, she saw more often, and with whom she had the longest relationship; and made her decisions accordingly.

From the therapist's perspective, it was tempting in part to act as Jan's representative within the health service, steering her towards her preferred family treatment in the specialist hospital. This had political implications because it meant turning a blind eye not only to the question of equity with other service users in the psychotherapy department, but also to the obligation to demonstrate Jan's eligibility for specialist referral. There were no guidelines outlining when it would be appropriate to make an expensive extra-contractual referral (ECR), or how to resolve disagreements between professionals about treatments and costs. In Jan's case the general practitioner and the psychiatrist had already made it clear that they were unlikely to endorse Jan's proposal. There were also moral issues (about collusion with a patient's denial) in view of Jan's reluctance to acknowledge her eating problems (the preferred programme did not offer treatment for eating disorders).

Jan did not get the desired treatment. After meeting the therapist just a few times she flounced out of the consulting room threatening to drive herself into a wall, and missed subsequent appointments. She was determined to acquire what she wanted. Jan was employed as a support worker, and took advice from work colleagues about welfare rights. When she deduced that there would not be an immediate recommendation for special financing she contacted an agency which advised on legal rights. She was convinced that her general practitioner and psychiatrist were trying to prevent her getting the treatment she wanted for financial reasons. However, she needed sanction from the therapist that local services could not help her, in order to warrant the specialist referral. She believed that the therapist was being weak with the doctors and later approached several more advice agencies to discuss her legal position.

Jan judged that collecting information about the different treatments was to be 'branding myself as bulimic! Even though I know these things are part of my difficulties, I will not put myself in that bracket'. In many ways, given the lack of trust Jan described in her formative experiences, her position here was reasonable: she should follow the advice of the person she trusted the most, her counsellor. It felt pointless, even unprofessional, for the therapist try to convince her that confrontation with fundholders was futile. The counsellor had tried this and failed. Britton (1989) has shown how the divisions in the family systems are often mirrored in the professional network when a patient's issues are complex and the potential for splitting is rife. Different professionals can assume alliances and positions which re-enact those taken by individuals in the family. In this case, it was possible to conjecture that the professionals (therapist, general practitioner, psychiatrist and counsellor) in her network might be mirroring some family pattern which Jan was trying to resolve in the present perhaps by repeating earlier traumas.

Adding financial constraints to these tensions imposed in Jan's case a further tier of complications between the user and the professional networks. This acted as an impediment to treatment, and increased Jan's mistrust. This was made more intractable by the absence of guidelines to help clinicians negotiate their ethical dilemmas by balancing the needs of the individual against those of other patients and potential patients. Without sufficient knowledge of how public funds are apportioned or from which budgets, it was impossible for the therapist to judge the fairness of Jan's wish to go to the hospital offering the family treatment. Yet Jan required the therapist's permission because the funders had stipulated that the psychotherapy department should demonstrate she was unable to receive therapeutic help from her local services. The competitive need to apportion limited resources effectively created in Jan's case webs of administration and bureaucracy, and caused delays. Market forces were corrosive of trust because they engendered unnecessary stress and provoked the second guessing of motives. This went on between all parties, not just between professionals, but also between the patient and service providers.

For patients like Jan who have survived abuse, trust in the treatment relationship is a precious commodity. At times the experience of trust and respect in the treatment relationship can be a patient's first experience of it. Hence they become bewildered and frightened, needing to find ways to test out this new confidence. Without trust and respect, relationships with those in authority can become semi-legal relationships, as happened when Jan resorted to the legal and advice agencies. Prior to marketisation, there was less confusion; less need for administration; probably fewer delays; and greater accessibility in service provision. Some of the moral dilemmas inherent for clinicians in working with a patient like Jan might be more easily resolved if it were possible to offer patients and potential users complete information about treatment outcomes.

THE MEASUREMENT OF OUTCOME IN RELATION TO THE
PRINCIPLES OF TREATMENT

It has been argued that the market places pressures on providers to increase their volume of care while reducing its cost, implying shorter-term treatment for a greater number. Fundholders, however, do not always appear to assess volumes or costs against likelihood of relapse or recurrence of illness. Financial restrictions could galvanise clinicians into greater clarity about what long- and short-term therapies can do, and how this differs from other treatments. This assumes that differentiations in outcome can be evaluated. In this respect, research such as that of Russell *et al.* (1987) ratifies the idea that in terms of anorexia nervosa some measures of outcome can be formulated. Other proposals of measurement and value have been drawn up; Fonagy and Higgett (1989), for example, outlined items of clinical audit and listed selection outcome measures (the views of patient, therapists, relatives, independent experts and so on). But as they comment, 'with over a thousand potential measures to choose from, and the experience of at least an equal number of previous studies to draw upon, the identification of a small number of outcome measures to be generally used within all units in the same service, remains primarily a question of logistics and goodwill!'.

Luborsky, Crits-Christoph, Mintz, and Auerbach (1988) have also considered who benefits from psychotherapy. They found that

> the final outcomes of psychotherapy are predicted significantly but only modestly from some types of initial information about the patient, while information about the therapist apart from the treatment adds relatively little to predictability. As long as the basis for prediction rests on pre-treatment evaluation, not much improvement in prediction seems likely because the more crucial predictive factors may not be apparent until the patient and therapist have had a chance to interact. Since most patients begin to show benefits in the course of psychotherapy, by examining sessions we should be able to discern when and how benefits develop. For patients who benefited most, but not for those who benefited least, an early working alliance developed.

Few pre-treatment pointers exist to help the clinician to identify the basis on which, or the stage at which, decisions are made about transfer of their users either to private services or to alternatives if health service funding is not forthcoming, or which settings are most conducive to the establishment of a working alliance. There is a paucity of provision filling the gap between privately and publicly funded services which is barely met by self-help or low cost services. It would be an abuse of the user and the various short-term focused methods if brief therapy or self-help manuals and groups become the covert basis for the reduction of services, or if clinicians are compelled by funders or funding systems to offer short term services.

Haley (1990) argues this has occurred in the United States. Like Vogler (1993), he makes a direct connection between the interests of funders and clinical decisions about thereapy. 'Obviously therapy is going to become shorter because of the ways it is financed. Just as it was discovered that hospitalisation could be more brief when the insurance companies decided that, so therapy will become briefer as insurance companies limit the length of therapy' (Haley, 1990). Resources tailored to limited and possibly insufficient budgets are comparable to trying to feed humans on starvation rations. Increased focus on short-term treatments could limit their effectiveness, because like all therapeutic strategies they are geared to producing change for specific patient groups. Therapists are often faced with the choice of offering a treatment (possibly short-term) which may be considered best use of available resources, but hardly tailored to the patient. The dynamics of supply and demand are not readily translatable into therapeutic terms; counting costs is a short-term preoccupation not always commensurate with a patient's long-term health.

It is the uncertainties of the therapeutic process, in particular the relational aspects of the treatment, which cause problems. There are patients who have been successful in accessing short term provision for therapy in a number of health care environments, generating a treatment history which is *ad hoc* rather than driven by their treatment needs. While some research findings offer guidance to the most expedient treatment strategies no clear methods exist for disseminating this information to users. Even on the rare occasions when those afflicted do encounter treatments that follow the research on outcomes, it is impossible to be sure that an accurate diagnosis can be made in the early stages or that estimations of the likely duration of the illness will be exact, as the following example demonstrates.

Clinical Example

Jo probably first began starving herself when she was about 11, but no one noticed how thin she had become until she was about 15. On the face of it her symptoms were neither serious or chronic. She was performing excellently academically and was a champion swimmer, but this locked her into an enmeshed relationship with her mother, who took her to competitions and training. Jo said later that part of her obsession with being thin came from some guidance a coach had given her, when she was 14, about achieving a weight well below average for Jo's height. Her family first began to suspect something was wrong when Jo was 15 because she could not sustain her usual stamina for swimming. Nonetheless it was not until after she was 18, when her maternal grandmother died, that Jo's starving became acute. Between 15 and 19 Jo received two lots of family therapy, first in an NHS hospital and then in a private hospital.

Her mother went to the family's general practitioner for advice. He was unusually well informed about eating problems, and had heard that family therapy was one of the better treatment options for adolescents, so the family were referred to the family therapy department at the local NHS hospital. Jo refused to allow her family to come to the sessions but was seen individually for 8 months. Her family felt their knowledge of what was happening with Jo was not valued by those trying to treat her. Their pique was exacerbated some years later, when Jo was nearly 18 and her weight fell to 32 kilos. These sessions ended unsuccessfully and Jo went to university only 'to flunk out 18 months later'.

When Jo left university the family were referred again for family therapy with different family therapists, this time to a private hospital where Jo had now to be an inpatient for a period because she had become so thin. In these later sessions the family were able to describe themselves as a 'high tech family' because everyone was adept with computers and other modern technologies. Jo spent much of her time in the hospital playing games on the computer. Later the family attributed this proficiency with machine technology to be 'their vehicle of self-reliance' and thought it reflected their ability and keenness 'to preserve their privacy, especially from professionals'. The family had interpreted Jo's individual attendance at the first lot of family therapy as a 'lack of concern by the helping systems' and this reinforced their 'suspiciousness of state interventions'. By the time they met the family therapists in the private hospital they had become more fixed in their convictions that those 'meant to be helping did not care enough to even find out what actually went on'.

Jo's father died when she was 18 months old and her mother felt compelled to work in a local authority nursery. Mother was appalled at the practices in this nursery, and this fostered in her the conviction that most children of single parents 'could be whisked away into care, just like that!'. Jo recounted on many occasions how she found her maternal grandmother supportive and caring, indulging her food fads and cooking her special meals. She characterised her maternal grand-father, however, as a 'drunken brute'. When Jo was five mother met John and married him. The reconstituted household included Jo, older sister Clare, mother, step-father John, the maternal grandparents and eventually a half-brother and half-sister, born from the second mar-riage. Jo oscillated in her feelings for Clare and John. Sometimes John would be considered 'thoughtful and restrained' and Jo dismissed her sister Clare as 'horrible and awful'. At other times the pattern could be inverted and John would be denigrated as 'weak and pathetic, not standing up to my mother' and her sister Clare elevated to someone 'who is getting on much better now she has stopped taking drugs'.

There seemed an approximate pattern to these fluctuating attach-ments and a strong possibility they were related to, or had an important bearing on, Jo's starving, because they had begun after a 'violent family row and acrimonious scene'. Everyone agreed this scene inaug-urated Jo's eating problems. Prior to this row, Jo was 'the good one swimming and studying' but afterwards Clare (who had been seen by mother as 'rebellious and awkward') settled down to a respons-ible job while Jo became 'anorectic and difficult'. Any attempts to unravel the meaning of these patterns of interaction in the family sessions went back to the acrimonious scene, pulled like a screen across the family's real story. Professionals speculated about the grandfather's possible abuse of Jo and her mother, but there were no explanations forthcoming of the bearing, if any, this might have had on Jo's anorexia.

In the second family therapy treatment these explorations and any references to abuse were referred to as 'Damocles' sword casting a shadow over everyone in the family'. The rapport with the family therapist was better but Jo protested she found more support and companionship with one of the nurses on the ward. Again Jo was determined not to be seen with her family; confiding to this nurse she felt that she was being forced to invite her family to the sessions. This time the family attended some sessions, but without Jo because she was so adamant. This fact of itself posed an ethical dilemma because Jo conceded in one breath she 'needed the family to come', and protested in the next that her agreement to their attendance was 'procured in a no-win situation about discharge from the hospital'. The sessions were held sequentially, usually with Jo alone followed by one or two sessions with Jo's mother alone; Jo's mother and stepfather, and one with sister Clare. All the therapeutic conversations were conducted mindful of the presence of others.

The family managed to conjure a sense that change could happen at any moment, but privacy and the maintenance of a system closed to outside interference was paramount. Alongside this was Jo's resolute maintenance of her low weight and her continued low calorie intake. The therapist was tantalised by the continuing hope of change. For example, the stepfather challenged Jo's mother about being over-involved with Jo's food shopping and cooking even now that Jo had managed to move into her own bedsit. On another occasion Jo summoned the courage to ask her mother long withheld questions about her father, only to be disappointed when her mother responded by saying 'give me a list of what things you want to know' rather than engaging in dialogue about her father.

By the time Jo was 22, other kinds of therapies, such as cognitive behavioural therapy and psychotherapy had to be introduced into her treatment programme because her eating problems appeared to have become so ingrained. In hindsight the overall picture was clearer: her problem was more pervasive than initially envisaged. The family were outraged and complained that when Jo first became ill they should have been more thoroughly appraised of the availability and effective-ness of different treatments which they equated with 'purchasing technical equipment, like a computer'. Neither Jo nor her family 'felt therapy played a part in her improved eating habits or weight gain'. They believed 'no one held overall responsiblity and there was no holistic assessment, just snatches here and there, depending on what could be funded'. They were dissatisfied that no full diagnosis had been made at the outset. The therapists felt hampered by the conflict-ing demands of their roles: the demand for them to provide treatment expediently in juxtapostion with the therapeutic obligation to tolerate uncertainty as part of the cure.

Giving the patient an experience that the therapist knows how to bear uncertainty may be an essential ingredient in recovery from anorexia nervosa, where bodily symptoms act as nerve centres regulating somatically processes which otherwise might be con-trolled dynamically or systemically. In this context the origin of the word burden (from the old English word *beran*, meaning to bear, labour or give birth) is evocative of the therapist's generative task.

THE CONTROVERSY ABOUT LONG TERM PROVISION

There seems to be a tacit controversy about the merits and shortfalls of long- and short-term therapy in the literature about therapy generally, as well as for anorexia nervosa specifically. In the public sector the availability of long-term treatment is limited and resources appear to be dominated by notions of 'short-term', 'cost-effective' and 'accountable'. The advocates of short-term treatment are epitomised by writers such as Bryant-Waugh and Lask (1995) who argue: 'There have been no studies demonstrating any benefits from long-term individual therapy'. They suggest further: 'In the present state of knowledge and particularly when there are financial constraints, preference should be given to shorter term treatments and cognitive techniques for adult patients, and family counselling and therapy for children and adolescents'. Watson and Ryle (1992) propound the introduction of universal attempts at brief therapy in the public arena as a first intervention for most patients who would benefit from psychological treatment. Such propositions are doubtless music to the controllers of the public budgets.

In the USA, it is already difficult to fund eating disorder treatments for adolescents. Anorexia nervosa tends to be treated as a psychiatric condition under health insurance policies and increasingly younger patients are being treated in paediatric or adolescent medicine facilities by 'behavioural paediatricians'. They can, customarily, expect relatively uncomplicated support from the parents of the patients, and do not have clear professional models for dealing with demoralised, psychologically disturbed, or problematic or confrontational parents. Family work (family therapy, family counselling) has been evolved either within child and adolescent psychiatry or in non-medical settings with non-medical practitioners. The long history of the clinical encounter between physicians and anorectic patients shows the hazards of collaboration between medical practitioner and parents, and it is rare in treatment programmes within paediatric or adolescent facilities to include family therapy, the one treatment shown by scientific evaluation to be effective in anorexia nervosa.

Brief solutions fit with financial constraints but hardly enlarge research or understanding in a field where all workers concur with the idea that no one has a precise answer as to either the causes or cure for anorexia. Dare and Crowther (1995) say: 'Trials of psychoanalytic psychotherapy are hard to fund, elaborate to execute and contradict some of the firmly held principles of the usual psychodynamic techniques. For this reason such trials are rarely undertaken, although currently most cases of anorexia nervosa are likely to require some form of psychotherapy'. Holmes and Lindley (1987) suggest that there is a paucity of therapeutic resources in the United Kingdom and that those that do exist are being eroded by cuts. Current market patterns mean that clinicians have fewer incentives either to pool their expertise or strive to develop their understanding of areas where their knowledge is more limited.

However, issues of measurement are fraught with difficulty. As the management academic Henry Mintzberg (1996) observes: 'Many activities are in the public sector precisely because of measurement problems: if everything was so crystal clear and every benefit so easily attributable, those activities would have been in the private sector long ago'. Mintzberg cites an example from the UK's National Health Service, in which a surgeon operated on ten liver transplant patients, of whom two died. The surgeon's measure of success was 8 out of 10. The nurses put the success rate at 3 out of 10, counting only the patients who had later been able to resume normal working lives. Other professionals had different estimates between the two. Mintzberg says: 'Picture yourself having to make your own assessment. Where is the magic envelope with the one right answer? You won't find it'. Mintzberg pinpoints precisely how recovery in health can be partial and protracted. A patient's overwhelming wish is usually to get well as quickly as possible, but it can take time for the awareness to dawn that the solution to mental health problems does not always come in days or weeks. How this understanding comes for the user varies but it is often formed in the nexus of communication between the provider and the patient. This is where issues of accountability and responsibility are negotiated. This nexus is subsumed in issues of values and ethics which at times can be paradoxical if patient and therapist are at loggerheads about treatment, as Jan's and Jo's stories illustrate. Even if the user and provider are in agreement about treatment under the market system the fear remains that there may be some other better treatment available that is being withheld for financial reasons. As argued earlier, this can jeopardise trust and possibly induces stress. The impact of stress as an impairing factor in recovery could be exacerbated by the increased emphasis on financial cost which itself has a price. This imposes an increased responsibility on clinicians to resolve any ethical dilemmas which might be evoked. For reasons of confidentiality this often has to be accomplished in professional semi-isolation. The new financial systems introduce an added level of secrecy associated with competitive business. Providers of services are limited only to dispensing treatment within their remit; workers realise they have to pitch against other service providers to remain competitive and protect their place in the market. This can give clinicians an incentive to be guarded about the information they disclose.

There seem currently to be few principles guiding therapists in evaluating the apportioning of existing expenditure, or in weighing the pecuniary balance in terms of overall provision between the benefits of longer term work, such as psychotherapy, against the advantages of shorter-term 'solution based' therapies. Nor (in the UK) does the Patients' Charter provide easy access to information about how the process of appeal against medical decisions works in practice or how to implement the leverage which can be exerted by requests for second opinions. Questioning treatment proposals presupposes that there are clear, agreed and accessible reports documenting the range of treatment options; there are not. Nor is there much recognition by health organisations in the UK, such as The Patients' Association or The College of Health, about the lack of information or the delays caused by negotiations about funding. Further, in some cases even where there should be no interference from administrators on clinical matters, decisions are questioned.

At best users have a formal right of appeal, or can try to exert leverage by an actual or an implied request for a second opinion. In such a context, even acquiring the information about how to do this, let alone its relevance or purpose, can become an insidious and rather covert practice. It can endanger reasonable working relationships between providers and users which may have taken some time to build. These working relationships can be damaged and may in worse cases complicate the potential for future treatments, especially if the course of treatment is not the patient's first preference.

Most resources in the public sector are oriented towards treatments of less than one or two years duration, and when someone has been unwell for a long period it is not always possible to complete the treatment in the time available. This causes lack of continuity and alterations in care programmes. This occurs in the private sector too, and patients may have to alter their treatment programmes when funds are no longer available. Consideration is not always given to how the severance of connections in relationships affect the continuity of a patient's treatment. For the patient, moving from one hospital or treatment centre inevitably means making a new set of relationships with clinical staff. Weaving an ethical course through the maze of money and medical cures can exacerbate these pressures.

At the outset the point was made about the life-threatening nature of anorexia nervosa. In this context it would seem critical to include a case which exemplifies the life and death nature of the therapist's clinical decisions when systems are failing. The case illustration which follows resulted tragically in the patient's death. In the professional literature few clinical examples document circumstances where patients are instrumental in bringing about their own end. The shame and isolation of such a deed is easily mirrored among the professionals who tend to shy away from public efforts to process the chains of actions and events which culminate in a patient's death.

Clinical Example

Kylie was admitted to a private hospital for eating disorders with an initial diagnosis of 'multi-impulsive bulimia'. She had a history of self-harming behaviour since she was 15 as well as depression and serious suicide attempts. There were no beds and no service in the NHS facility, so she was admitted under a specialist funding referral for treatment of her eating disorder. She responded well to the hospital regime and her disordered eating behaviour rapidly diminished. But during her admission there were problems in obtaining funding and pressure was exerted by the Health Commission (which monitors funding) to transfer her to the NHS facility.

Her condition began to deteriorate and she displayed depressive and possibly psychotic symptoms. Professionals and family, who were grappling with treatment strategies, complained of feelings of isolation and of lack of liaison between previous and future therapists. Her parents intimated that Kylie had no energy to form relationships with professionals because she had 'lost faith that any relationships would be sustained for more than a few months' and there were mutterings about second opinions. The lack of finance seemed a metaphor for a lack of security for her in her treatment programme. No liaison with the NHS staff was forthcoming, leaving staff caring for her uncertain and anxious about her. Anxiety about her placement, status in hospital, and her treatment worsened her clinical condition.

The following letter written by her parents conveys their mood at the time: 'Kylie was admitted for bulimia. Considerable progress has been made, particularly in recent weeks, in overcoming the problem. This had been due to the special care and attention from the doctors and staff at the private hospital. The underlying cause of the eating disorder had more recently been identified as clinical depression for which Kylie is now being treated. Throughout her treatment she has found the psychotherapy sessions invaluable in helping to identify the underlying reasons for her depression. Her key nurse has been very kind and supportive throughout as have all the other staff under the expert guidance of her consultant. We are very concerned at the possibility of our daughter having to move to another hospital to continue her treatment. It has taken her a long time to begin to talk to staff following her admission. We feel that a move would have a very detrimental effect on her present state of mind and progress to recovery.'

This patient's despair and depressive symptoms became increasingly evident with some psychotic features. She was treated with neuroleptic agents and anti-depressants and was making progress, but the underlying concern in the staff was the need to treat her quickly before funding was withdrawn. Treatment as a day patient was hastened. During her two weeks as a day patient she became increasingly anxious and agitated with psychotic elements to her beliefs. Her mood was so low that she was re-admitted with suicidal intent as an emergency. At this point she was allowed only one week's stay pending transfer to NHS care. It was impossible to treat her in a week, and clinical decisions were being delayed by the uncertainty of her placement. There was no smooth transition arranged. After one week's assessment the clinical decision was made pragmatically that it must be assumed she would stay in the private hospital for her treatment until clarification about the financial arrangements was forthcoming. She was clearly suicidal at the time. Her sleep was disturbed with bad dreams, but there was no recurrence of eating disorder.

Kylie was suicidally depressed again two weeks later and there was still no clarity about the financial decisions. This meant clinical decisions had to be made on an interim basis, while controversies within the professionals and between family and professional networks were highlighted. She was closely observed for the next month and her mood began to brighten. The close observation (15 minute checks) necessitated an increase in staff and thus an increase in payment by the Health Commission. Pressure for explanations and queries about the length of such observation led to a climate of uncertainty about the likely continued support.

It seemed to the therapists that the instability created by the delays in the financial decision making went on too long. Only a fraction of the negotiations surrounding the monitoring (i.e. alterations in the intensity of observation by staff) can be documented here, but it should be noted that the effect on those working closely was evidently wearing. In her last days she was still felt to be at risk, so she was again placed on intensive close observation. When her mood was brighter, she began discussing Christmas and her future at college. Things changed when a nurse observed that there was redness around her neck, and Kylie said that momentarily she used the cord of her dressing gown to try to strangle herself. Again she was closely observed at her own request. She then spent the remainder of the day with her mother, went to bed without incident and was looking forward to her father coming to pick her up the following morning. She was checked at 10 pm by the staff nurse. At 10.15 the staff nurse entered the room and found her hanging from the shower curtain metal rail. At that point Kylie lost consciousness and required resuscitation. She died a few days later, never having regained consciousness.

There is little doubt that the insecurity engendered in staff, family and patient contribute to a metaphor of illness and funding. 'Starvation' of funding can lead to early discharge and hasty decisions. 'Bingeing' on funds can lead to a short and over-full programme. Suspicion, anger and uncertainty within staff does not convey to patients the sense of calm which is required in many psychiatric cases. There are also needs to be addressed in relation to the necessary passage of time for minds to heal. We know that in treatment of anorexia nervosa, the real cure comes when the thinking surrounding food is abated, not when the anorectic reaches target weight.

The family and professionals involved are still trying to assimilate the shattering impact of Kylie's death. On rare occasions they construct from the shards fragments of understanding. For example, some professionals have pondered about connections between her death and the transgenerational links connecting Kylie's realistic fantasies that her mother and maternal grandmother's family lost many relatives in the holocaust. Indeed including her story in this chapter is an attempt to provide one such strand developing the theoretical thinking about patient deaths.

CONCLUSION

A therapist cannot work in isolation from society, disconnected from the forces which shape their world and that of their patients. These forces include those which shape health provision and, more generally, changes in the expectations that patients bring to the therapeutic process, together with changes in the structure of society itself. At the same time, it is reasonable to assert that there are core values to which therapists must try to remain attached in framing their work. The core value identified in this chapter as being under threat from the current changes in the structure of health services is that of trust. It is fundamental to the therapeutic process, and without it, some would say, our work is built on sand.

Analysing similar phenomena Hildebrand (1976) predicted that 'a psychoanalytic variant of Gresham's Law would come into operation with bad work driving out good, and the result would be ... a lowering of ethical standards at great cost to patients and analysts'. He suggested then that psychotherapists and psychoanalysts should combine in 'a patrician posture of simultaneous attachment and acceptance'. The changes in the intervening twenty years have reinforced Hildebrand's prediction. Organisations which used to operate as clubs, held together by the shared assumptions of peer groups, no longer do so (Carmichael, 1995). But the ethical rules which have replaced them are at best poorly articulated and at worst unclear. Today's organisations are flatter and thinner. Above all, they have less time. Now, the adoption of a similar position of 'attachment and acceptance' might require a therapist to find ways of combining psychotherapy with brief therapy. Looking ahead ten years, or less, the integration into these processes of digital and network technology seems certain, with the possible implication of counselling by videophone, or even by e-mail. How this integration will impact on treatments such as eating disorders, where non-verbal cues are intrinsic, is unclear.

While one should not resist unnecessarily the use of new technology (support groups for those with eating disorders can already be found on the internet) one has to be concerned about the effect of a disembodied relationship in therapy, which runs counter to the human and personalised spirit of the endeavour. In treating anorexia nervosa, such disembodiment would collude with one of its inherent contradictions; that life and human relationships can be conducted without prerequisite bodily experiences such as food and nurture.

The speed of change (financial, managerial, and technological) will increase, and therapists need to be able to respond on different levels. The first level is purely pragmatic: that which can be done in hospitals and community services to reduce ethical conflicts and identify them. Inside hospitals, an evaluation of possible conflicts of interest between the duty of care to the patient and the responsibility of the organisation to its funders could be added to the assessment process for each patient, making it necessary for discussion and evaluation of the issue for each individual patient as they enter the system. Further, it needs to be possible for patients to find and trust information. Therapists need to find ways of evaluating the advice which they give to potential patients for its self-interest (organisational or personal); effectiveness; and its contribution to their patient's overall health. More needs to be known about the routes which patients find into therapy (a barely researched area). Information about therapy, both generally and specifically, could be improved. Therapists need to be aware of the existing information resources (usually print-based) and the potential of new ones (such as the electronic World Wide Web, an effective way of publicising material at low cost). None of these, however, are a substitute for the larger, tougher, project of protecting and developing the ethical frameworks within which therapists operate. The critical issue is that the introduction of market systems fragments health services and forces professionals to focus on their own unit and its continuing organisational survival. In this structure it is harder to hold onto either the ethical frameworks essential to health care or even the values of the health system as a whole. Competition replaces co-operation. Trust is reduced to individual exchange.

The question, therefore, in the face of fragmentation, is who, or what, holds on to the values which are essential to the well-being of the system as a whole. The non-market values underpinning health care are being destroyed by the spread of market values within health institutions. Traditionally, the professional organis-ations encouraged therapists to reflect the sentiments of the Hippocratic oath which were encoded and often realised at a pragmatic and clinical level in consistency; the comradeship of peer support; respect; the rewards of job satisfaction; and faith. Now, the evaluation of treatment tends to reflect what can be done with the available cash.

The attack on the ethical base of therapeutic work represented by the market, and the decline of trust that follows it, cause real costs to health services. It should not be the task of therapists – individually or collectively – to carry that cost for the system as a whole. This should be done by funders, at the highest possible level in the system. It is, though, the job of therapists and clinicians to articulate the problem so that fundholders can recognise it and act to change the structures of the system. If they do nothing the very core of their profession could be washed away.

REFERENCES

Belbin, R.M. (1981) *Management teams*, Oxford: Butterworth-Heinemann.
Britton, R.S. (1981) 'Re-enactment as an unwitting professional response to family dynamics.' In Box, S. (ed.), *Psychotherapy with families*, London: Routledge Kegan Paul.
Bruch, H. (1973) *Eating disorders: Obesity, anorexia nervosa, and the person within*, New York: Basic Books.
Bryant-Waugh, R., and Lask, B. (1995) 'Eating disorders and overview.' *Journal of Family Therapy*, 17: 13–31.
Carmichael, S. (1995) *Business ethics: The new bottom line*, London: Demos.
Dare, C. and Crowther, C. (1995) 'Living dangerously: Psychoanalytic psychotherapy of anorexia nervosa.' In Szmukler, G. et al. (eds) *Handbook of eating disorders: Theory, treatment and research*, Chich-ester-New York: John Wiley.

Fairbairn, C. (1995) *Overcoming bulimia*, London and New York: Guilford Press.

Fallon, P., Katzman, M.A., and Wooley, S.C. (eds) (1994) *Feminist perspectives on eating disorders*, London-New York: Guilford Press.

Fukuyama, F. (1995) *Trust*, London: Hamish Hamilton.

Fonagy, P. and Higgett, A. (1989) 'Evaluating performance of departments of psychotherapy.' *Psychoanalytic Psychotherapy*, 4: 2121–53.

Gray, J. (1993) *Beyond the New Right*, London: Routledge.

Gresko, R.B. and Karlsen, A. (1994) 'The Norwegian program for the primary, secondary and tertiary prevention of eating disorders.' *Eating Disorders*, 2: 57–63.

Haley, J. (1995) 'Why not long term therapy?' In Zeig, J.K. and Gilligan, S.K. (eds) *Brief therapy: Myths, methods and metaphors*, New York: Brunner/Mazel.

Handy, C.B. (1989) *The age of unreason*, London: Business Books.

——(1993) *Understanding organisations* (4th ed), London: Penguin.

Harris, J. (1987) 'Qualifying the value of life.' *Journal of Medical Ethics*, 13: 117–23.

Hildebrand, P. (1967) 'Reflections on the future of psychoanalysis.' *International Review of Psychoanalysis*, 3: 323–30.

Holmes, J. and Lindley, R. (1989) *The values of psychotherapy*, Oxford: Oxford University Press.

Hutton, W. (1995) *The state we're in*, London: Jonathan Cape.

Jaggar, A. and Bordo, S. (eds) (1989) *Gender/body/knowledge: Feminist reactions of being and knowing*, New Brunswick, NJ: Rutgers University Press.

Luborsky, L., Crits-Cristoph, P., Mintz, J. and Auerbach, A. (1988) *Who will benefit from psychotherapy?*, New York: Basic Books.

Mintzberg, H. (1996) 'Managing government, governing management.' *Harvard Business Review*, Spring/Summer.

Morgan, G. (1993) *Imaginization*, London: Sage Publications.

Mulgan, G. (1993) 'Re-inventing the BBC.' In Mulgan, G. and Paterson, R. (eds) *Re-inventing the organisation*, London: British Film Institute.

Office for National Statistics (1994) *Vital statistics*, 3, London: HMSO.

Organisation for Economic Co-operation and Development, (1995) *New directions in health care policy* (Health Policy Studies No 7), Paris: OECD.

Ormerod, P. (1994) *The death of economics*, London: Faber and Faber.

Orbach, S. (1986) *Hunger strike*, New York: Avon.

Parston, G. (1993) 'Public service, public management and the BBC.' In

Mulgan, G. and Paterson, R. (eds) *Re-inventing the organisation*, London: British Film Institute.

Peters, T. (1994) *The Tom Peters seminar*, London: Macmillan.

Ratnasuriya, R., Eisler, I., Szmukler, G. and Russell, G. (1991) 'Anorexia nervosa: Outcome and prognosis after twenty years.' *British Journal of Psychiatry*, 158: 495–502.

Ruark, J.E., Raffin, T.A. and Stanford University Medical Center Committee on Ethics (1988) 'Initiating and withdrawing life support.' *New England Journal of Medicine*, 318: 25–30.

Russell, G., Szmukler, G., Dare, C. and Eisler, A. (1987) 'An evaluation of family therapy in anorexia nervosa and bulimia nervosa.' *Archives of General Psychiatry*, 44: 1047–50.

Schmidt, U. and Treasure, J. (1995) *Getting better bit(e) by bit(e)*, London: Lawrence Erlbaum.

Shaoul, J. (1996) *NHS Trusts – a capital way of operating*, Unpublished paper: University of Manchester Department of Accounting and Finance.

Vandereycken, W. and van Deth, R. (1995) *From fasting saints to anorexic girls*, London: Athlone Press.

Vogler, R.J.M. (1993) *The medicalisation of eating: social control in an eating disorders clinic*, London: JAI Press.

Watson, J. and Ryle, A. (1992) 'Providing a psychotherapy service to an inner London catchment area.' *Journal of Mental Health*, 1: 176–96.

CHAPTER ELEVEN

Treatment of eating disorders in the context of managed health care in the United States: A clinician's perspective

Arnold E. Andersen

INTRODUCTION

The term managed care is shorthand in the United States for the true phrase, management of the costs of health care. Many currently accepted life style norms for doctors of medicine including high status and high income, modes of payment for doctors (third party payment instead of payment by patients directly), and location of treatment (hospitals not homes), have been present for only about fifty years. A radical rethinking of health care finance in the United States is essential because of multiple changes in medical care including an exponential increase in the costs of health care, increasingly effective but expensive diagnostic and therapeutic procedures, an aging population, costly technical means to extend life, the expense of AIDS, and the increased number of poor, immigrant, and minority populations who have inadequate or no health care coverage. Traditional benefactor financing for hospital deficits is no longer possible.

Many recent changes in the financing of medical care are positive or neutral, timely, and rational, including coverage of lives rather than fee for service payment, transition from inpatient to outpatient location for most treatment and teaching, and a restoration of a more equal balance between generalists and specialists. Intermixed with these positive or neutral and rational trends have been predatory, inhumane and irresponsible changes based on the assumption that health care is simply a business commodity. The unethical trends in profit-orientated managed care corporations include maximization of income for health maintenance organizations (HMOs) through minimization of patient care, deceptive contract practices, skimming off ('cherry picking') of healthy patients for contracts while avoiding the chronically ill, and setting up abusive behavioral and financial disincentives for clinicians in order to obtain approval for care for patients and just compensation for themselves, while rewarding doctors for not providing expensive options, often concealing these facts through contact clauses requiring secrecy.

The out of date and unscientific division of illnesses into medical versus psychiatric can no longer be defended or tolerated. The under-funding of disorders labeled 'psychiatric' must be discontinued since major psychiatric disorders are more biological in origin than the major chronic adult medical illnesses such as heart disease and cancer. Eating disorders have been especially ravaged by United States managers of health care financing because of the frequent need for extended treatment and because of efforts to trivialize these disorders as not being serious disorders. A mandate is required for parity in funding of mental and psychiatric disorder in general, and for the utilization of combined medical and psychiatry benefits for the care of eating disordered patients in particular. More radical solutions such as single party (government) payment and the rationing of care for all illnesses are on the American horizon.

Fears of excessive use of psychiatric benefits leading to increased health care costs have been shown to be unfounded. Adequate psychiatric care at parity with medical care for funding actually decreases overall health care expenses for corporations. Depression, for example, is recognized to be an economic burden second only to heart disease in national health costs. A tradition of humane and scientific care will negotiate a healthy balance between national health care needs and present economic realities, between realism and idealism, between rights and responsibilities for all parties concerned. Managed care denial of health benefits for patients provokes stressful psychological responses in caregivers. The moral tradition of medicine will reject 'gag' rules that deny frank discussions with patients of all beneficial treatments,

Table 1: Recent Trends in Health Care and Financing in the United States 1945–1995.

- Relatively recent rise over the last 50 years in the status and especially the income of physicians.
- Rapid proliferation of specialties, with the income of technical/invasive specialties twice that of family practice.
- Compensatory decrease in the number of primary care physicians.Increased role of government in many areas of life, including the economics of health care and supervision of practice.
- Increased expectations for doctors to cure disease and to prevent death.
- Perceived decrease in physicians as compassionate and caring.

financial conflicts of interest between giving care and being compensated, or unnecessary disclosure of confidential information about patient care.

The topic of managed care in medicine in general, in psychiatry specifically, and in eating disorders in particular, has aroused concern, anxiety, anger, and a variety of distressing behavioral and psychological responses from administrators, clinicians and patients. The evolving recent changes in the financing of medical care in the United States are best understood by appreciating the broader perspective of paradigm changes in the financing of American medicine over the last half century. The challenge of dealing with managed health care is only one change in modern medical life, but one which demands the perspective of history, and a pro-active rather than a re-active or passive response.

HISTORICAL REVIEW

Paul Starr, in his historically rigorous book *The Social Transformation of American Medicine* (1982) describes the tremendous changes that have occurred in American medicine from 1760 to the present, with special emphasis on the recent half-century. Many of the features of the current practice of medicine that are being threatened by managed health care are, in fact, rather new aspects of medicine. Table 1 summarizes some of these recent changes. It is only in the last fifty years, since the end of World War II, that the status and even more so, the income of physicians, have risen significantly. Before that time, while physicians were often respected members of a community, they were usually modestly compensated, sometimes in kind by food, as physicians made rounds to patients' homes and offered comfort if not cure, for many illnesses.

Since World War II there has been a rapid development of medical specialties, with the result that specialists practicing invasive or technological procedures earn approximately twice as much as primary care practitioners. Third party payer insurance was originated primarily by the need for reimbursement in surgical treatments and for inpatient hospital care. Along with the increase in specialists and subspecialists has come a decrease in the number and status of primary care practitioners, but with some signs of reversal of this trend in the past ten years. Currently, 70 per cent or more of most university medical center residency training focuses on producing specialists instead of generalists. Basic training in the primary care fields of pediatrics and internal medicine often leads to additional training in subspecialties.

Intermixed with these changes in status, income, and the balance between primary versus specialty care, has come an enormous increase in the role of government in many areas of life, including the process of medical reimbursement, the extension of health care to more people, and increasingly, the monitoring of medical practice. The public, additionally, has changed from its past view of seeing physicians as helpers at the entrances and exits of life, offering care, compassion, and occasionally effective treatment, to increasingly demanding from them, impossible expectations for cure and avoidance of death. At the same time, the general public increasingly perceives physicians as less compassionate, more greedy and emotionally unavailable. Whether the 'good old days' were basically rotten, as Margaret Mead is reported to have suggested, or whether they were in fact, a more humane, tender, and caring time, remains a subject for historians. It is a fact, however, that those past days, good or bad, will never return.

Medicine has changed dramatically in its effectiveness. Enormous economic issues are now involved in health care, and, finally, a state of tension between hope and cynicism, anger and trust, permeates modern medical practice for both patients and practitioners alike. Few issues are more sensitive to most physicians than the economics of medical care. No other profession requires the extraordinary length of training, expense of training, denial of short-term rewards, or the intense, arduous and focused daily life, than the practice of medicine. It would be illogical to demand that physicians not receive reasonable compensation for their past training and current practice, but therein lies the rub. Should physicians be compensated for their training and difficulty of practice entirely by standard market forces? What is the role of ethics and morals in practice? Is being a provider of medical care the same as being a provider of manufactured goods, of entertainment, or modern services of convenience? American medicine has a very complex and contradictory history in its response to the need for change in financing. At its highest expression of practice, physicians have given expert care and accepted sliding fees, or no fees, according to the income of the patient. It is not too many decades ago that our family primary physician visited the elderly sick at home. Unfortunately, the issues of greed and power, status and privilege, have characterized American medicine at its worst. The American Medical Association reflects this complex mix of morality and baseness, in its previous resistance to virtually every improvement in the availability of lower-cost medical care for Americans, while at the same time advancing standards of technical expertise. Recently, it has become slightly more reflective and reasoned in its former resistive attitude to change.

The changes in society that have required changes in medical financing are multiple. The costs of medical care during the 1970's and 1980's escalated exponentially, driven by many factors including belated recognition of the need for adequate salaries for support personnel in hospitals, by more effective but expensive improvements in diagnostic testing, by drying up of benefactors to pay off hospital deficits. In contrast, there has been a plateau or regression in actual income of the average citizen adjusted for inflation. American medicine has simply become too expensive for many people. The disparity in availability of good medical care that exists for different people has not always been related to economics but sometimes relates to geography. The poor in some US cities received superb care from teaching institutions, while in other cities were relatively neglected in treatments of the same disorders, a situation of geographic disparity that is no longer accepted. National standards of practice, not local standards, are now required. The recent influx of immigration, both legal and illegal, has additionally overloaded the medical care system and placed a disproportionate burden on big city hospital facilities. The increasing health care burden of AIDS, the extension of the quantity of life in the elderly and terminally ill through heroic means, and the decrease in the willingness of the wealthy to make up for deficits in the budget of medical centers, have all contributed to the crisis in financing of medical care in the 70s and 80s, requiring change as an inescapable necessity, not an option.

NEUTRAL OR POSITIVE CHANGES IN HEALTH CARE FINANCING

Until the 1980s, management of medical care costs care was viewed with suspicion by the American Medical Association. The managed costs approach was functional only in parts of the country and for a small minority of individuals. The Kaiser Permanente System, for example, was one of the first to provide managed health care. Beginning in the 1980s however, broader changes occurred nationwide. Some of these changes are described by Sharfstein and Goldman (1989). These neutral or progressive trends in medical financing, such as thoughtful managed care, and in other aspects of health care, are summarized in Table 2. These neutral or positive trends grew out of the conviction that costs for medical care must be and can be reduced, primarily by changing from fee for service to the concept of coverage of individuals at a fixed fee for comprehensive medical care. Associated with this fundamental change was a need for a restoration of a more equal balance between primary care physicians and specialists. There is increasing recognition, in addition, that health care has to be rationed in one form or another, because the total monies available for health care are finite. While explicit rationing of care has previously been rejected, there has always been de facto rationing without using the term because of its political or emotional unacceptability.

Another neutral, but in fact a positive trend, has been increasing emphasis on the prevention of illness and early illness recognition rather than treatment of established and chronic disease. Hospitals and outpatient facilities have increasingly moved toward development of teams for health care in place of the previous hierarchy of care based on the status of the physician on top of the pyramid.

Table 2: Neutral or Positive Trends in Managed Economics of Health Care and Health Care Training

- Conviction that costs can be reduced.
- Change from fee-for-service to coverage of lives.
- Restoration of the balance between primary care physicians and specialists (50:50).
- Explicit or implicit rationing of care based on cost effectiveness and priorities within total health care funds available.
- Emphasis on prevention and early recognition of disease.
- Integrated teams for care in place of a hierarchy based on high physician status at the top.
- Increased research and accountability for the delivery of health services and outcome documentation.
- Critical rather than indulgent attitude toward teaching hospitals.
- Encouragement of competition.
- Better regulation of practice within the medical profession to avoid the threat of increased regulation from government.
- Rapid and unpredictable changes in health care financing methods for an indefinite time.
- Emphasis on deliver of care and teaching in the ambulatory, outpatient setting not the inpatient context.

The American National Institutes of Health have recently allocated funds for the first time for research studies on the delivery of health care services and for outcome documentation, in contrast to traditional areas of research only in the basic science and clinical research. A much more critical attitude has developed in the public and government toward teaching hospitals, with simultaneous incompatible demands being made on them for parity of funding between teaching hospitals and community hospitals, but at the same time recognizing the need for some differential costs to teaching hospitals to compensate for the training needs and for complexity of patient illness in these referral centers.

Competition between physicians for cheaper care has increasingly been encouraged. Demands for stricter limits on the costs of practice have come from within the medical profession, to some extent, but primarily have come from ever increasing governmental regulations. There has been a steady shift in the location of medical care and teaching, from inpatient beds to the outpatient setting, with integrative ambulatory care being the norm, rather than the traditional fractionated and specialized inpatient services.

NEGATIVE (REGRESSIVE) CHANGES IN HEALTH CARE FINANCING

None of these neutral or positive changes noted above are irrational, invidious, or incompatible with the highest traditions of expert affordable care for all individuals. Unfortunately these neutral or positive changes have been accompanied by much less positive, more destructive changes. American physicians during this period of 1945–1995 have, for example, tended to unbundle their charges in response to reduced fees so that literally every suture of an operative procedure was counted as a separate cost. A complex chess-like game of us-versus-them took place in the past decade between clinicians and insurance payers. What did not happen between 1945 and 1996 was development of any parity between medical and psychiatric disorders or greater confidence by the public in the medical establishment. The idealistic premise behind President Johnson's 'Great Society' mandate in regard to psychiatric disorders was to empty patients from the large state psychiatric institutions and to restore these 'freed' individuals to life in their local communities where psychiatric care could be given in neighborhood mental health centers. The eviction of patients from the large state psychiatric institutions took place promptly, but the redirection of moneys to local mental health facilities never occurred, a tragic travesty of a political promise followed by a cynical lack of fulfillment. The result has been a large increase in the homeless mentally ill without care anywhere.

Psychiatry became increasingly medicalized in the last decade. Medicare (government payment of medical costs for persons over 65) benefits for psychiatry were expanded for the first time, in 1987, but only for purely medical management of psychiatric disorders. Psychological treatments were correspondingly undermined. There has been a continued, almost unquestioned, acceptance of the exclusionary insurance policy for mental health care, usually limited to 30 days a year, or to a fixed number of days allowed for a lifetime, with no similar limits on chronic medical disorders. Co-payments now required by patients for psychiatric disorders are usually 50 per cent but generally only 20 per cent for medical disorders, despite lack of rational reasons behind this distinction. Unfortunately, too many physicians have passively agreed with these negative, prejudicial changes in health care financing for psychiatric disorders by making changes in their practice entirely for reasons of economic incentive.

The trend away from non-profit third party payers as sources of health care financing to profit-centered managed care corporate-model organizations accelerated in the 1990's. The *Wall Street Journal* has documented the enormous profits accumulated by health maintenance organizations selected by industry to decrease their corporate costs for medical care (Quint, 1995). The assumption behind the change to managed health care costs instead of fee for service, was that managed health care creates incentives to provide less expensive care. The publicly stated goal was to provide comprehensive pre-paid health care for an increased number of citizens at less cost to the patient and to the employer. In fact, patients generally received decreased service, physicians earned less, and for-profit HMO's became wealthy at the expense of patients and doctors. The concept of letting market place forces operate resulted in a new 'golden rule' of managed health care as summarized by DeAngelis: 'Manage a lot and care not' (quoted in Silber, 1994). The system of management of care costs through coverage of lives by fixed annual fees led to the introduction of Draconian 'gatekeepers' with little or no improvement in health care for patients, but, instead, the generation of an enormous new bureaucracy, causing waste of clinical time in order to argue with managed care gatekeepers.

The concern expressed by corporations that comparable reimbursement for psychiatric disorders on a par with medical services would cause a huge increase in the cost of comprehensive health care simply has proven to be unfounded, undocumented, and disproven. There is no evidence that individuals will seek unlimited care for psychiatric disorders more than for medical disorders. Good psychiatric care usually results in an overall reduction in health costs and decreased loss of employment time.

It is time to require that all medical practice, of psychiatric or physical disorders, be guided by valid and reliable scientific studies demonstrating the effectiveness of treatment in place of archaic distinctions between mental and physical. Unfortunately, there exists between medical and psychiatric coverage an 'uneven playing field.' The care of generally untreatable medical disorders such as pancreatic cancer, remains unquestioned despite the fact that 95 per cent of cases will die rather promptly, while the care for treatable major, so called 'mental' disorders remains inadequate, despite enormous data demonstrating the effectiveness of care for most of these conditions. Studies have documented the fact that the cumulative economic burden of depressive illnesses on the United States economy is as great as that for cardiac disease, yet economic coverage for care of depression is generally half that of medical symptoms produced by heart disease (Mintz et al., 1982). Clearly, most of the health care financing for psychiatric disorders is not driven by rational, scientific or humane reasons, but is driven instead by profit-based economic motives, by studied ignorance, and disregard of scientific treatment studies. There is no way to avoid asking the ethical-political question of whether delivery of health care is comparable to the production and delivery of widgets, or whether it requires special consideration based on Western moral traditions.

EATING DISORDERS TREATMENT FUNDING

Eating disorders have been singled out for disproportionate and ruthless limitations of the costs of health care, despite the fact that they represent combined medical and psychiatric disorders and should logically be covered by both medical and psychiatric insurance. Eating disorders involve profound, often life-threatening, alterations in biology, psychological suffering, social interactions, and family functioning. They are, however, generally highly treatable, with multiple studies demonstrating the treatment effectiveness of programs utilizing a multidisciplinary program of nutritional rehabilitation, behavioral relearning, and specific validated forms of psychotherapy in appropriate combinations for anorectic and bulimic syndromes. No rational individual would deny surgical care for a patient who self-inflicts a head wound with a firearm, secondary to depressive illness. The appropriate surgical and medical care would be given first and then treatment of the depressive disorder would follow.

Eating disorders, likewise, result in multiple organ system medical symptomatology, which require expert medical evaluation and care. Yet the basis for funding eating disorders remains

Table 3: Special Problems of Eating Disorders and Managed Health Care

- Longer stay often required, providing tempting target for cost-cutters.
- Intrinsic combination of medical and psychiatric components within eating disorders.
- Belief that eating disorders are not 'real' illnesses but faddish preoccupation.
- Misuse of eating disorder diagnosis to admit simple obesity, by a minority of practitioners, has led to generalized suspicion of caregivers.
- Unscientific demand by HMO's for change in treatment goals from comprehensive biopsychosocial improvement to improvement in serious medical aspects only.
- Lack of adequate scientific paradigm by HMO's for understanding of the multifactorial etiology and multidisciplinary team approach required for treatment for eating disorders.
- Insufficient public outrage to generate legislative requirements for combined use of medical and psychiatric benefits.

limited, usually restricted by unscientific, out of date views, that these are purely psychological disorders, with an implicit bias that these illnesses are really fads, not serious conditions, perhaps not illnesses at all. The major unstated reason for difficulty in obtaining adequate funding for care of eating disorders is the fact that treatment of these disorders may be longer, more expensive than some other illness and may require inpatient care, especially for anorectic states. The real issue should not be how long a hospital stay is required or how intensive care is required (outpatient or inpatient), but whether care can be demonstrated on a scientific basis to be effective and to be enduring. Table 3 summarizes some of the special economic problems eating disorders face in the context of managed health care.

The treatment response potential of eating disorders is more likely than the treatment response of many chronic medical conditions, with greater possibility for sustained improvement. Robust confirmation exists for the enduring effectiveness of cognitive behavioral therapy of bulimia nervosa, and there is increasing evidence for its effectiveness in the treatment of anorexia nervosa. Restoration of body weight to a healthy range in anorexia nervosa is life-saving and leads to decreased relapse. Definitive inpatient treatment of eating disorders followed by intensive outpatient follow-up stops the revolving door pattern of inadequate inpatient treatment followed by relapse requiring repeated admission and chronic lowered quality of life. Many valid questions do exist about the optimum treatments of eating disorders, as well as questions about their etiology and mechanism, but no more questions than in other serious health problems we treat. It is the symptomatology of the illness not the presumed etiology, that should guide treatment. The following legal cases illustrate this principle. Full day programs are increasingly important in care of serious eating disorders, reducing costs substantially (Kaplan and Olmsted, 1997)

LEGAL CASES AND THE COVERAGE OF TREATMENT COSTS

The following are two recent and very pertinent court cases in which disputes over coverage of costs for inpatient treatment of anorexia nervosa were resolved in favor of patients (see also Andersen, 1996).

FIRST CASE: SIMONS VS BLUE CROSS AND BLUE SHIELD OF GREATER NEW YORK, 536 NEW YORK STATE 2d 431 (AD I DEPT. 1989)

Facts: The insured sued for denied costs incurred by daughter's treatment for malnutrition secondary to anorexia nervosa. She was admitted at 72 3/4 pounds (a loss of 30 per cent) and with a blood pressure of 72/62, significantly dehydrated. Treatment included nasogastric feeding and intravenous infusions. Medical tests included computer tomographies. Discharge diagnoses: Malnutrition, hypotension, bradycardia, chronic weight loss, and atypical eating disorder.

Court decision: 'The Supreme Court, Appellate, Division, Milonas, J., held that hospitalization for treatment of malnutrition was not subject to the limitation of coverage applicable to in-hospital care for psychiatric disorders, even though the malnutrition was caused by a psychiatric disorder.' The motion was granted to recover costs for the treatment of malnutrition and other medical complications of anorexia nervosa.

Judicial reasoning:
a. Hospitalization was because of malnutrition and hypotension. It was not to a psychiatric unit.
b. Care included nasogastric feeding directed at reversing weight loss and physical symptoms.
c. The malnutrition did not have to be severe.
d. Patients admitted for a physical condition may also receive psychiatric counseling. Psychotherapy does 'not negate the fundamental nature of the treatment as being medical.'
e. 'It is axiomatic that ambiguities in an insurance policy are to be construed against the insurer, particularly when found in an exclusionary clause.'

Implications:
a. 'The fact that ... physical disability was the result of the psychiatric condition known as anorexia nervosa does not transform what is customarily medical treatment into psychiatric treatment.'
b. 'It is the physical condition and the treatment required to deal with that condition which is crucial, not the reason for the disorder.'
c. 'Any person suffering from malnutrition would have received the same or comparable treatment.'

Comment: There is no reason to consider physical consequences of anorexia nervosa differently from other psychiatrically related medical/surgical conditions, such as drug overdose or a gunshot wound from a suicide attempt.

SECOND CASE: MANNHEIM VS TRAVELERS INSURANCE COMPANY, UNITED STATES DISTRICT COURT, EASTERN DISTRICT OF NEW YORK [92-CV-5466 (JG)](FROM A TRANSCRIPT OF BENCH TRIAL).

Facts: The plaintiff's daughter was hospitalized for anorexia nervosa, weighing 72 pounds at 5'2". She manifested intense fear of weight. During the hospitalization of five months, she received psychiatric and medical treatment in a psychiatric hospital. The

Travelers Insurance Company paid for 30 days and refused the remaining four months.

Court decision: The patient warranted medical benefits for treatment until she reached 85 per cent of her ideal weight. 'Over time, as her physical condition improved, the psychiatric care became the primary purpose of her hospitalization.' The plaintiff received a judgment in the amount of $31,360, covering the time between admission until 85 per cent of target weight.

Judicial reasoning: The standard set by the Simons case was invoked. The court rejected the view that treatment was completely medical or psychiatric, choosing a 'bright line' of 85 per cent of healthy weight, at which point it was judged that treatment became primarily psychiatric. 'To put the issue in clearer relief, I have posed to the parties the following hypothetical: An insured person suffering from clinical depression jumps out a window and breaks every bone in her body. For the ensuing 6 weeks she received indisputably necessary inpatient treatment for her broken bones and indisputably necessary psychiatric treatment for her depression. Defense counsel has candidly ... stated that the exclusion cause does not address such dual-treatment hospitalizations, and it seems to me, pursuant to the principles I have already mentioned, this ambiguity in the contract must be resolved in favor of the insured.'

Implications: Again, ambiguity must be resolved in favor of the insured. Treatment in a psychiatric institution does not invalidate medical benefits. The condition treated was the determining factor of treatment methods. When medical treatment stops and psychiatric care begins is, to some extent, arbitrary but can be decided.

Comment: The weight at which treatment becomes primarily psychiatric could be argued to be higher, until nutritional rehabilitation is fully complete, but 85 per cent is an improvement over many current benefits. The undisputed ruling in this case, however, is that medical benefits apply to a substantial portion of the treatment. The context of a psychiatric hospital does not invalidate medical benefits.

REVIEW AND INTEGRATION OF THESE CASES

A number of positive shared features of these cases are potentially applicable to other cases of anorexia nervosa which is appropriately treated as a complex psychiatric disorder with profound medical complications. The logic of comparing its integrated treatment to the condition of broken bones from a suicide attempt caused by depression is persuasive. A disorder is treated according to its symptomatology by appropriate methods rather than by its causation. Nutritional rehabilitation, intravenous liquids, medical testing to rule out tumors, medical consultations, etc. are all medical treatments.

Adjunctive psychotherapy does not invalidate the application of medical benefits. Exclusion clauses for health care must be scrutinized much more strictly than inclusionary clauses. Any ambiguity be construed against the insurance company and in favor of the insured. Most contract holders do not know these facts.

A number of limitations are also evident from these court cases. The first case was adjudicated in the Appellate Division of the New York State Supreme Court serving as a precedent in New York. It certainly can be cited out of New York State. Perhaps more importantly, the reasoning can be applied elsewhere in the United States. In the second case, a federal district court was chosen because the insurance company was multi-state. The transcript of the bench trial was not published in the Federal Supplement and therefore is not a precedent. It certainly can be referred to, and the logic invoked, but has less authority than the 30 per cent or so of federal cases whose decisions are formally published.

It is doubtful whether any managed care company will acknowledge, or refer to these cases. It would not be surprising if they attempted to invalidate, marginalize, or dispute them if cited, because cost minimization guides these companies. The irony is that brief hospitalization not only leads to rehospitalization of severely underweight anorexsic patients, but may also be more expensive (Baran, Weltzin and Kaye, 1995).

ETHICAL DIMENSIONS TO MANAGED HEALTH CARE

How do we balance market forces with academic imperatives? How are we to solve the current health care financing crisis, and simultaneously carry out our missions of giving excellent comprehensive care, teaching future physicians, and adding to knowledge through research? The answer begins by asking more questions. The first question to ask is whether the delivery of medical services is the same as, or fundamentally different from, the delivery of other products or services. Traditionally, medically care has been viewed as having intrinsic ethical demands, with the historic Western ethical code dating back to Hippocrates and other ancient sages. If medical care has an intrinsic ethical and moral dimension, then it cannot be viewed by the same principles underlying the production of tires, computer games, and rock music: let the market forces rule. Lip service is often given to the ethical beliefs concerning medical care, but in the end, only ethical behavior counts, which often means making financial decisions on a broader basis than market forces alone.

SPECIFIC ETHICAL CHALLENGES AND CONFLICTS

Shore and Beigel (1991) examined the reductionistic consequence of managed behavioral health care. They note the ongoing transition in treatment goals from comprehensive improvement and prevention of recurrence, to a more limited treatment goal of simply returning patients to marginal improved functioning, and getting them out of danger. There is decreased funding for long-term intensive psychological treatment, for example, for definitive psychotherapy, with the newer replacement goal of just sufficient decrease in current symptoms to leave the hospital or get off the outpatient rolls. Woodward (1994) states the implication of the computer-based patient record as an essential aspect of managed health care systems. Confidential medical records become, in fact, semi-public, accessible records without privacy, leading to an erosion of the confidentiality barrier in a managed health care system. Not uncommonly, details completely unrelated to approval for treatment funding are requested by non-trained, non-clinicians, for purely economic reasons. Finally, insurance coverage for mental disorders is often 'carved out' from health coverage for 'medical disorders' and subjected to more scrutiny and more limitations without scientific basis. Many myths and stigmas persist about psychiatric disorders being ineffective, endlessly sought, and unnecessary. The fact is that the public too seldom seek care of psychiatric disorders, rather than too often.

Physicians practicing in a managed care environment incur multiple ethical and moral conflicts. Signing a 'gag rule' that prevents a physician from describing the most effective care means the patient's welfare takes second place to the financial benefits of the insurance company or the physician. Recommendations for specialty consultation must be made on the basis of patient need rather than on loss of funds to the HMO because of referral. There is increasing recognition that physicians in a managed health care environment have responsibilities to appeal decisions unfavorable to their patients, especially when necessary coverage is denied (Hoge, 1995). Child and adolescent psychiatry have special ethical demands on them in the context of managed health care, because of the minority status of their patients. Geraty, Hendren and Flaa (1992) disagree with the suggestion that medical personnel should be 'value-neutral'. Grappling with ethical dilemmas and conflicts is essential for good medical care, especially for the care of children. Sukol (1994) summarizes the ethical basics of practice as being: truthful speech, respectful relationship, acknowledgment of limitations, and focus on patient welfare above all other interests.

Most interactions with managed health care center on behavioral practices by the managed care organizations designed to discourage care givers from asking for treatment funding. Many times, the first interaction with the HMO is through telephone contact with an unqualified individual having no clinical or research expertise in the disorders upon which they are pronouncing judgments regarding their worthiness for insurance coverage. The exculpatory clause in the contracts and correspondence of HMO's that denial of benefits does not constitute denial of care is, in fact, a fraud and a lie. For the vast majority of individuals, the denial of coverage of health care costs is the denial of care.

Having a thoroughly prepared, rational, calm, organized interaction with managed health care workers remains the soundest basis for obtaining positive responses. In general, it helps to deal only with those HMO employees who are a position to make funding decisions based on adequate clinical training. All interactions ideally, should be tape-recorded by the caregiver, with a request for confirmation of and rationale for decisions in writing. An in-depth understanding of the patient's case, as well as the scientific evidence for the effectiveness of the requested treatment,

Table 4: Possible Psychological Responses to Managed Health Care Interactions.

NEGATIVE	POSITIVE
Powerlessness	Becoming empowered
Emotional distress	Rational responses
Transference unrecognized	Transference dealt with
Feelings of abandonment and ineffectiveness	Empathy with caregivers and patients
Splitting into good and bad parties	Shades of gray recognized
Diversion of energy from patient care	Increased enthusiasm for care
Isolation of affect and alienation	Group support and reintegration
Admitting defeat	Pursue 'win-win'
All or none thinking	Seek incremental benefits for patients and self
Wishful thinking	Work to change the system
Unreflected responses	Altruism toward opponents
Being part of the problem	Being part of the solution

are mandatory. Understanding the historical background to managed health care and especially the broader national and historic recent changes in health care financing constitute an essential part of health care training. The enormous time, energy, and psychological cost for physician interaction with managed health care are realities in today's world, and must therefore be adequately taught in training programs. Not surprisingly, there is diversity among HMO's with an encouraging minority seeking out and providing funding for treatment of eating disorders in programs of excellence.

The interaction by physicians and other health care givers may be highly stressful. Table 4 summarizes some of the possible negative psychodynamic responses to managed care interactions experienced by clinicians as well as suggestions for more positive alternatives. A pervasive sense of powerlessness and ineffectiveness resulting from denial of requests for treatment costs is common because the professional who gives health care is generally not trained in the relentless, time consuming, and burdensome business tactics necessary to interact with these powerful economic forces. On the positive side, the interaction with managed health care may give the physician some empathy with the feelings of many patients about the medical establishment in general, towards which they often feel helpless and ineffective. Gabbard et al. (1991) apply psychodynamic principles to the review process, first examining the psychological dangers of splitting or worsening outcome, with advocacy of a balanced view of all legitimate concerns.

FUTURE CHANGE: A MANDATE

What does the future hold and what changes should be advocated in the economics of medical care especially of eating disorders, in the United States? A rational revision of health care financing is essential because there are simply not enough dollars to give everyone unlimited care, especially with availability of new, more expensive, diagnostic and treatment procedures, with an aging population and the possibilities for the extension of quantity, if not quality, of life. Many economic models are needed for the varied aspects of health care. The legal and ethical issues of health care must be continually reviewed. Managed care companies are usually directed by corporate administrators with many layers of legal advisors. It is only fair and just to suggest to patients that where inappropriate denial of benefits has taken place, that they seek legal counsel regarding what basically is the interpretation of complex contracts. Health care contracts are among the most important contracts an individual signs, many times exceeding in importance, other contracts such as mortgages, that are regularly scrutinized before commitment. Health care often comes down to the legal area of contract law. Courts often take a much more consumer oriented view of the health care contract benefits than do those whose profits depend on the denial of benefits. Providers must be willing to work through multiple denials in order to reach the more reasoned response of administrative law judges or other courts.

It is imperative for physicians to ask patients to carefully review their health care benefits contracts before signing them. Physicians must weight the ethical dilemmas present in signing contracts for services. At a minimum, a full disclosure of the true nature of the proposed health care contract, should be mandatory. This disclosure would include illustrative examples of the costs and benefits, extent and duration of coverage, for the most common and severe, acute and chronic, medical and psychiatric conditions, with calculations of costs and description of benefits available in clear language and non-confusing mathematics. There is nothing unethical about an individual agreeing to a low cost for a very reduced level of minimal health care benefits coverage, provided this decision is based on true informed consent, rather than deceptive advertising. The problem usually arises when slick advertising recruits patients by implying more extensive coverage than those covered by the fine print of the actual contract. One positive note has been the finding in some studies (Rosenberg et al., 1991) that utilization review has a moderate, but not necessarily adverse, effect on patient care.

At a minimum, there needs to be a legislative mandate for parity between medical and psychiatric disorders. The division between medical and psychiatric disorders is archaic and unscientific. Eating disorders need to be appreciated as representing combined medical and psychiatric disorders for which funding will logically be a combination of medical and psychiatric benefits. Until the individual anorectic patient is above 90 per cent of ideal weight, the care of eating disorders is primarily medical, and therefore the financing of care until 90–95 per cent restoration should be under medical coverage. The location for care of eating disorders is often the department of psychiatry because of its ability to manage the behavioral and psychopathological, as well as medical, complications of eating disorders but may be in pediatrics or general medicine, with psychiatric consultation and guidance.

The least effective method of changing unfair HMO practices is case-by-case discussion with the insurance companies. The next most effective is positive court decisions which set precedent. Real, enduring, change requires legislative action, both state and federal, to assure joint funding with medical, plus psychiatric benefits for eating disorders, or preferably, removal of out-of-date distinctions between physical and mental. A federal law is scheduled to take effect in 1998 to bring equality to medical and psychiatric funding. The example of a consolidated response to cuts in post-partum care leading to federal legislation requiring a minimum of 48 hours is encouraging.

CONCLUSION

The financing of health care is in a process of change, of critical review, and reformulation. It is not overly dramatic to say there is a crisis in health care financing. The meaning of the word crisis, however, needs to be appreciated. It is not wholly negative – crisis in Greek means a time of danger and a simultaneous time of opportunity. Because huge economic forces are at work, because the quality of life for physicians, including, but not limited to compensation aspects, is at stake, because modern health care involves large personal and corporate expenditures, it is not surprising that conflicted and passionate views on all sides are present in regard to health care financing and additional changes (Glass, 1995). Understanding the historical growth of cost management of health care financing and the most effective methods to work within the system as well as when to work outside of the system, are essential for care of eating disordered patients.

REFERENCES

Andersen, A.E. (1996) 'Third party payment for inpatient treatment of anorexia nervosa.' *Eating Disorders Review*, 7(6): 1–5.

Baran, S.A., Weltzin, M.D. and Kaye, W.H. (1995) 'Low Discharge Weight and Outcome in Anorexia Nervosa.' *American Journal of Psychiatry*, 152: 1070–72.

Gabbard, G.O., Takahaski, T., Davidson, J., Bauman-Bork, M. and Ensroth, E. (1991) 'A psychodynamic perspective on the clinical impact on insurance review.' *American Journal of Psychiatry*, 148: 318–23.

Geraty, R.D., Hendren, R.L. and Flaa, C.J. (1992) 'Ethical perspectives on managed health care as it relates to child and adolescent psychiatry.' *Journal American Academic Child Adolescent Psychiatry*, 31: 398–402.

Glass, R.M. (1995) 'Mental disorders quality of life and inequiality of insurance coverage.' *Journal of the American Medical Association*, 274: 1557.

Hoge, S.K. (1995) 'Your legal responsibilities in a managed health care environment.' *Journal of Practical Psychiatry and Behavioral Health*, 2: 62–8.

Kaplan, A.S. and Olmsted, M.P. (1997) 'Partial Hopitalization.' In Gamer, D.E. and Garfinkel, P.E. (eds) *Handbook of Treatment for Eating Disorders*, New York: The Guildford Press, 354–71.

Mintz, J., Mintz, L.I., Arruda, M.J. and Hwang, S.S. (1992) 'Treatments of depression and the functional capacity to work.' *Archives of General Psychiatry*, 49: 761–8.

Quint, M. (1995) 'Health plans force changes in the way doctors are paid.' *New York Times*, February 9.

Rosenberg, S.N., Allen, D.R., Handt, J.S., et al. (1995) 'Effect of utilization review in a fee-for-service health insurance plan.' *New England Journal of Medicine*, 333: 1326–30.

Sharfstein, S.S. and Goldman H. (1989) 'Financing the medical management of mental disorders.' *American Journal of Psychiatry*, 146: 3.

Shore, M.F. and Beigel, A. (1996) 'The challenges posed by managed behavioral health care.' *New England Journal of Medicine*, 334: 116–18.

Silber, T.J. (1994) 'Eating disorders and health insurance.' *Archives of Pediatrics and Adolescent Medicine*, 148: 785–8.

Starr, P. (1982) *The Social Transformation of American Medicine*, New York: Basic Books.

Sukol, R.B. (1995) 'Teaching ethical thinking and behavior to medical students.' *Journal of the American Medical Association*, 273: 1388–89.

Woodward, B. (1995) 'The computer-based patient record and confidentiality.' *New England Journal of Medicine*, 333: 1419–22.

Index